PRAISE for *Good Morning Messages*

"Katherine Merkle and her husband, Ken, have been my friends for over twenty years, and I have seen what God has done in and through her. She leads a remarkable spiritual life. It has been about nine years since God began this work in her life, and she has devoted her life to reaching hundreds of souls online every day with these powerful daily devotion teachings which have both encouraged my life and changed my faith into being more practical in doing the Word of God and not only hearing, as Jesus said in Matthew 7:24-25.

I recommend this book of Daily Devotions to everyone who will carefully read and act upon the Scripture and words of encouragement Katherine Merkle has put together by the help of the Holy Spirit. I know her, and she teaches what she lives. The Bible is her lifestyle.

Read these pages again and again until the truth of each daily devotion soaks through to your innermost consciousness and your spirit being. Let these words of daily devotion become part of your life, and you will never remain the same.

I send my blessings to my friend, sister in Christ Katherine Merkle and whoever allows this book to land unto their hand and heart."

Bishop Lawrence Owino
Gospel Harvest Ministries, Kenya, East Africa

"In this beautiful book, *Good Morning Messages*, the author has captured the characteristics of God, His love, mercy, forgiveness, compassion, and everlasting presence with us. Daily she gives us Scriptures and prayers that often speak to our needs that very day. She speaks often of the joys and delights that only God gives."

Susan Jungman
Author of *The Mountains and Valleys of My Life*

"*Good Morning Messages* is an encouraging and simply beautiful daily reminder of the gospel in our lives! I appreciate the personal connection to these devotionals. Katherine does a great job at presenting everyday moments around following Jesus. *Good Morning Messages* will encourage and challenge you to know what it means to follow Jesus. Be encouraged by the gospel, God's Word, and prayer as you enter every day."

Pastor Joel Gregory
Grace Brethren Church, Barberton Campus, Ohio

"Katherine Merkle has been encouraging many people for years with Daily Devotions through text messages. Now, with her new book, *Good Morning Messages: Prayer, Praise, and Love From Above*, many more will be reached and impacted for the Kingdom of God. *Good Morning Messages* devotional book is an inspiring way to begin a New Year. Starting each morning with a word from God prepares us to have an uplifting successful day. This book awakens the inner man to seek God early in the day and serves as a reminder throughout the day that God is with us.

Katherine has captured the essence of just "being still and knowing that He is God" (Psalm 46:10). We can trust Him at all times and in all things (Psalm 62:8). God is progressive; He moves forward to build His Kingdom. *Good Morning Messages* spiritually inspires readers to study God's Word, share His message of Love, Peace, and Faith, and will impact many lives. I applaud you, Katherine, and I praise God for this well written, soul-searching devotional book. God bless."

Dalia Tucker
Mentor and Friend

"These devotions have touched my spirit in the most positive way. Katherine's story is similar to many of us in our spiritual walk with the Lord Jesus. Her God-given ability to weave the Scriptures with life experience is refreshing and encouraging.

The devotions are a collection of spiritually impactful, awe-inspiring bursts of Holy Spirit encounter. Each devotion has a message to help us through difficulties we may experience on an everyday basis.

Each message is a great spiritual breakfast to empower us for a successful day! Thank you, Katherine!"

Elizabeth Knepper
Friend and Pastor John Knepper's Wife

"*Good Morning Messages* is an encouraging read for those looking for a daily devotional and those not realizing they could use one. Each day is set apart, allowing readers to focus on God and His Word, standing on its own. It's amazing how often the message relates with my other studies and challenges me to view God differently, praise Him more completely, and follow Him more closely."

Lorraine K.

"Great Daily Devotional! I've used this book in the mornings with the kids, and we have been able to discuss daily life issues and how the Bible has the answers to these issues. *Good Morning Messages* is a great devotional, not only for the new believer, but for those who have studied the Bible for years!! Great gift idea."

Sheryl Eberhart
Amazon Customer

"Messages from the Heart! This book is not like the other daily devotional books with just Bible verses and one liners. It contains devotionals written with enriched messages that are easy to apply and personalized through the author's heart. I am eager for each new day to read them. A must have!"

Lori H.
Amazon Customer

"*Good Morning Messages* is an encouraging and simply beautiful daily reminder of the gospel in our lives! I appreciate the personal connection to these devotionals. The author does a great job at presenting everyday moments around following Jesus. *Good Morning Messages* will encourage and challenge you to know what it means to follow Jesus. Be encouraged by the gospel, God's Word, and prayer as you enter every day."

Anonymous
Amazon Customer

"Content is easily relatable and the author is so transparent. Absolutely love the book and the messages."

Dan Tucker
Amazon Customer

"Such an amazing book!"

Kaylee V.

"God is so good. This book gives you a reason to wake up and want to read."

Kelly
Amazon Customer

Good Morning Messages

Good Morning Messages

Prayer, Praise, and Love from Above

Katherine Merkle

Bestwine Press
Indianapolis, Indiana

Bestwine
Press

A BESTWINE PRESS BOOK

© 2024 Katherine Merkle

https://authorkatherinemerkle.com
ksmerk@authorkatherinemerkle.com

Unless otherwise marked, all Scriptures are taken from THE HOLY BIBLE, NEW INTERNATIONAL VERSION®, **NIV**® Copyright © 1973, 1978, 1984, 2011 by Biblica, Inc.® Used by permission. All rights reserved worldwide.

Other versions used are marked as follows:

CSB: The Christian Standard Bible. Copyright © 2017 by Holman Bible Publishers. Used by permission. Christian Standard Bible®, and CSB® are federally registered trademarks of Holman Bible Publishers, all rights reserved.

ESV: ESV® Bible (The Holy Bible, English Standard Version®). ESV® Text Edition: 2016. Copyright © 2001 by Crossway, a publishing ministry of Good News Publishers. All rights reserved. Used by permission.

KJV: KING JAMES VERSION, public domain.

NKJV: NEW KING JAMES VERSION (NKJV): Scripture taken from the NEW KING JAMES VERSION®. Copyright© 1982 by Thomas Nelson, Inc. Used by permission. All rights reserved.

ISBN: 979-8-9921838-0-1

PRINTED IN THE UNITED STATES OF AMERICA

Good Morning Messages is

DEDICATED to ...

All the people searching for God who feel as if He is hiding or possibly doesn't even exist, to those who feel they aren't worthy of Him or who think they're too far gone, and to those who have a desire to know Him better or deepen their faith.

> *Therefore the Lord waits to be gracious to you,*
> *and therefore He exalts Himself to show mercy to you.*
> *For the Lord is a God of justice:*
> *blessed are all those who wait for Him.*
>
> ISAIAH 30:18

———

God actively desires to show grace and mercy to those who seek Him. God loves us more than we could ever fathom, but He waits for us to come to Him so He can show us His love and compassion. My prayer is that each reader of *Good Morning Messages* would come to a deeper understanding of who God is and surrender their lives to the One who sets us free to experience life in and through Christ Jesus.

> *For God so loved the world that He gave His one and only Son,*
> *that whoever believes in Him shall not perish but have eternal life.*
> *For God did not send His Son into the world to condemn the world,*
> *but to save the world through Him.*
>
> JOHN 3:16-17

ACKNOWLEDGMENTS

The Lord deserves the most credit and thanks, not only for giving me the privilege of writing *Good Morning Messages* but for every word written. Each morning as I studied God's Word and spent time in other devotional works, God guided and directed me through topics and supporting Scriptures, deepening my knowledge of and faith in Him. I am eternally grateful for who He is in my life and the mighty work He has done (and continues to do) in me. Thank You, Jesus!

Of course, my husband, Ken Merkle, is my greatest supporter. He is a faithful man, knowledgeable in God's Word, and an encouragement to me as I pursued writing the book God put on my heart. Once it was written, Ken read every word straight through, and his input prompted a few welcome edits. Through his ever-friendly, talk-to-everyone personality, Ken was also the one who first met and introduced me to the book's publisher, Mary Jo Gremling. The Lord knew what he was doing when He put us together, and I'm so blessed Ken is my husband. Much of *Good Morning Messages* is a result of our journey together. Thank you, my dear sweet husband. I love you, my Special K.

My pursuit of Jesus was ignited by my mentor and dear friend, Miss Dalia Tucker. There will never be sufficient words for me to describe how special she is to me and the gratitude I have in my heart for the gift she gave me. Through her example, Miss Dalia taught me the importance and value of time spent with the Lord—in His Word and in prayer and fellowship with other believers. She demonstrates what it looks like to love like Jesus, represent Him well, and lead a Spirit-filled life in Him. Thank you, Miss Dalia, for allowing God to rule in your life and to unreservedly serve Him.

And then there is Phoebe Wagler, the always willing responder to my pleas for creative inspiration and design help. Phoebe is an incredibly talented woman with a gentle kindness about her that I truly appreciate. Her patience with my out-of-the-blue requests and endless revisions do not go unnoticed. Phoebe, you are very special to me in all you do and who you are. Thank you for being a part of my life and for your perfect cover design for *Good Morning Messages*.

A special callout to my publisher (can't believe I can say that), Mary Jo Gremling, for your patience and guidance through the crafting of *Good Morning Messages*. This would never have happened without your expertise and dedication to every detail. You are truly gifted in what you do. Thank you for sharing that gift with me.

And lastly, for the many readers of the past decade of my daily devotions who encouraged me to pursue publishing a book, as well as family and friends who have prayed over me. Without your encouragement, I might never have embarked on this journey. I am so grateful for each one of you and pray the Lord continues to bless you as you pursue a deeper knowledge of and faith in Him. Thank you for encouraging me. I hope you enjoy *Good Morning Messages*.

Katherine Merkle

INTRODUCTION

Because of the LORD's great love we are not consumed, for His compassions never fail. They are new every morning: great is Your faithfulness.

LAMENTATIONS 3:22-23

This devotional is an expression of my love and gratitude for all that God has done in my life. He rescued me from the depths of sin and rebellion and gave me a new life in Him. The most powerful impact we can make in changing our lives is through building our relationship with God through the Lord Jesus Christ.

Each morning, we are given the gift of a new day, an opportunity to grow into the person God created us to be. An important part of my journey has been and continues to be spending time daily in morning devotionals, studying God's Word, prayer, praise, and experiencing His presence and love.

God desires for us to know Him, to have a deep personal relationship with Him, and an established devotional time daily is a great place to begin or a practice to continue in. In the morning, *Lord, You hear my voice; in the morning I lay my requests before You and wait expectantly* (Psalm 5:3). There is no better time of day than morning to give ourselves over to God, to surrender all to Him, to listen for His voice, and to allow God to lead and direct our path. *But seek first His kingdom and His righteousness, and all these things will be given to you as well* (Matthew 6:33).

Our Heavenly Father knows best. I pray we all will devote ourselves to the daily pursuit of knowing Him more and serving Him, as well as others in and through Him. May His will be our priority.

God is good, all the time!

Katherine Merkle

authorkatherinemerkle.com

May these words of my mouth and this meditation of my heart be pleasing in Your sight, Lord, my Rock and my Redeemer (Psalm 19:14).

January

JANUARY 1ST

This is the day which the LORD hath made; We will rejoice and be glad in it.

PSALM 118:24 KJV

Good morning! New Year's Blessings to you and yours! It is not just "this day," but all of our days—the yesterdays, todays, and for all eternity. We can choose to live in this truth! We can choose Jesus and live victoriously! When we start each day in prayer and praise, we start the day off in the right direction.

Praise the Lord! Praise God in His sanctuary; praise Him in His mighty heavens! Praise Him for His mighty deeds; praise Him according to His excellent greatness! Praise Him with trumpet sound; praise Him with lute and harp! (Psalm 150:1-6).

We can choose another year of battling through, trying so hard to control our circumstances and other people, places, and things, and we'll continue to get the same results. OR we can surrender our lives to the One who is truly in control, who loves us beyond anything we could ever imagine (Psalm 36:5-7) and *who is able to do immeasurably more than all we ask or imagine* (Ephesians 3:20).

The best resolution we can make has nothing at all to do with earthly matters. It is not about weight loss, quitting bad habits, or forcing temporary changes into our lives. It is all about Jesus!

Do not be anxious about anything, but in every situation, by prayer and petition, with thanksgiving, present your requests to God. And the peace of God, which transcends all understanding, will guard your hearts and your minds in Christ Jesus (Philippians 4:6-7). Let's choose to follow Jesus more closely and grow deeper in faith as our New Year's resolution.

Lord, we thank You for another New Year and praise You for who You are in our lives. This year, Lord, we desire to follow you more deeply, to shift our priorities to Yours. It is in our surrender that we are set free and will find our resting place in Your promises of love, healing, and peace. Thank You, Jesus. Amen.

JANUARY 2ND

If you love Me, keep My commands. And I will ask the Father, and He will give you another advocate to help you and be with you forever—the Spirit of truth. The world cannot accept Him, because it neither sees Him nor knows Him. But you know Him, for He lives with you and will be with you.

JOHN 14:15-17

Good morning! I woke up early this morning to sit with God alone in the peace and quiet of our living room. Whatever the circumstances of our lives, *God is with us.* When we really consider, know, and believe in the truth of these four precious words, our lives are forever changed. We know Him, for He lives with us and in us! God exists with us in a whole new way because of Christ's death and resurrection. Do not live a defeated life—claim the victory of Christ. Experience His presence with you.

The Lord is my Shepherd, I shall not want [I lack nothing]. He makes me to lie down in green pastures, He leads me beside still waters, He restores [refreshes] my soul. He guides me along the paths of righteousness [the right paths] for His Name's sake. Even though I walk through the valley of the shadow of death [the darkest valley], I will fear no evil, for You are with me; Your rod and Your staff, they comfort me (Psalm 23:1-4 NKJV).

There is no one like our God. There is no alternative to Him, no other way, no better way. His grace abounds, His mercy is endless, and He waits for us to come to Him.

Lord, thank You for loving us with a deep, from-the-inside-out, life-changing, life-saving love. A love we don't deserve, could never earn, and that never changes. You are our All in all, and we gladly surrender our lives to You. Thank You, Jesus. Amen.

JANUARY 3RD

*Now faith is confidence in what we hope for and assurance about what
we do not see. This is what the ancients were commended for.*

HEBREWS 11:1-2

Good morning! Why are we so obsessed with understanding and
explaining before believing what God's Word says? Faith is
based on past experiences with God—that His new and fresh
surprises will surely be ours. *Jesus Christ is the same yesterday, and
today, and forever* (Hebrews 13:8). Jesus Christ is unchangeable! Our
faith starts with believing that God is who He says He is—believing
in His character. Everything we need to know is found in God and in
His Word.

*I am the Lord, and there is no other; apart from Me there is no God. I will
strengthen you, though you have not acknowledged Me, so that from the
rising sun to the place of its setting people may know there is none besides
Me. I am the Lord and there is no other* (Isaiah 45:5-6).

God will anoint whomever He chooses to do the work He gives them
to do. We can have confidence in God and what His Word says. It is clear,
and it leaves nothing to question. Who are we to rewrite what God
spoke? To doubt what He said? Would we not be better off to study His
Word for a deeper knowledge that leads to understanding?

*Do your best to present yourself to God as one approved, a worker who
does not need to be ashamed and who correctly handles the word of truth*
(2 Timothy 2:15). Let us build our lives on His Word and His Word into
our lives.

*Lord, we desire a deeper relationship with You. Increase our faith and open
our hearts and minds to Your Word. May we intentionally pursue after You
with a renewed fervor and love. Thank You, Jesus! Amen.*

JANUARY 4TH

Grow in grace, and in the knowledge of our Lord and Savior Jesus Christ.

2 PETER 3:18

Good morning! Are we content in our knowledge of the Lord Jesus Christ? Let it never be so! We should never be content to rest on our laurels when it comes to our Lord. Charles Spurgeon wrote, "Absence from Christ is hell; the presence of Jesus is heaven."[1] We are to grow and mature in our understanding and our knowledge of Christ. Why? Because this is the most important thing to us. If we have experienced and know the love of Christ, we will yearn to go deeper with Him.

As the deer pants for streams of water, so my soul pants for You, my God. My soul thirsts for God, for the living God. When can I go and meet with God? (Psalm 42:1-2).

No matter where we are in our spiritual journey, no matter how mature we are in our faith, this sinful world will continue to challenge us with corruption and false teachings. Every day, we must find time with Him, to draw closer to Him, so that we will be prepared to stand in truth in any and all circumstances.

"I am the vine, you are the branches. If you remain in Me and I in you, you will bear much fruit; apart from Me you can do nothing" (Matthew 15:5). Apart from Christ our efforts are unfruitful. The only way to live a fully good life is to stay close to the Lord.

Lord, we thank You and praise You! There is nothing and nobody like You! We pray for a more perfect understanding of who You are, of Your love, and that we would continue to grow in all grace—in faith, humility, knowledge, and love. Thank You, Jesus! Amen.

---

1. Charles Spurgeon, *Morning and Evening*, Updated Edition, (Grand Rapids: Discovery House Publishers, 2016), 14.

JANUARY 5TH

Whatever you do, work at it with all your heart, as working for the Lord, not for human masters, since you know that you will receive an inheritance from the Lord as a reward. It is the Lord Christ you are serving.

COLOSSIANS 3:23-24

G ood morning! We live in a world overly concerned about status and position, always looking for recognition for everything we do. God's recognition is worth so much more than any human praise we will ever earn or receive! Jesus does not encourage us to pursue recognition and position. On the contrary, we are not to live for the approval of others, but to be humble in everything we say and do.

"*But when you give to the needy, do not let your left hand know what your right hand is doing, so that your giving may be in secret. Then your Father, who sees what is done in secret, will reward you*" (Matthew 6:3-4).

Our motive for whatever we do is to be without selfish intent, done without a show ("done in secret") and with no expectation of reward or praise. God sees everything, and it is Him we aim to please. "*Be careful not to practice your righteousness in front of others to be seen by them. If you do, you will have no reward from your Father in heaven*" (Matthew 6:1). Our motive should come out of humility and a desire to serve God and others.

Lord, thank You for the privilege of serving You and others. May we commit all we do to You, trusting in You and finding our fulfillment in Your purpose for our lives. All we need comes from Your hand, and our ultimate desire is to please You. Thank You, Jesus! Amen.

JANUARY 6TH

May the favor of the Lord our God rest on us; establish the work of our hands for us—yes, establish the work of our hands.

PSALM 90:17

Good morning! One touch of God's favor can turn lives around. Without His favor, we will find it difficult to face the atrocities, wickedness and corruption abounding in this world. Our days are numbered, and we should want our work to count, to be effective and productive. The favor of God takes a believer to places where money and qualifications cannot. The favor of God will bring opportunities into our lives that skill and hard work cannot bring. If all we have has come only through toil and sweat, then we are leading a very difficult life. If we feel dissatisfied with this life and its imperfections, we must remember God's favor. Favor is God's grace in our lives. We can't earn His favor, and we aren't entitled to it. But for those who walk with the Lord, life will be fruitful, *like a tree planted by streams of water* (Psalm 1:3).

Keep His commandments. Walk in His Spirit. Be compassionate, tenderhearted, full of His grace, mercy, and love. If we do these things, our lives and our ministry will be a blessing to others. Fruitful living is not gauged by earthly measures, but by how we further the kingdom of God on earth.

Lord, we want to be diligent in obeying Your will and living in Your favor. May we always seek to please You, to never let go of who You are and of Your promises, that we would be a blessing to others. May the measure of our success always be for Your kingdom, honor, and glory. Thank You, Jesus! Amen.

JANUARY 7TH

He has shown you, O mortal, what is good. And what does the Lord require of you? To act justly and to love mercy and to walk humbly with your God.

MICAH 6:8

Good morning! Are we in the place where God wants us to be? Micah 6:8 gives us a clear and simple statement of what God wants of us—God wants changed lives. He wants His people to be fair, just, merciful, and humble.

Therefore, I urge you, brothers and sisters, in view of God's mercy, to offer your bodies as a living sacrifice, holy and pleasing to God—this is your true and proper worship. Do not conform to the pattern of this world, but be transformed by the renewing of your mind. Then you will be able to test and approve what God's will is—His good, pleasing and perfect will (Romans 12:1-2).

God wants us to become living sacrifices for Him, living rightly. He has perfect plans for our lives. In our efforts to please God, to be where God wants us to be, we must ask ourselves: Are we fair in our dealings with others? Do we show mercy to those who wrong us? Are we learning humility? It is impossible to follow God consistently without His transforming love in our hearts and an active intentional desire to follow Him. We need to be transformed, offering ourselves, daily laying aside our own desires to seek after Him and His will. Trust Him and He will guide us.

Lord, may we be a people after Your own heart—fair, just, merciful, and humble. Thank You for providing Your Word as our guidebook to show us what it means to live rightly. Teach us and show us through Your Word and give us willing hearts to follow You. Thank You, Jesus! Amen.

JANUARY 8TH

See, forget the former things; do not dwell on the past. See, I am doing a new thing! Now it springs up; do you not perceive it? I am making a way in the wilderness and streams in the wasteland.

ISAIAH 43:18-19

G ood morning! Do we believe that God will make a way? When we are faced with the hauntings of our past, the circumstances we don't understand, or when life seems too much to handle, God will make a way. God is not limited by our past or our circumstances, nor is He surprised by them. He will make a way when and where there seems to be no way. He works in ways we cannot see and do not understand. He is God—and we are not.

You will keep in perfect peace those whose minds are steadfast, because they trust in You. Trust in the Lord forever, for the Lord, the Lord Himself, is the Rock eternal (Psalm 26:3-4).

With God, we can know perfect peace even in our times of turmoil. What are you facing today that is challenging your faith in God's sovereignty? Release it *to Him who is able* (Ephesians 3:20).

Trust in the Lord with all your heart and lean not on your own understanding; in all your ways submit to Him, and He will make your paths straight (Proverbs 3:5-6). Trust God to be God in your life, in all circumstances. Watch and see what He will do.

Lord, we surrender all to You, trusting in Your all-sufficient grace, Your enabling power, and Your sovereign working in our lives. We know You are able, and Your ways far exceed our own. Lord, we submit to Your will and choose to follow where You lead. Thank You, Jesus! Amen.

JANUARY 9TH

And a voice from heaven said, "This is My Son, whom I love;
with Him I am well-pleased."

MATTHEW 3:17

Good morning! What fills God's heart should also fill our hearts. Is Jesus Christ the desire of our heart? Are we spending personal time with the Lord, deepening our understanding of and passion for who He is?

While he was still speaking, a bright cloud covered them, and a voice from the cloud said, "This is My Son, whom I love, with Him I am well-pleased. Listen to Him!" (Matthew 17:5).

There is no one like Jesus. He is not just a good speaker, an influential leader, or a great prophet. He is the Son of God, and God commanded us, "Listen to Him!" The Lord is pleased with His Son because His Son listened to Him. Jesus did nothing without His Father's bidding—even though they are One and the same.

The Son is the image of the invisible God, the firstborn over all created. For in Him all things were created; things in heaven and on earth, visible and invisible, whether thrones or powers or rulers or authorities; all things have been created through Him and for Him. He is before all things, and in Him all things hold together (Colossians 1:15-17).

If we understand this profound truth, our response should be nothing less than the highest worship. Our hearts should belong to Him, and we should desire nothing more than to praise Him and to "Listen to Him!"

Lord, You are the Sustainer of life. We humbly bow before You, Lord, with a sacrifice of praise and hearts full of love. Just as You were One with Your Father, may we be one with You and do what pleases You. Thank You, Jesus! Amen.

JANUARY 10TH

"Come, follow me," Jesus said, "and I will send you out to fish for people."

MATTHEW 4:19

G ood morning! How have we responded to Jesus' invitation to follow Him? Peter and Andrew, James and John, responded immediately: *At once they left their nets and followed Him* (Matthew 4:20). There were others Jesus invited that didn't accept His invitation—the rich young ruler, for example.

"Sell everything you have and give to the poor, and you will have treasure in heaven. Then come, follow me." When he heard this, he became very sad, because he was very wealthy. Jesus looked at him and said, "How hard it is for the rich to enter the kingdom of God!" (Luke 18:22-24).

Jesus' call to follow Him is an invitation to a spiritually productive life, to become more like Him, with our thinking anchored in God's Word. *Whoever says he abides in Him ought to walk in the same way in which He walked* (1 John 2:6).

To walk today as Jesus did, we must obey His teachings and imitate His example of complete obedience to God and loving service to others. And because Jesus is the image of God in human form (Colossians 1:15; Hebrews 1: 3), as we become more and more like Him, the image of God is increasingly restored in our lives. Our lives are being transformed by the renewing of our minds (Romans 12:2). We no longer conform to the ways of this world but to the one Way that pleases God.

Lord, open our hearts and minds to following You. May we gain a clearer knowledge of You, growing in faith and love, by first trusting to follow You as Messiah, Son of God, and then living it out in our everyday lives in all we think, say, and do. Thank You, Jesus! Amen.

JANUARY 11TH

Praise be to the God and Father of our Lord Jesus Christ,
the Father of compassion and the God of all comfort,
who comforts us in all our troubles, so that we can comfort those
in any trouble with the comfort we ourselves receive from God.

2 CORINTHIANS 1:3–4

Good morning! The seeds of comfort take root in the soil of adversity. When our lives seem to be falling apart, God is there. We may not escape the adversity, but God—we find His comfort. Being comforted doesn't always mean our troubles vanish, but it can mean we receive strength, encouragement, and the hope necessary to deal with our troubles. And through every trial we endure, we are equipped to comfort others who suffer a similar situation.

"Comfort, comfort My people," says your God (Isaiah 40:1). God told Isaiah to "comfort" and "speak tenderly" to Jerusalem in their years of trouble. Our tests make up our testimony; our mess creates our message. The experiences of our lives are used for our benefit AND the benefit of others. The most substantial comfort we have is the encouragement of God's Word, hope for today, and the knowledge we will one day be with God.

Lord, thank You for our trials, Your comfort, and the comfort we are able to share with others. May we have eyes to see, ears to hear, and hearts filled with Your compassion and love for others, that we would share the comfort we receive from You. Thank You, Jesus! Amen.

JANUARY 12TH

Consequently, faith comes from hearing the message,
and the message is heard through the word about Christ.

ROMANS 10:17

Good morning! It is impossible to believe in something or someone we've never heard of. Those who hear the good news of the gospel and redemption in Jesus can have faith in Christ and accept His eternal salvation. Faith is God's gift poured into the hearts of the hearers through the power of the Holy Spirit.

For it is by grace you have been saved, through faith—and this is not from yourselves, it is the gift of God—not by works, so that no one can boast (Ephesians 2:8-9).

Faith is one of the fruits of the Spirit (Galatians 5:22-23). The Spirit produces these character traits that are found in the nature of Christ. They are the by-products of Christ's control—we can't obtain them by trying to get them without His help. If we want faith to grow in us, our lives must be joined to Christ.

So then, just as you received Christ Jesus as Lord, continue to live your lives in Him, rooted and built up in Him, strengthened in the faith as you were taught, and overflowing with thankfulness (Colossians 2:6-7). God expects us to have faith, to grow in faith, and to remain connected to Him. He is our source of growth and faith.

Lord, we believe You are who You say You are. We believe in Your promises. We believe You will do what You said You will do. Lord, grow our faith as we lean into You and Your Word. May we live out the faith that comes from You and our belief in You. Thank You, Jesus! Amen.

JANUARY 13TH

You were taught, with regard to your former way of life, to put off your old self, which is being corrupted by its deceitful desires; to be made new in the attitude of your minds; and to put on the new self, created to be like God in true righteousness and holiness.

EPHESIANS 4:22-24

Good morning! New year, new self? We're nearing mid-January. has our enthusiasm for spiritual growth waned like so many of our New Year's resolutions? If we are believers in and followers of Christ, people should see a difference in the way we live. Living the Christian life is a process that takes intentional effort and a strong desire. We must put our old way of thinking and our bad habits behind us as we seek and listen to God. We must make a daily commitment to change because although we have a new nature, we don't automatically think good thoughts and express right attitudes.

Follow God's example, therefore, as dearly beloved children and walk in the way of love, just as Christ loved us and gave Himself up for us as a fragrant offering and sacrifice to God (Ephesians 5:1-2). Our love for others should go beyond simple affection, to imitate the self-sacrificing love of Christ.

Lord, may we grow more like You each day. Thank You for loving us so much that You sacrificed Yourself so we might live. We pray our love for You would continue to grow and manifest itself into love for others, a love like Yours—a love that goes beyond affection to self-sacrificing service. Thank You, Jesus! Amen.

JANUARY 14TH

You are my hiding place; You will protect me from trouble and surround me with songs of deliverance. I will instruct you and teach you in the way you should go; I will counsel you with My loving eye on you.

PSALM 32:7-8

Good morning! We have a Shepherd who loves us, who guides, leads, and protects us. We have no reason to fear what lies ahead; He's been there, and He knows the way. *"I am the good shepherd. I know My own sheep and My own sheep know me—just as the Father knows Me and I know the Father—and I lay down My life for the sheep"* (John 10:14-15).

What is our fear, our anxiety? He is the Mighty One, and He is with us always. God longs to guide us with His love and His wisdom. He offers to teach us and show us the way we should go. But oh, how stubborn we are!

Do not be like the horse or the mule, which have no understanding but must be controlled by bit and bridle or they will not come to you (Psalm 32:9).

God offers us the best way to go, and He longs to guide us with His love and wisdom. What is keeping us from Him today? Are we stubbornly insisting on our way? If we want to lead effective, productive lives for Him, it starts with accepting and obeying God's Word. Follow the Good Shepherd, for He loves us.

Lord, You alone are God, holy and good. Lord, we repent of our stubbornness and turn to You. Teach us and guide us, Lord. Your ways are higher than ours. "You order our steps, and we find delight in Your way" (Psalm 37:23). Thank You, Jesus! Amen.

JANUARY 15TH

What I mean, brothers and sisters, is that the time is short.

1 CORINTHIANS 7:29

Good morning! Time is moving fast—it's already mid-January. It seems the older we get, the faster time goes. Are we making the most of our time for what really matters? Paul is urging all believers to make the most of their time before Christ's return. Every person in every generation should have a sense of urgency about knowing and sharing the gospel with others.

Paul went on to urge believers not to regard the things of this world as the ultimate goals for our lives. *For this world in its present form is passing away* (1 Corinthians 7:31). Yes, we need to take care of earthly responsibilities, but we should make efforts to keep life modest and manageable. When material possessions, vacations, and living beyond our means become our lifestyle, we will quickly lose proper perspective and be weighed down by it all. God created us for a purpose—His "goal."

We are God's handiwork, created in Christ Jesus to do good works, which God prepared in advance for us to do (Ephesians 2:10). God has numbered our days and will fulfill every purpose He has for us. *I cry out to God Most High, to God who fulfills His purpose for me* (Psalm 57:2). However, our choices and actions also really matter. We must be mindful of our priorities and the purpose God has set before us.

Lord, thank You for each new day that You give to us. May our hearts overflow with Your love, our minds be set on You, and our desire be fixed on doing the work You set before us. We pray our priorities to be established on what Your purpose is for us to do. Thank You, Jesus! Amen.

JANUARY 16TH

*And we know that in ALL things God works for the good
of those who love Him, who have been called according to His purpose.
For those God foreknew He also predestined to be conformed to the image of
His Son, that He might be the firstborn among many brothers and sisters.
And those He predestined, He also called; those He called, He also justified;
those He justified, He also glorified.*

ROMANS 8:28-30

Good morning! Do you know how special you are? All that happens isn't good, but God knows and is able to turn every circumstance around for our long-range good. God loves us so much that His desire is to use everything in and about our lives to grow us for our good. God is not working to make us "happy" but to fulfill His purpose. This promise is not for everyone. It is claimed by those who love Him and those the Holy Spirit moves in and through. We have a new perspective, trusting in God, not for life's treasures, but for the security found in heaven. God's ultimate goal is to make us like His Son, Jesus Christ, that we will become more and more like Him.

See what great love the Father has lavished on us, that we should be called children of God! And that is what we are! (1 John 3:1). Let us be more intentional in discovering who God intended us to be and what He has purposed for each one of us—for we are His children, loved, saved, and redeemed.

Lord, we thank You for Your everlasting love, beyond our comprehension. We are known by You, our Creator, and You have a purpose for each one of us. Lord, we pray Your Spirit to guide us and protect us until the day we stand in Your presence praising and worshiping You. Thank You, Jesus! Amen.

JANUARY 17TH

But I trust in You, Lord; I say, "You are my God." My times are in Your hands; deliver me from the hands of my enemies, from those who pursue me.

PSALM 31:14-15

Good morning! Are we living in faith with trust and zeal or unbelief in what God will do because of who He is and what He says? The difference between Zechariah's and Mary's responses given to the angel was that Zechariah responded with unbelief and Mary said, *"Let it be to me according to your word"* (Luke 1:38).

Peter, when awakened by the angel while imprisoned by Herod, thought he was dreaming or having a vision when the angel came to free him. But once in the streets outside the prison after the angel left, Peter knew *"for certain that the Lord has sent His angel, and has delivered me ..."* (Acts 12:11).

When Peter knocked on the door at the house of Mary to let them know of his escape, the young servant, Rhoda, displayed faith in the midst of the doubts of all the rest gathered there. *She ran back without opening it and exclaimed, "Peter is at the door!" "You are out of your mind," they told her* (Acts 12:14-15a). Despite the fact they had been ceaselessly praying to God for Peter's release! Rhoda insisted she had seen Peter at the door, but the people had no faith at all. *"It must be his angel"* (15b).

How many times have we prayed and doubted the answer God gave to us? He wants us to have an inward *amen*—a mighty, moving *amen*. This *amen* says, "It is, because God has spoken."

Lord, help our unbelief! May we have an energy and enthusiasm about our faith, confident that nothing is impossible for and with You. We know who You are and whose we are: we belong to You. May our answer always be "Yes" in You and "Amen" to Your glory! Thank You, Jesus! Amen.

JANUARY 18TH

We have this hope as an anchor for the soul, firm and secure.

HEBREWS 6:19a

Good morning! We are so fickle—blown and tossed about by our circumstances and trials as though we have no anchor at all. But God! Yes, Jesus is our hope and anchor who will keep us in the midst of our storms. He is the One who is able to keep us steadfast and unmovable in spite of the tides of life.

God is not blown about like us. He is not moved by all that affects us. The more we get to know God and understand His nature, the more we realize His immensity, and we begin to praise Him through our storms. *I will praise You, Lord my God, with all my heart; I will glorify Your name forever* (Psalm 86:12).

There is no one like our God! He is alive and able to do mighty things for those who put their hope and trust in Him. He is our Father who loves us, and He is faithful to His promises.

Therefore, my dear brothers and sisters, stand firm. Let nothing move you. Always give yourselves fully to the work of the Lord, because you know that your labor in the Lord is not in vain (1 Corinthians 15:58). If we feel as though we are being blown about or sinking in the muck of life, we should call out to the One who saves. He is with us and will not forsake us.

Lord, we need You in our lives to lead us and guide us through the circumstances and trials of this life that can be overwhelming, oftentimes leaving us blowing about like tall grasses of the fields or the waves of the sea. You are our anchor, our strong tower and deliverer. We praise You for who You are, the Lord God Almighty. We put our hope and faith in You. Thank You, Jesus!

JANUARY 19TH

We wait in hope for the Lord; He is our help and our shield. In Him our hearts rejoice, for we trust in His holy name. May Your unfailing love be with us, Lord, even as we put our hope in You.

PSALM 33:20-22

G ood morning! Where are we placing our hope? God is in control of all things, and confidently knowing and believing that allows us to wait and securely put our hope in Him. He is always there to strengthen and help us.

So do not fear, for I am with you; do not be dismayed, for I am your God. I will strengthen you and help you; I will uphold you with My righteous right hand (Isaiah 41:10). We are secure in Him because He never changes. *I the Lord do not change* (Malachi 3:6). *Jesus Christ is the same yesterday and today and forever* (Hebrews 13:8).

His love for us is beyond measure: and to know this love that surpasses knowledge—that you may be filled to the measure of all the fullness of God (Ephesians 3:19).

When we know Jesus, we know we have hope. We can look at life with the assurance of and confidence in Him Who cares for us. *May the God of hope fill you with all joy and peace as you trust in Him, so that you may overflow with hope by the power of the Holy Spirit* (Romans 15:13). All trials and troubles are relieved through our enduring hope in who God is, His love, and ultimate salvation.

Lord, we find our hope in You. You alone are God, worthy of all honor, glory, and praise. In You we find all we need to face each day with confidence in who You are and Your love for us. Thank You for choosing us, saving us, and loving us. We are Yours. Thank You, Jesus! Amen.

JANUARY 20TH

Yet You, Lord, are our Father. We are the clay,
You are the potter; we are all the work of Your hand.

ISAIAH 64:8

Good morning! Have you ever watched a potter at the wheel? The potter works and molds the clay into what he intends it to become. At times the potter has to refashion his work, taking out the offending parts and reshaping his creation. And so it is with us in the hands of God! We were created by God and predestined for His purpose.

Our best efforts without Him are tainted with the sin of man. It is by faith in Jesus Christ that we are made whole, perfected by the hand of God. This necessitates being moldable, pliable, and submissive to God's divine will. Our lives are the work of God's hands. Just like clay in the hands of a potter, He molds and makes us, even breaks us when necessary. God uses all things in our lives to refine us and to shape us into the image of His Son, Jesus Christ.

"Can I not do with you, Israel, as this potter does?" declares the Lord (Jeremiah 18:6). Just as the potter has power over the clay, God has power to reshape us to conform to His will and purpose. Do not fight the Maker's hands, but fully trust in Him. Our God makes no mistakes!

Lord, have Your way! Like clay in the hands of a potter, mold us as You will, that we would be vessels for You. Fill us, Lord, with Your living water, that we would be springs that pour water over Your fields and quench the thirst of Your flock. All the praise, glory, and honor are Yours forever. Thank You, Jesus! Amen.

JANUARY 21ST

"The King will reply, 'Truly I tell you, whatever you did for one of the least of these brothers and sisters of Mine, you did for Me.'"

MATTHEW 25:40

Good morning! Are we doing our best in service to others? We are presented opportunities each and every day to bring Jesus to other people. How do we respond? Are we embracing them the way we would if it were Jesus standing in front of us?

The parable Jesus told in Matthew 25 shares what it means to be ready for His return and what our posture and activity should be until He comes. *"For I was hungry and you gave Me nothing to eat, I was thirsty and you gave Me nothing to drink, I was a stranger and you did not invite Me in, I needed clothes and you did not clothe Me, I was sick and in prison and you did not look after Me"* (Matthew 25:42-43).

We have no excuse to neglect those in need. The acts of mercy Jesus described are not dependent on wealth, ability, or intelligence. They are simple needs to be met by compassionate hearts who freely give. Jesus demands our personal involvement in caring for each other. We are to love every person and serve anyone we can, as though they were Jesus Himself. *"Truly I tell you, whatever you did for one of the least of these brothers and sisters of mine, you did for Me"* (Matthew 25:40). Such active love for others glorifies God by reflecting our love for Him and demonstrating His love for us.

Lord, where would we be if it weren't for Your grace, mercy, forgiveness, and love? As You have freely given to us, may we, too, give generously in serving others. There is always something we are able to do for another to share Your compassion and love. Thank You, Jesus! Amen.

JANUARY 22ND

Consider it pure joy, my brothers and sisters, whenever you face trials of many kinds, because you know that the testing of your faith produces perseverance. Let perseverance finish its work so that you may be mature and complete, not lacking anything.

JAMES 1:2-4

Good morning! Embrace your trials as friends. They are intended for our growth and maturity that we cannot get any other way. The point is not to pretend our way through as though nothing were happening, and we are not to fall into "stinking thinking."

Our attitude impacts our circumstances and their results. When we have a positive outlook ("consider it pure joy"), we recognize what trials can produce in our lives. Turn hardships into times of learning. We don't know the depth of our character until we see how we react under pressure.

Not only so, but we also glory in our sufferings, because we know that suffering produces perseverance; perseverance, character; and character, hope (Romans 5:3-4). God desires to make us mature and complete, and we know He is using life's difficulties to build our character and deepen our trust in Him. We don't get to choose life's trials, but we can choose our response to be in Christ Jesus.

Lord, teach us how to respond to our trials with an attitude befitting of You, with perseverance and confidence that these are opportunities to grow. Help us to deal with them in Your strength. We are trusting in You, that in all things You work for the good of those who love You (Romans 8:28). Thank You, Jesus! Amen.

JANUARY 23RD

Finally, brothers and sisters, whatever is true, whatever is noble, whatever is right, whatever is pure, whatever is lovely, whatever is admirable—if anything is excellent or praiseworthy—think about such things.

PHILIPPIANS 4:8

Good morning! If we are to be transformed to become more like Jesus, we need to reflect His character. There is a principle in computer science that says, "garbage in, garbage out," which essentially means the quality of system output is determined by the quality of the input. And so it is with our minds. What we put into our minds determines what comes out in our words and actions. If we are not programming our minds with quality thoughts, the results will be impure thinking and actions. To become more like Jesus, we must replace harmful input with wholesome material.

In your relationships with one another, have the same mindset as Christ Jesus (Philippians 2:5). Jesus was humble and surrendered to His Father's will, giving up His rights in order to obey God and serve others. *For those God foreknew He also predestined to be conformed to the image of His Son, that He might be the firstborn among many brothers and sisters* (Romans 8:29). The more closely we follow Jesus, the more we will be like Him, and that is God's ultimate goal for us.

Lord, help us to focus our minds on what is good and pure. Help us to be transformed into the men and women You are calling us to be—that You designed us to be. We want to be more like You, that our lives would bring honor and glory to You and draw others to know You. Thank You, Jesus! Amen.

JANUARY 24TH

See to it, brothers and sisters,
that none of you has a sinful, unbelieving heart that turns away
from the living God. But encourage one another daily, as long as it is called
"Today," so that none of you may be hardened by sin's deceitfulness.

HEBREWS 3:12-13

Good morning! Our unbelief robs us from the blessings God has promised, and we miss out on our inheritance. Our hearts are turned away from God when we stubbornly refuse to believe Him. If we persist in our unbelief, God will eventually leave us alone in our sin. The Israelites wandered the desert for forty years as a result of their unbelief. They did not believe that God could help them. One way to prevent having an unbelieving heart is to remain in fellowship with other believers, sharing in mutual faith, being aware of the deceitfulness of sin that divides and destroys, and encouraging each other with love and concern. *Therefore encourage one another and build each other up, just as in fact you are doing* (1 Thessalonians 5:11).

Having Christian fellowship is vital in our daily lives to provide accountability and encouragement as we grow in our belief and develop faith. A word of encouragement at the right time can make a big difference in the midst of difficulty, and a listening ear is often a welcome help. Being sensitive to those around us and aware of another's needs can open doors to conversation and create opportunities to share Jesus at just the right time.

Lord, thank You for the opportunities You give us to encourage one another in faith and to share in accountability with each other. Forgive us when our hearts are weak in faith. May we remain firm in our belief and strong in encouragement toward others. We are grateful for the fellowship of believers and the chance to share You with others. Thank You, Jesus! Amen.

JANUARY 25TH

I am not saying this because I am in need, for I have learned to be content whatever the circumstances. I know what it is to be in need, and I know what it is to have plenty. I have learned the secret of being content in any and every situation, whether well fed or hungry, whether living in plenty or in want. I can do all this through Him who gives me strength.

PHILIPPIANS 4:11–13

Good morning! Did you ever notice our tendency to be dissatisfied or discontent, to covet the things we don't have? When we're short, we want to be tall, and the tall want to be short. Curly-haired people long for straight, and those with straight hair "would do anything" for curls or waves. When we're young, we want to be older, and the old long for their younger years. We're never content with the changing seasons, complaining that it's too hot, too cold, too wet, too dry. We upsize, then turn around and downsize our homes, and flip the bigger car we traded up only to trade down for smaller. The list is endless, and none of it proves to be of any gain.

Paul learned how to be content in ALL circumstances because he relied on the power of Christ Jesus for strength. Paul's priorities were in proper order. He was grateful for everything God provided, and his focus was on eternity. *And my God will meet all your needs according to the riches of His glory in Christ Jesus* (Philippians 4:19). We can trust God to always meet our needs, not necessarily our wants. Our contentment lies in the security of knowing whose we are, not in what we have.

Lord, all we need is found in You. Forgive us, Lord, for complaining and having a disgruntled demeanor. Lord, we put our trust in You, accepting Your provision with a grateful heart and a deeper desire to live for You. Thank You, Jesus! Amen.

JANUARY 26TH

Because of the Lord's great love we are not consumed, for His compassions never fail. They are new every morning; great is Your faithfulness.

LAMENTATIONS 3:22-23

Good morning! Each day is a new beginning, a gift, and an opportunity to start again. I've heard it said that each morning we start with two things for which to praise God—our two eyes opening to see another day. God gives mercy for each day, and it is refilled and refreshed each morning. We should wake up excited for the possibilities God is going to lay out before us each day and embrace the life He's given us. *This is the day the Lord has made; let us rejoice and be glad in it* (Psalm 128:24).

The beauty of the day is not that it is new, but that we are being made new. The glory of the day is not that it marks a change, but that we are being changed. If we choose to set our eyes on what God is doing and join Him in His activity, the change continues, and more is revealed.

For it is God who works in you to will and to act in order to fulfill His good purpose (Philippians 2:13). Whatever we have, wherever we are, God gives us the desire and the power to do what pleases Him. The secret to a changed life is to submit to God's control and let Him work.

Lord, may we embrace this day with our eyes fixed on You, with an attitude of gratitude, and willing hearts to go wherever You send us. This day is Yours— You made it, You invite us into it, it belongs to You. Help us to make the most of it, centered in Your will and Your way. Thank You, Jesus! Amen.

JANUARY 27TH

"If you can?" said Jesus. "Everything is possible for one who believes."

MARK 9:23

Good morning! What is stronger—your faith or your doubting? Do you fully believe what Jesus says? Our battle with Satan is real. It is a difficult and ongoing struggle. Our victory over sin and temptation comes through faith in Jesus Christ, never through our own efforts.

The attitude of trust and confidence that the Bible calls belief or faith (Hebrews 11:1, 6) is not something we can obtain without help. Faith is a gift from God. *For it is by grace you have been saved, through faith—and this is not from yourselves, it is the gift of God—not by works, so that no one can boast* (Ephesians 2:8-9).

No matter how much faith we have, we never reach the point of self-sufficiency. Faith is not stored away like money in the bank. It is alive and active. Growing in faith is a constant process of renewing our trust in Jesus. God desires to bring us to a definite place of unswerving faith and confidence in Him, and Him alone. *Immediately the boy's father exclaimed, "I do believe; help me overcome my unbelief!"* (Mark 9:24.) Let us not be hindered by doubt but strengthened in faith.

Lord, Your plan is for us to believe and to be saved. Your word says if we will believe, we will see Your glory (John 11:40). We pray for Your work and will to be done in and through us. May we not be a people that frustrates You with our wavering ways, but that we would be amongst those You call Your "good and faithful servants." Thank You, Jesus! Amen.

JANUARY 28TH

So Christ Himself gave ... to equip His people for works of service,
so that the body of Christ may be built up until we all reach unity in the faith
and in the knowledge of the Son of God and become mature,
attaining the whole measure of the fullness of Christ.

EPHESIANS 4:11-13

Good morning! We live in a competitive world where each person plots and plans how best to get ahead, to gain the promotion, to earn the larger salary, to get the best education, to win the grand title. But God! What does He say? We need to "build others up"! God uses people to do His work. And He is the One who gives us the talents and the resources to do that very thing He is calling us to do!

We have different gifts, according to the grace given to each of us (Romans 12:6). Everyone has some special gifts and talents to be used for the building up of others and in service to God in the building up of His kingdom. Our role is to be faithful and to seek ways to serve according to the gifts we've been given. *Each of you should use whatever gift you have received to serve others, as faithful stewards of God's grace in its various forms* (1 Peter 4:10).

Our abilities are not intended for our own enjoyment but to be used for others and for God's glory. Take time to discover the gifts and talents God's given and use them as a method of praising God for all He has done, is doing, and will continue to do in and through us.

Lord, You have equipped us with unique gifts and talents to serve alongside fellow believers and to serve others. Help us to know who we are and the gifts You've given us for Your service, Lord. We pray that we use Your gifts wisely, pleasing and glorifying You. Thank You, Jesus! Amen.

JANUARY 29TH

"Therefore, if you are offering your gift at the altar and there remember that your brother or sister has something against you, leave your gift there in front of the altar. First go and be reconciled to them; then come and offer your gift."

MATTHEW 5:23-24

Good morning! Broken relationships and hardened hearts are a hindrance in our life to our relationship with others and with God, and they keep us from receiving the blessing of His peace. The problems and grievances we hold in our hearts, justifying them through repeating old tapes and bad memories, are the very ills that hold us captive and block the freedom of a living relationship with our God.

Jesus is able and wants to set us free! We cannot love God from a heart that is poisoned with sin, hatred, anger, and resentment. Our attitudes toward others reflect our relationship with God. We are of little value—like salt with no flavor (Matthew 5:13) or a light covered by a bushel (Matthew 5:15)—when we are content to justify wrong thinking and marginalized living. If we are too much like the world, we are of little or no use to build God's kingdom. We are not meant to blend into the sameness of society, but to stand out for and in Christ. Our lives should demonstrate Christ's character and positively impact the people around us.

Lord, cleanse our hearts from the sin that blocks us from being effective witnesses for You. Give us a boldness to speak up, to not "go with the crowd," but to shine brightly and positively impact others who so desperately need You. Thank You for loving us so much that You came to save us and set us free at a cost to Yourself that we can never fully comprehend or repay. Thank You, Jesus! Amen.

JANUARY 30TH

You do not delight in sacrifice, or I would bring it;
You do not take pleasure in burnt offerings.
My sacrifice, O God, is a broken spirit;
a broken and contrite heart You, God, will not despise.

PSALM 51:16-17

Good morning! There is a question we need to ask ourselves: are we just being religious or are we truly in Christ? The Pharisees and religious leaders were obsessed with religion, and following rules and laws, but they missed the Savior right in their midst. We can never please God by following rules and by outward appearances and actions if our inward heart attitude is not right. God looks at the condition of our hearts! Are we repentant of our sin? Do we genuinely desire oneness with and in Christ? Are we sincere about turning away from our idols that draw us away from our relationship with Jesus?

Create in me a pure heart, O God, and renew a steadfast spirit within me. Do not cast me from Your presence or take Your Holy Spirit from me. Restore to me the joy of Your salvation and grant me a willing spirit, to sustain me (Psalm 51:10-12).

Born as sinners, our natural inclination is to please ourselves rather than God. As we invite God in and ask Him to cleanse our hearts and fill us with His thoughts and desires, we become open for right conduct and God's right way of thinking to enter in. God is not interested in rule followers. His desire for us is a deep relationship with Him, for us to experience the full and complete life He's planned for us.

Lord, we repent of our sinful ways and wrong thinking, of our concern for following rules that lead us away from focusing on a living relationship with You. Thank You, Lord, for never leaving us or giving up on us. Forgive us and renew us, Lord, in Your Spirit. Thank You, Jesus! Amen.

JANUARY 31ST

The Lord delights in those who fear Him,
who put their hope in His unfailing love.

PSALM 147:11

Good morning! If there is one whom we should want to delight, it should be the Lord our God! We muddle around trying to figure ourselves out—to understand what we want, how we feel, what's wrong with us, or what we should do about things. And yet all the while, God's understanding has no limit—He understands us fully. *Great is our Lord and mighty in power; His understanding has no limit* (Psalm 147:5).

Let us take our minds off ourselves and focus them on God. The more we lean into God and His ways, the better we will understand ourselves. And our efforts to know God more increase our striving to become more like Him. God desires our reverence (fear) and trust. Why? Because when He has those, He is able to use our skills and strengths in the ways He intends—for our good and far better, even greater, than we could ever imagine.

Give praise to the Lord, proclaim His name; make known to the nations what He has done. Sing to Him, sing praise to Him; tell of all His wonderful acts. Glory in His holy name; let the hearts of those who seek the Lord rejoice. Look to the Lord and His strength; seek His face always (1 Chronicles 16:8–11). Let us find ways to delight in the Lord. God's presence surrounds us, and that alone is reason to praise Him!

Lord, we delight in Your presence, and we want to honor You, to bring delight to You! Lord, may our lives be a testimony to You, to Your works in and through us. Thank You, Jesus, for loving us, for saving us. May we serve You faithfully. Thank You, Jesus! Amen.

February

FEBRUARY 1ST

All Scripture is breathed out by God and profitable for teaching, for reproof, for correction, and for training in righteousness, that the man of God may be complete, equipped for every good work.

2 TIMOTHY 3:16-17

Good morning! God's Word is not a buffet line from which we pick and choose. It takes all the truth to make it God's Word. Even if no man ever read or believed one word of it, the Bible would still be, is, and will always be completely true and right. The Bible is God's Word! *For the word of the Lord is right, and all His work is done in truth* (Psalm 33:4). All God's Word can be trusted and is reliable. God cannot and does not lie. He doesn't change His mind or ignore His Promises. *"So is My word that goes out from My mouth: It will not return to Me empty, but will accomplish what I desire and achieve the purpose for which I sent it* (Isaiah 55:11).

We must study and know God's Word so we are able to withstand the devil and his schemes. *Study to show thyself approved unto God, a workman that needeth not to be ashamed, rightly dividing the word of truth* (2 Timothy 2:15). We will never be effective disciples, ministers of God's Word, if we don't know what it says, lack understanding, and are not able to stand firm in our faith.

Thank You, Lord, for Your Word that teaches, rebukes, corrects, and equips us to do the work You prepared in advance for us to do. Protect us that we would not compromise on Your Word; that we would not add or take away from Your Truth but abide in You and in every Word You speak. Thank You, Jesus! Amen.

FEBRUARY 2ND

And Jesus answered him, saying, "It is written, that man shall not live by bread alone, but by every Word of God."

LUKE 4:4

Good morning! A challenging question to consider: if we have enough time to post daily updates to social media, scroll through endless reels, binge watch favorite shows or whatever else we consume, how can we say "I don't have enough time" or "I'm too busy" when it comes to reading the Bible, praying or spending time with God? While we do have responsibilities to fulfill and daily needs to tend to, where does God fit in?

We do not spend time with God to feel invigorated, to make us ready to face the day, or to get us through whatever we are facing. We spend time with God to equip ourselves for this life, to face this world and all that comes from living in it—that we might stand firm, be a light in the darkness, a hope for the lost.

Now may the God of peace ... equip you with everything good for doing His will, and may He work in us what is pleasing to Him, through Jesus Christ, to whom be glory for ever and ever. Amen (Hebrews 13:20-21). Be intentional about time with God and He will change us from within and then use us to serve Him and others.

Lord, may our priority always be You first! Instill in us the desire to seek You, to spend time with You in silence, in prayer and in Your Word. All of life makes more sense with, in and through You. Thank You for loving us, saving us and giving us life through You! Thank You, Jesus! Amen.

FEBRUARY 3RD

Very early in the morning, while it was still dark, Jesus got up, left the house and went off to a solitary place, where He prayed.

MARK 1:35

Good morning! We can learn so much from Jesus—our teacher and Lord. Jesus, the very Son of God, felt it necessary to get up "very early" to go "off to a solitary place, where He prayed." This was a pattern in Jesus' earthly life, to seek time away alone with His Father. Time away from distractions and demands and crowds and noise. "Why?" we might ask. Jesus is God in the flesh. Why did He need and choose to prioritize prayer?

Jesus prayed because He was dependent on His Father, in constant relationship and regular communion with Him. He was one with Him. Clearly prayer was important to Jesus—it was His lifeline and His connection to the Heavenly Father. It equipped Him for the battles He had to face and decisions He had to make. It kept alive the intimate relationship that sustained Him. And it revealed to Him God's desires and direction. So if prayer was this important to Jesus, then it must be even more important for us, His followers. What is our prayer life like? Pray—even if you have to get up very early in the morning to do it!

Lord, may we choose to seek You before we jump into our day, before the busy schedules dominate our thoughts and take over our day. Help us, Lord, to find a quiet place, secluded from the noise and distractions that prevent us from focusing on You. Make a way for us, Lord. We want to be nearer to You, to be still and to listen for Your voice. Thank You for the privilege of prayer and communion with You. Thank You, Jesus! Amen.

FEBRUARY 4TH

"Truly I tell you, if you have faith the size of a mustard seed, you can say to this mountain, 'Move from here to there,' and it will move. Nothing will be impossible for you."

MATTHEW 17:20-21

Good morning! It is the power of God, not the size of our faith, that moves mountains, but faith must be present to do it. When we are feeling weak or powerless, we need to stop and examine our faith, for without it, we can do nothing. *And without faith it is impossible to please God, because anyone who comes to Him must believe that He exists and that He rewards those who earnestly seek Him* (Hebrews 11:6). This verse tells us that even those who act in faith based only on the knowledge of God that they have, will be rewarded.

But God doesn't want us to stop at simply acknowledging He exists. Believing is just the beginning of our life with Christ Jesus. *So then, just as you received Christ Jesus as Lord, continue to live your lives in Him, rooted and built up in Him, strengthened in the faith as you were taught, and overflowing with thankfulness* (Colossians 2:6). God wants our trust, He wants our faith, and He wants our faith to lead us to a deep, personal relationship with Him.

Thank You, Lord, for Your power in our lives. May we diligently seek after You with a faith that trusts and is active, doing what You call us to do. Nothing is impossible with You. Thank You, Jesus! Amen.

FEBRUARY 5TH

Oh, the depth of the riches of the wisdom and knowledge of God! How unsearchable His judgments, and His paths beyond tracing out! "Who has known the mind of the Lord? Or who has been His counselor? Who has ever given to God, that God should repay them?" For from Him and through Him and for Him are all things. To Him be the glory forever. Amen.

ROMANS 11:33-36
(Doxology: prayer of praise for the wisdom of God's plan)

Good morning! God's ways are not our own. His methods and means are far beyond our understanding. The richness of His love is graciously shared and never-ending. Everything we are and everything we have comes from the hand of God. He is in control, and ultimately, we are absolutely dependent on Him. We yield ourselves to Him, knowing He is God.

And He passed in front of Moses, proclaiming, "The Lord, the Lord, the compassionate and gracious God, slow to anger, abounding in love and faithfulness, maintaining love to thousands, and forgiving wickedness, rebellion and sin" (Exodus 34:6-7).

God's glory is revealed in His mercy, grace, compassion, faithfulness, forgiveness, and justice. We did nothing to earn His love, and yet He gave it fully. We could never understand the magnitude of who He is and all He has, is, and will continue to do. God is beyond deserving of our praise.

Lord, You are bigger and greater than anything we could ever imagine. Open our hearts to adore You: fill our souls with a greater love for who You are and all You do. Make us more like You. We worship, praise, and glorify You, our mighty and majestic God. Thank You, Jesus! Amen.

FEBRUARY 6TH

And we know that in all things God works for the good of those who love Him, who have been called according to His purpose.

ROMANS 8:28

Good morning! We have all experienced difficulties, trials, and times of waiting. But how many of us stop to see God's hand in the midst of them? We've been given God's promise, as saved believers who have put our trust in Jesus Christ and love God, that *in all things God works for the good.*

God's ultimate good for us is not just about this world and our conditions here, but true fulfillment and eternal joy in eternity with Him. We live out God's promises through faith, loving God, and living in Christ. We are called to fulfill God's purpose as He works in and through us. *For it is God who works in you to will and to act in order to fulfill His good purpose* (Philippians 2:13).

Nothing we endure in this life is wasted. It is all meaningful for those living in Christ, even through the painful moments and waiting. God's promises are true—yes and amen (2 Corinthians 1:20). There is nothing in this world that God can't use for His good purpose. We put our faith, hope, and trust in Him, the One *who is able to do immeasurably more than all we ask or imagine, according to His power that is at work within us* (Ephesians 3:20).

Lord, we trust the times of trials and troubles will be used for our good. Help us to increase our trust in You and not the things of this life. We know our security is in heaven, and we know the pain of this world is temporary. You are with us, and one day we will join You in eternity. Thank You, Jesus! Amen.

FEBRUARY 7TH

He replied, "My mother and brothers are those
who hear God's Word and put it into practice."

LUKE 8:21

Good morning! God is so, so good! He invites us into a personal relationship with Him. What is Jesus inviting us into through this one statement? Jesus loved His mother (Luke 19:25-27), and He loves us. So much so that He offers us the intimacy of a family relationship with Him, and He tells us how to get it—His family are those who hear and obey God's Word.

For those who are led by the Spirit of God are children of God. The Spirit you received does not make you slaves, so that you live in fear again; rather, the Spirit you received brought about your sonship. And by Him we cry, "Abba, Father." The Spirit Himself testifies with our spirit that we are God's children (Romans 8:14-16).

We have a new relationship with God, adopted into His family. His inward presence, the Holy Spirit, reminds us who we are and encourages us with God's love. Are we experiencing the presence and power of God's love in our lives? If not, if something is lacking, it is not God who has moved; He never leaves His children. He is waiting with open arms for us to return to Him. We are God's children. What a privilege!

Thank You, Lord, for Your invitation into a personal relationship with You. You made a way for us to be called Your sons and daughters, children of God. We surrender our lives to You, in obedience and love, hearers and doers of Your Word. Thank You, Jesus! Amen.

FEBRUARY 8TH

Finally, be strong in the Lord and in His mighty power. Put on the full armor
of God, so that you can take your stand against the devil's schemes.
For our struggle is not against flesh and blood, but against the rulers,
against the authorities, against the powers of this dark world
and against the spiritual forces of evil in the heavenly realms.

EPHESIANS 6:10-12

Good morning! Do we know the enemies we face? They are not the
people we struggle to agree with, don't understand, or find
challenging to get along with. To withstand the real enemies'
attacks, we must depend on God's strength and every piece of His
armor. *Therefore put on the full armor of God, so that when the day of*
evil comes, you may be able to stand your ground, and after you have
done everything, to stand (Ephesians 6:13).

We face a powerful enemy (an army) whose goal is to defeat Christ's
church. Our real enemy will try every device to turn us away from Christ
Jesus and back into sin. But God. *If God is for us, who can be against us?*
(Romans 8:31). There is no one and nothing that can overcome God's
love for us. He must be our priority as we center our lives around His
desires and His teachings, so that our very lives become a constant
prayer, and our strength is grounded in Him. Our victory is already won
in Christ Jesus.

Lord, we stand on Your Word and Your Truth—the victory is already won. The
devil is a defeated foe prowling around with lies and deceit. We put on Your
armor and stand firm on Your rock of salvation. Thank You, Jesus! Amen.

FEBRUARY 9TH

The true light that gives light to everyone was coming into the world.
He was in the world, and though the world was made through Him,
the world did not recognize Him. He came to that which was His own,
but His own did not receive Him.

JOHN 1:9-11

Good morning! Not everyone is prepared to hear and accept the Truth, but we are called to share God's Word and the message of Jesus. God's own creation did not recognize or accept His Son, Jesus Christ. The people chosen by God, who were to prepare the way for Jesus, rejected Him.

"If the world hates you, keep in mind that it hated me first" (John 15:18). The fact is, not everyone will receive the message of Christ. We will offend people, and we will be hated for the Truth. *"If anyone will not welcome you or listen to your words, leave that home or town and shake the dust off your feet"* (Matthew 10:14). The gesture of "shaking the dust off one's feet" signified separation, that the people they were leaving were making a wrong choice.

We strive to speak lovingly and graciously but not apologetically. We must stand firm in our faith and bold in our continuing to share the gospel with others. Some, possibly many, will reject what we are sharing. In essence, they are rejecting God and His Son. Pray for their hearts to be softened and changed, that they would come to a saving knowledge of the Lord Jesus Christ.

Lord, may we boldly share Your Truth without fear of rejection or offense,
trusting You to penetrate the hearts of those who are ready to hear and accept
Your Word as Truth. Open our eyes to see others as You see them, our hearts to
love, and our mouths to speak the Truth You give us to share. Thank You,
Jesus! Amen.

FEBRUARY 10TH

*Praise the Lord, my soul; all my inmost being, praise His Holy Name.
Praise the Lord, my soul, and forget not all His benefits—who forgives all
your sins and heals all your diseases, who redeems your life from the pit and
crowns you with love and compassion, who satisfies your desires
with good things so that your youth is renewed like the eagle's.*

PSALM 103:1-5

Good morning! Count your blessings! In a world and lifetime filled
with difficulties and challenges, we often lack gratitude for
God's great love for us and the rich, undeserved blessings He pours
over us. In many of the psalms that David wrote, his focus was on
praising God for the good things the Lord was doing, even in the
midst of David's most challenging times. We, too, instead of
complaining about life with an Eeyore "woe-is-me" attitude, must
choose to be grateful and give thanks to God.

*Great is the Lord and the most worthy of praise; His greatness no one can
fathom* (Psalm 145:3). We have endless reasons for a grateful heart and
to praise God as we receive His many blessings without deserving any of
them. No matter how difficult our journey, whatever circumstances we
are experiencing right now, we must always count our blessings and
praise our God!

*Lord, we thank You for Your loving kindness and Your steadfast love. May our
hearts be filled with love and thanksgiving for who You are, what You do and
will continue to do in our lives. Our response will always be loving You and
hearts filled with gratitude, praise, and thanksgiving for Your love and many
blessings. Thank You, Jesus. Amen.*

FEBRUARY 11TH

You have searched me, Lord, and You know me. You know when I sit and when I rise; You perceive my thoughts from afar. You discern my going out and my lying down; You are familiar with all my ways.

PSALM 139:1-2

Good morning! God knows everything, and yet many still do not believe in Him and the Son, Jesus, whom He sent. Let it not be so! Biblically, the "heart" refers to our inner moral and spiritual life. God knows our hearts because He knows the motives behind every action. Jesus knew all people thoroughly, their hearts and their thoughts. *Immediately Jesus knew in His spirit that this was what they were thinking in their hearts* (Mark 2:8).

There is no one who perplexes Jesus. No thought or action is unintelligible to Him. He knows its origin and end. And He knows all things that will come to pass. Jesus foretold many things His friends and enemies would do. *"I am telling you before it happens, so that when it does happen, you will believe that I am who I am"* (John 13:19).

Jesus is the divine Son of God—the "I AM" of Exodus 3:14. He is our "All in all"—omnipresent (exists everywhere all at once), omnipotent (all-powerful), and omniscient (all-knowing). God knows everything, has the power to do anything, and is perfectly good.

Lord, we believe You are who You say You are, and You do what You say You will do. In our moments of weakness, Lord, strengthen us with Your Word. Increase in us our faith, that we would "be called oaks of righteousness, a planting for the display of Your splendor" (Isaiah 61:3). Thank You, Jesus! Amen.

FEBRUARY 12TH

"You unbelieving and perverse generation," Jesus replied, "how long shall I stay with you? How long shall I put up with you? Bring the boy here to me."

MATTHEW 17:17

Good morning! Jesus spoke these words to His disciples when they asked Him why they weren't able to heal the demon possessed boy. Stop and think about Jesus' words for a moment, and more importantly, to whom He was speaking. This was His response to His disciples—the very men He was closest to. The men who walked with Him every single day for the three years of His earthly ministry. The men who witnessed firsthand His presence, power, and miracles. The very men He was teaching to take the charge of spreading the gospel, to *"Go into all the world and preach the Good News to everyone"* (Mark 16:15).

So what was Jesus saying here? The disciples had been given the authority to do the healing, but they had not yet learned how to appropriate the power of God. Jesus' frustration is with the unbelieving and unresponsive generation. His disciples were merely a reflection of that attitude in this instance. Jesus' purpose was not to criticize the disciples, but to encourage them to a greater faith.

Faith is believing in the Word of God. There is no "if" in faith, but "when." It is the power of God, not our faith, that moves mountains, but faith must be present to do so. There is great potential in even the smallest amount of faith when God is with us. Surrender your whole selves to the power of God—believe and be set free to do the things He's called you to do! Examine your faith, making sure you are trusting not in our own abilities to produce results, but in God's.

Thank You, Lord, for who You are in our lives. Lord, increase our belief, grow our faith. You must increase in us as we decrease. Make us effective in growing Your Kingdom by Your Word and Power in us. Thank You, Jesus! Amen.

FEBRUARY 13TH

And the God of all grace, who called you to his eternal glory in Christ,
after you have suffered a little while, will Himself restore you
and make you strong, firm and steadfast.

1 PETER 5:10

Good morning! Sunshine-filled days are always appreciated more after we've experienced the clouds and the rain. And that's how it is with our faith—it increases through experiencing the tough times. When we are suffering and faced with adversity, we often feel as though our pain will never end—that the clouds and rain are here forever. Peter's words offer us the encouragement that compared to eternity, our suffering lasts only "a little while."

Jesus is the only answer! All of God's faithful followers are assured of an eternal life where there will be no suffering, no pain, and no tears. *The Lord is close to the brokenhearted and saves those who are crushed in spirit. The righteous person may have many troubles, but the Lord delivers him from them all* (Psalm 34:18-19). God promises to be "close to the brokenhearted," to be our source of power, courage, and wisdom, helping us through our problems (the clouds and the rain). There is no brighter son-shine than Jesus!

Lord, we put our hope and trust in You! We admit that we need You and we thank and praise You for being with us through the storms. You are our hope, our strength, our Light in the darkness. "And we know that in all things God works for the good of those who love Him, who have been called according to His purpose." (Romans 8:28). Thank You, Jesus! Amen.

FEBRUARY 14TH

Jesus answered, "I am the way and the truth and the life.
No one comes to the Father except through Me."

JOHN 14:6

G ood morning! Jesus is the answer to every hard problem of the heart! This is one of the most basic and important passages in Scripture—the answer to the question: "How can we know the way to God?" Only through Jesus! Some would argue that this way is too narrow. In reality, it is wide enough for the whole world if the world chooses to accept it!

"*Enter through the narrow gate. For wide is the gate and broad is the road that leads to destruction, and many enter through it. But small is the gate and narrow the road that leads to life, and only a few find it*" (Matthew 7:13-14). The narrow gate leads to eternal life. It is narrow not because of the size of its width or its difficulty, but because there is only One Way— believing in Jesus. He is our only Way to Heaven, to the Father, to God, because Jesus alone died for our sins and made us right before God.

The only way we can know that we are on that narrow way and that we will make it through that narrow gate is when we are in union with Christ, when we have Christ's righteousness as our own by grace through faith, clothed in it, and in union with Him.

Lord, thank You for making a way for us, sinners saved by grace, forgiven and set free by Your mercy. You paid the price that we might choose the narrow path set before us. Thank You for providing a sure Way to get to God, Your Father, and to our eternal home. You are the only living Way! Thank You, Jesus! Amen.

FEBRUARY 15TH

*Let us not become weary in doing good, for at the proper time we will reap
a harvest if we do not give up. Therefore, as we have opportunity, let us
do good to all people, especially those who belong to the family of believers.*

GALATIANS 6:9-10

G ood morning! What is our motivation for doing good? It can be
discouraging to continue to do right and receive no word of
thanks or see no tangible results. Paul was challenging the Galatians
(and us) to keep on doing good and to trust God for the results. As
soon as we let our expectations enter in, we set ourselves up for
disappointment and open the door to resentment.

"*And if you do good to those who are good to you, what credit is that to
you? Even sinners do that? But love your enemies, do good to them, and lend
to them without expecting to get anything back. Then your reward will be
great, and you will be the children of the Most High ...*" (Luke 6:33, 35).

It takes intentional, concise effort to do good regardless of the
recipient's attitude and posture. What is our ultimate goal? Is it to bless
others, to share the love of Christ, freely given to us, with others? "*Be
merciful, just as Your Father is merciful*" (Luke 6:36). Great joy comes from
a generous spirit, giving freely, without expectations of anything in
return. In due time, we will reap a harvest of blessings from God.

*Lord, may we continue to plant seeds of goodness, love, peace and joy that are
pleasing to You. The harvest we will reap comes from Your Hand and will be
beyond our expectations. Lord, may we represent You well. Thank You, Jesus!
Amen.*

FEBRUARY 16TH

To those who through the righteousness of our God and Savior Jesus Christ have received a faith as precious as ours: Grace and peace be yours in abundance through the knowledge of God and of Jesus Christ our Lord.

2 PETER 1:1-2

Good morning! We all like to hear about and receive the benefits, but are we willing to put in the efforts and work required? "Grace and peace in abundance"—oh, yes please!!! But are we willing to put forth the effort to gain the "knowledge of God and His Son Jesus"? We want the privileges without getting to know Him better through the study of His Word, devotionals, and time in prayer.

His divine power has given us everything we need for a godly life through our knowledge of Him who has called us by His own glory and goodness. Through these He has given us His very great and precious promises, so that through them you may participate in the divine nature, having escaped the corruption in the world caused by evil desires (2 Peter 1:3-4).

The power to grow doesn't come from within us, but from God. We don't have the resources to be truly godly. God allows us to "participate in the divine nature" in order to keep us from sin and help us live for Him. Take time to be with the Lord in study, prayer, and listening for His voice.

Lord, we seek more knowledge of who You are, to be in a living relationship with You. Thank You for our rebirth, for Your Spirit in us, and for Your Grace, peace and love. More of You, less of us. Thank You, Jesus! Amen.

FEBRUARY 17TH

But as for you, continue in what you have learned and have become convinced of, because you know those from whom you learned it, and how from infancy you have known the Holy Scriptures, which are able to make you wise for salvation through faith in Christ Jesus.

2 TIMOTHY 3:14-15

Good morning! We must take away the things from our lives that interfere with our relationship with God. Smith Wigglesworth said, "We need a conscience that does not allow one thing to come into and stay in our lives to break up our fellowship with God and shatter our faith in Him."[2]

We must not allow "stinking thinking" and the lies that surround us in our society to distort or crowd out God's eternal truth. Spend time each and every day reflecting on the foundation of our Christian faith found in God's Word, the great truths that build up and into our lives. We put our lives into God's Hands, finding confidence in His strength and protection.

But I trust in You, Lord; I say, "You are my God" (Psalm 31:14). We set our hearts and minds on Christ Jesus who strengthens us. *Since then, you have been raised with Christ, set your hearts on things above, where Christ is seated at the right hand of God. Set your minds on things above, not on earthly things* (Colossians 3:1-2). We strive to put heavenly priorities into daily practice, concentrating on things eternal rather than the temporal of this world. Don't be fooled by lies and hypocrisy but stand firm in your faith. No matter what comes your way, be tenacious in faith!

Lord, our victory is won in and through You. We stand firm in faith, confident in belief, and ready to fight the battles, knowing they're already won! Lord, may we live lives pleasing to You, and do the work You've set before us well. Thank You, Jesus! Amen.

---

2. Smith Wigglesworth, *Smith Wigglesworth Devotional* (New Kensington: Whitaker House, 1999), 88.

FEBRUARY 18TH

Arise and eat.

1 KINGS 19:5 KJV

G ood morning! Depression and despair can paralyze us, and both are a reality of life. Oswald Chambers says of depression that "a human being is capable of depression, otherwise there would be no capacity for exaltation."[3] The answer is simple: we have to do the next thing and do it in the inspiration of God. The angel did not give Elijah a vision, or explain the Scriptures to him, or do anything remarkable. If we are focused on doing something to overcome depression, we are more likely to deepen the depression. But God! Let His Spirit fill us, guide us, and lead us into His action. Our focus is moved, and healing begins.

And for despair, we find ourselves saying, "It is all done, there is no use trying." The disciples went to sleep when they should have been watching. When they realized what they had done, it produced despair. We've all experienced situations like that in our lives. But Jesus said, *"Rise, let us be going"* (Matthew 26:46). Jesus responded with a spiritual initiative against despair—"get up (arise) and do the next thing." We mustn't let depression and despair stop us or block us from the Power of God in our lives.

What is the next thing? To trust Him absolutely and to pray on the ground of His Redemption. *Trust in Him at all times, you people; pour out your hearts to Him, for God is our refuge* (Psalm 62:8). Give everything to the Lord and see what He will do. *Commit your way to the LORD; trust in Him, and He will act* (Psalm 37:5). We provide a surrendered heart, and God provides the outcome of our stories. "I can't. He can. Let Him."

Lord, whatever we face, we never face it alone. You are with us in the midst of it all, inviting us to do the next thing, and to do it confidently in and with You. We are never alone. Thank You, Jesus! Amen.

---

3. Oswald Chambers, *My Utmost for His Highest* (Grand Rapids: Discovery House, 2017).

FEBRUARY 19TH

For the Spirit God gave us does not make us timid,
but gives us power, love and self-discipline.

2 TIMOTHY 1:7

Good morning! We limit the power of God at work in and through us due to our lack of belief. Don't believe the lies that neutralize our effectiveness for God. The power of the Holy Spirit can help us to overcome obstacles and fears so we can continue to do God's work. The three characteristics of an effective believer Paul mentioned to Timothy (power, love, and self-discipline) are available to us because the Holy Spirit lives in us. *But he said to me, "My grace is sufficient for you, for my power is made perfect in weakness." Therefore I will boast all the more gladly about my weaknesses, so that Christ's power may rest on me. That is why, for Christ's sake, I delight in weaknesses, in insults, in hardships, in persecutions, in difficulties* (2 Corinthians 12:9-10).

It is by God's grace we are made strong and His power rests in us. *I can do all things through Christ who strengthens me* (Philippians 4:13). Whatever we are facing, our strength and our success come from the Lord. His Spirit is in us and works through us. *"Have faith in God," Jesus answered. "Truly I tell you, if anyone says to this mountain, 'Go, throw yourself into the sea,' and does not doubt in their heart but believes that what they say will happen, it will be done for them. Therefore I tell you, whatever you ask for in prayer, believe that you have received it, and it will be yours"* (Mark 11:22-24).

Lord, increase our faith, our belief in what You have said. More of You, less of us. Move in and through us, Lord, that we would be mighty advocates for You, that Your power would increase, and many will be saved by Your hand. Lord, we believe! Remove our unbelief. Thank You, Jesus! Amen.

FEBRUARY 20TH

"This, then, is how you should pray: Our Father in heaven, hallowed be Your name, Your kingdom come, Your will be done, on earth as it is in heaven."

MATTHEW 6:9-10

Good morning! I am convinced there are times I lack faith to fully believe, as if I need a fallback position in case things don't happen as I prayed. And therein lies the problem! Our prayers are not about our will at all! When we pray "Your will be done," we are not resigning ourselves to fate, but praying God's perfect purpose will be accomplished in this world as in the next. And how does God accomplish His will on earth? In part, through people willing to obey Him. We offer ourselves up as doers of God's will. We believe and we trust in His plans and give the outcomes to Him. God's will for our lives has meaning and purpose. And it is not always what we think, want, or choose. Are we truly seeking His will or are we looking for God to rubber stamp "yes" on our will and our plans?

If we are interested in knowing God's will and His plan for our lives, we need to develop a trusting relationship with Him. Before He reveals His will, we must be committed to doing whatever it is He desires for us to do. Like Shadrach, Meshach and Abednego, we need to believe *the God we serve is able to deliver us ... but even if He does not*, we won't give in to despair, we *won't serve other gods* (Daniel 3:17-18). We will stand firm in our faith that God gives *exceedingly abundantly above all we ask or think* (Ephesians 3:20). Pray with confidence, "God's will be done."

Lord, forgive our weakness and the doubting of our faith. Renew in us, Lord, a zeal and fervor for You and trust in Your will. Continue to increase our faith and grant that we would be surrendered, obedient servants to Your calling. Thank You, Jesus! Amen.

FEBRUARY 21ST

By faith in the name of Jesus, this man whom you see and know was made strong. It is Jesus' name and the faith that comes through Him that has completely healed him, as you can see.

ACTS 3:16

Good morning! There is such power in the name of and relationship with Jesus! Have we experienced and found Him? Jesus heals us from the disease of sin and the sentence of death. *If My people who are called by My name humble themselves and pray and seek My face and turn from their wicked ways, then I will hear from heaven and will forgive their sin and heal their land* (2 Chronicles 7:14). We need first to recognize our need for Jesus!

If My people who are called by My name HUMBLE themselves. We are falsely proud, relying on faulty human capabilities when we have a perfect Lord who desires relationship with us. Call out to Him!

And PRAY. Have a conversation with Jesus. He is our advocate to the Father (1 John 2:1-2). There is no human conversation we'll ever have that can even come close to producing the results equal to prayer. Our answers are found in Jesus.

And SEEK My face. He invites us into a relationship with Him, to experience His healing power and His peace. Determine to walk away from the sin that binds us.

And TURN FROM their wicked ways. Jesus promises He hears our calling, and He will respond.

Then I WILL HEAR from heaven and WILL FORGIVE and HEAL their land. Is there anything that keeps you from allowing His power to work in your life? We all need healing, and Jesus is the only sure way!

Lord, we call out to You, "forgive us our trespasses" and make us whole again in You. We desire to know You and to walk with You. We thank You for who You are and all that You have, are, and will continue to do in our lives until the day You call us home. Thank You, Jesus! Amen.

FEBRUARY 22ND

I remain confident of this: I will see the goodness of the Lord in the land of the living. Wait for the Lord; be strong and take heart and wait for the Lord.

PSALM 27:13-15

Good morning! Patience is one of the fruits of the Spirit that seems to be slow in coming for so many of us! We have plenty of opportunities to practice as we wait—in lines, in traffic, for answers, for results—the list is endless. So where is our confidence while we wait? David was sixteen when he was anointed king, but he didn't become king until thirty. During his time of waiting, he was chased through the desert by the jealous King Saul. And we think we have challenges in our times of waiting!

Waiting for God is not easy, but there is no greater reward to be found than the answers and results from Him. God is our ray of hope filled with mercy and grace. *Because of the Lord's great love we are not consumed, for His compassions never fail. They are new every morning; great is Your faithfulness. I say to myself, "The Lord is my portion; therefore I will wait for Him"* (Lamentations 3:22-24).

In our impatience we can miss what God does in the times of waiting. He is in control and is worth waiting for. He uses waiting to refresh, renew, prepare, and teach us. Our time belongs to Him. *Wait for the Lord; be strong and take heart and wait for the Lord* (Psalm 27:14). Patience is a worthwhile virtue to have and to exercise. Trust in the Lord and wait for Him!

Lord, may we exercise patience and make good use of our times of waiting by discovering what Your desire is for us, what You are revealing and teaching us. Thank You for Your goodness, faithfulness, grace, mercy, and love. Thank You, Jesus! Amen.

FEBRUARY 23RD

"Come to Me, all who labor and are heavy laden, and I will give you rest.
Take My yoke upon you and learn from Me;
for I am gentle and lowly in heart, and you will find rest for your souls.
For My yoke is easy, and My burden is light."

Matthew 11:28–30 ESV

Good morning! The trouble is that we don't come to Him. We do not ask Him for what He is more than willing and able to do. We toil and we fret, fuss, and complain; all the while we have One who is waiting for us to turn and give it all to Him. Jesus frees us from our burdens. His rest is love, healing, and peace with God. A relationship with God changes meaningless, wearisome toil into spiritual productivity and purpose. And we are invited into this relationship by the Lord Himself: *"Come to Me."*

The challenges we face in this life and world are real. They weigh us down, sometimes even within the effort of staying true to God. But Jesus' yoke remains easy compared to the crushing alternative. He shares our burdens, with the weight falling on much broader shoulders than our own. Jesus has more pulling power and is in front helping us. *"Everything is possible for one who believes"* (Mark 9:23).

So what keeps us from partnering with the One who can help us to do all things? *"I can do all things through Christ which strengtheneth me"* (Philippians 4:13 KJV). Turn to Jesus, who never changes and is always able.

Lord, we can prevail in victory over any circumstance when we trust and rely on You and Your strength. Thank You for inviting us to share our burdens with You. You are unchanging—"the same yesterday, today and forever more" and always with us. We can be at peace in our circumstances when our trust and hope are stayed on You. Thank You, Jesus! Amen.

FEBRUARY 24TH

You were taught, with regard to your former way of life,
to put off your old self, which is being corrupted by its deceitful desires;
to be made new in the attitude of your minds; and to put on the new self,
created to be like God in true righteousness and holiness.

EPHESIANS 4:22-24

Good morning! We would not frequent an establishment where we felt unwelcome, had a poor experience, or were repeatedly turned away. Yet in our very own lives we will continue to repeat behaviors and thinking that have terrible results or consequences and potentially bar us from our heavenly home! There is One answer to our dilemma—and His name is Jesus! Over 2,000 years ago, God Himself gave us His answer to make a way out of our mess and secure our home with Him. *For God so loved the world that He gave His one and only Son, that whoever believes in Him shall not perish but have eternal life* (John 3:16).

Jesus is the only answer to every problem we have—our sin, our rebellion, and the hopelessness found in this world. God promises us new life in Christ Jesus. *Therefore, if anyone is in Christ, the new creation has come: The old has gone, the new is here!* (2 Corinthians 5:17).

What keeps us from God's promises is ourselves! Our sin nature, our self-centeredness, and our fears. But God! He made a way for us to experience new life, welcoming us into the family of believers, and our identity from being fallen is made new in Christ Jesus. God desires for all to be saved, to be set free from sin, death, and destruction, and live in eternity with Him.

Lord, thank You for making a way for us out of our sin and into new life in You. Forgive us when we rebel and disobey, when we think more of ourselves than we should. Lord, we want to know You more, to be surrendered to You and to live in a way that pleases You. Thank You for Your promise of new life and for loving us. Thank You, Jesus! Amen.

FEBRUARY 25TH

The Lord is near to the brokenhearted
and saves those who are crushed in spirit.

PSALM 34:18

Good morning! It has been said that from our tests comes our testimony and out of the mess is our message. I know that is true for me. Smith Wigglesworth wrote, "You cannot take people into the depths of God unless you have been broken yourself."[4]

The Pharisees and the religious people of Jesus' day did not understand Jesus, why He would keep company with sinners and the "unclean." *Jesus answered them, "It is not the healthy who need a doctor, but the sick. I have not come to call the righteous, but sinners to repentance"* (Luke 5:31-32).

Jesus chose not to spend time with the proud, self-righteous religious leaders but with people who sensed their own sin and knew they were not good enough for God. But God! That is exactly who He sent Jesus to save! In order for us to come to God, we must recognize our need and repent—recognize our sin for what it is and renounce it. Out of our mess comes our message! *So the man went away and told all over town how much Jesus had done for him* (Luke 8:39).

Tell everyone what Jesus has done for you! We all need a Savior and He is the One, Jesus Christ. He didn't come for those who believe themselves sinless. He came for those who recognize their need for Him and surrender themselves to Him.

Lord, may we care for the spiritually needy, just as You have cared for us out of our mess. Please may it be so—that we would look around us and see so many in need of Your Grace, Your love and Your mercy, even as we recognize our own need. Lord, help us to shine Your Light in the darkness just as You have illuminated our lives. Thank You, Jesus! Amen.

---

4. Smith Wigglesworth, *Smith Wigglesworth Devotional*, 99.

FEBRUARY 26TH

Is anyone among you in trouble? Let them pray. Is anyone happy? Let them sing songs of praise. Is anyone among you sick? Let them call the elders of the church to pray over them and anoint them with oil in the name of the Lord. And the prayer offered in faith will make the sick person well; the Lord will raise them up. If they have sinned, they will be forgiven. Therefore confess your sins to each other and pray for each other so that you may be healed. The prayer of the righteous person is powerful and effective.

JAMES 5:13–16

Good morning! My faith is being recharged by the encouragement given through the writings of Smith Wigglesworth: "Oh, beloved, may God help us to get our eyes off the conditions and symptoms, no matter how bad they may be, and get them fastened on Him. Then we will be able to pray 'the prayer of faith.'"[5]

Stop looking at the problems, the symptoms, the person(s) and the circumstances. Look at Jesus Christ! He is the only answer we ever need. *Fixing our eyes on Jesus, the pioneer and perfecter [author and finisher] of faith* (Hebrews 12:2). Our faith comes from Jesus and He is the one who brings it out to its full potential and completion. When we focus on the mole hills of life (our troubles), they become mountains. And what moves mountains? *"Truly I tell you, if you have faith as small as a mustard seed, you can say to this mountain, 'Move from here to there,' and it will move. Nothing will be impossible for you"* (Matthew 17:20). There is tremendous power in the "prayer of faith."

Lord, You are the author of our faith and the source of all things good. You showed us what it means to trust our heavenly Father, and You gave us the gift of prayer. May we lift our prayers to You in faith, believing You hear and answer them in Your will and timing. Thank You for the privilege of prayer. We trust that Your will be done. Thank You, Jesus! Amen.

---

5. Smith Wigglesworth, *Smith Wigglesworth Devotional*, 101.

FEBRUARY 27TH

In Him we have redemption through His blood, the forgiveness of sins,
in accordance with the riches of God's grace that He lavished on us.

EPHESIANS 1:7-8

Good morning! Ain't nobody like Jesus! So why are we living marginalized lives as if He doesn't exist? Jesus is real, and He is alive! Jesus is Messiah, Jehovah, Emmanuel, Redeemer, the Holy One of Israel, Wonderful, Counsellor, Mighty God, Everlasting Father, and Prince of Peace. He is our Healer, Savior, Son of God, Way Maker, Miracle Worker, Light in the darkness. Whatever we are facing, Jesus is our answer. Job 19:25 tells us that Jesus is our Living Redeemer who stood on the earth. Jesus is the One whose hands and feet were pierced on the cross. Jesus is the Son of God who descended from heaven to save us and ascended to be our advocate. Do we really know Him? The One, the ONLY One who came to save us?

But He was wounded for our transgressions, He was bruised for our iniquities; The chastisement for our peace was upon Him, And by His stripes we are healed (Isaiah 53:5). Jesus paid the ultimate price, His very life on the cross, that we would be set free, to have life, life abundant and eternal. Are we living the life Jesus came and died to give us? "The thief comes only in order to steal and kill and destroy. I came that they may have life, and have it in abundance [to the full, till it overflows]" (John 10:10). Be encouraged by who Jesus is, why He came. Run into His arms and make Him yours!

Lord, we cannot possibly understand and know the sacrifice You made for our freedom, redemption and salvation. But we know it to be true and we believe You are the only Way, Truth and Life. We give ourselves wholly to You today, that we might be vessels for sharing Your love, compassion and kindness. Thank You, Jesus! Amen.

FEBRUARY 28TH

*Be very careful, then, how you live—not as unwise but as wise,
making the most of every opportunity, because the days are evil.
Therefore do not be foolish, but understand what the Lord's will is.*

EPHESIANS 5:15-17

Good morning! Praise the Lord for another new day! As our eyes have opened to see this day, we have new opportunities before us and should not allow the negative to deter us from what God has planned. There is a sense of urgency in Paul's message: *the days are evil.* Be aware and recognize the difficulties we face. But God! He doesn't leave us to face anything alone. He prepares us and equips us to face each moment strengthened in Him. *I can do all things through Him [Christ Jesus] who strengthens me* (Philippians 4:13). It is with God's strength and empowerment that we are able to tackle challenges and seize opportunities—we are able to accomplish what may seem impossible.

What is our attitude today? *The steadfast love of the Lord never ceases; His mercies never come to an end; they are new every morning; great is Your faithfulness* (Lamentations 3:22-23). Each morning is a new opportunity to reflect on God's work in our lives, a chance to share who He is and what He's done for us with others. Each and every day, our slate is wiped clean by Jesus' sacrifice on the cross, and we are given an opportunity to share His truth with someone who needs to hear it for the first time or be reminded of it again. What will we choose to do with the gift of this day?

Lord, open our eyes to see You and our hearts to receive Your love. Then set us on our way into this day—Your day—with intentionality for sharing You with others, that everyone we meet will see the Christ in us and ask, "What must I do to have Christ in me?" Thank You, Jesus! Amen.

FEBRUARY 29TH

But may the righteous be glad and rejoice before God,
may they be happy and joyful. Sing to God, sing in praise of His name,
extol Him who rides on the clouds; rejoice before Him—
His name is the Lord.

PSALM 68:3-4

Good morning! We are blessed with another day to either praise the Lord or choose to muddle through it. What benefit do we gain from the latter? The best response to each new day is one of gratitude and praise. God is worthy of our praise. He is our Hope, the Defender of the weak, our Healer and Restorer. If our eyes are fixed on our circumstances, we will miss what God is doing.

Enter his gates with thanksgiving, and his courts with praise! Give thanks to him; bless his name! For the Lord is good; his steadfast love endures forever, and his faithfulness to all generations (Psalm 109:4-5). Praise invites God's presence and our spirits are refreshed and renewed. Praise brings us closer to God. It changes us and helps us grow in our faith. Praise reminds us who God is. A life filled with praise places us in a position to receive God's blessings. Praise leaves no room for complaining and negativity.

God knows our hearts. And He cares about all that concerns us. Praise focuses on Him, distracting our attention from our struggles. Remember what the Lord has done. Rejoice and give Him praise!

Lord, there is no one like You! You are worthy to be praised! We magnify You and honor You. We fix our eyes on You alone and our hearts in steadfast love toward You. Where would we be without You in our lives? We shudder to think! Thank You, Jesus, for saving us! Amen.

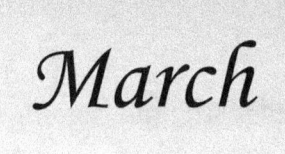

March

MARCH 1ST

*Be alert and of sober mind. Your enemy the devil prowls around
like a roaring lion looking for someone to devour. Resist him, standing firm
in the faith, because you know that the family of believers throughout the
world is undergoing the same kind of sufferings.*

1 PETER 5:8-10

Good morning! There is not one of us who isn't beyond the devil's grasp. We're walking along; life is going well. God is moving in our lives; we're ministering to others and engaged in fellowship. And it seems "all of the sudden" we're hit with a personal problem, or an argument explodes. What just happened? Our enemy is the devil, and he desires to devour us, to cause real and lasting harm. But our place in eternity is secure through our belief in Jesus Christ, and the devil can do nothing to take that from us. *"I give them eternal life, and they will never perish, and no one will snatch them out of My hand. My Father, who has given them to Me, is greater than all, and no one is able to snatch them out of the Father's hand"* (John 10:28-29).

The devil will do whatever he can to damage our faith, and he knows our personal relationships, marriage, and family are opportunities for creating divisiveness. *Submit yourselves, then, to God. Resist the devil, and he will flee from you* (James 4:7). We must live in humility toward God and each other, standing firm in faith and trusting our Father who cares for us. Stay alert and remain clear-minded, watching for the enemy who seeks to destroy us.

Lord, thank You that we do not walk in and through this life on our own. You are with us and guard us. Help us to recognize our deep need and dependence on You and to be alert to the enemy's deception and lies. Our hope and trust are in You always. Thank You, Jesus! Amen.

MARCH 2ND

Before the mountains were born or You brought forth the whole world,
from everlasting to everlasting You are God.

PSALM 90:2

Good morning! There is no beginning and no end to God; He is eternal. He has always existed, and He always will. It is impossible for us to wrap our minds around or fully understand the magnitude of God. *"I am the Alpha and the Omega," says the Lord God, "who is, and who was, and who is to come, the Almighty"* (Revelation 1:8).

Without God we have nothing that is eternal, nothing that can change our lives, and nothing that can save us from sin. How many times in life do we separate ourselves from God, acting as if we don't need Him, or that we can do life on our own? It's just not so. Without Him, no real good can come from our lives.

Pastor Rick Warren wrote in his book *The Purpose Driven Life*, "Without God, life has no purpose, and without purpose, life has no meaning. Without meaning, life has no significance or hope."[6]

But our God pursues us! *For God so loved the world that He gave His one and only Son, that whoever believes in Him shall not perish but have eternal life. For God did not send His Son into the world to condemn the world, but to save the world through Him* (John 3:16-17).

There is nothing that compares to our God, nor will there ever be. He sent His Son, Jesus Christ, our Savior, that we would be one with Him.

Lord, You are our All in all! Everything we will ever need we find and have in You. Thank You for the great sacrifice You made that we would have abundant life in You. Lord, may we constantly seek after You with hearts and minds set on You. Thank You, Jesus! Amen.

---

6. Rick Warren, *The Purpose Driven Life* (Nashville: Zondervan, 2002), 30.

MARCH 3RD

Consequently, faith comes from hearing the message,
and the message is heard through the word about Christ.

ROMANS 10:17

Good morning! We see something transformed with our own eyes
and we believe; we may even seek after it for ourselves. Yet how
often do we find ourselves doubting that God is able to transform
broken, shattered lives—ours or someone we love? Where is our
faith? Yes, Jesus is in the transformation business of impacting and
changing lives. Is our faith only strengthened by seeing? That is not
faith at all! *Thomas said to Him, "My Lord and my God!" Then Jesus told
him, "Because you have seen Me, you have believed; blessed are those
who have not seen and yet have believed"* (John 20:28-29). Jesus said
there is a greater blessing for those who believe when they cannot
see.

When your heart is aching and nothing appears to be going right and
yet you still believe God is Sovereign and good, then you are blessed.
*Blessed is the one who perseveres under trial because, having stood the test,
that person will receive the crown of life that the Lord has promised to those
who love him* (James 1:12).

Are we like Thomas, needing to see to believe? Has not the change
God has made in our lives visible proof enough? God is our Deliverer—in
that we can believe.

*Lord, You take lost souls and breathe new life into them—Your Life. You
transform what is broken and lost into new creations in You. Lord, may our
faith increase, so that no matter what, we will believe in You and the Truth of
Your message. Thank You, Jesus! Amen.*

MARCH 4TH

Lord, I know that people's lives are not their own; it is not for them to direct their steps. Discipline me, Lord, but only in due measure— not in Your anger, or You will reduce me to nothing.

JEREMIAH 10:23-24

Good morning! We are not our own, to live as though we have no God, no Lord or Savior. Jeremiah's prayer is so bold and beautiful! We are children of God, loved beyond measure (Ephesians 3:18). God's ability to direct our lives is infinitely beyond our ability. Sometimes I think we fear God's power and His plans because we know if He chose to use it against us, He could easily crush us. But God! Don't fear the Lord's plans. He is the source of all wisdom and strength and knows what's best. *Trust in the Lord with all your heart and lean not on your own understanding; in all your ways submit to Him, and He will make your paths straight* (Proverbs 3:5-6).

We live our lives as though we have control over everything, when in reality that just isn't true. *"For My thoughts are not your thoughts, neither are your ways My ways," declares the Lord. "As the heavens are higher than the earth, so are My ways higher than your ways and My thoughts than your thoughts"* (Isaiah 55:8-9).

God spoke all creation into existence (Genesis 1) and then formed man from dust and breathed life into him (Genesis 2:7). God made us! We can have and make our plans, but ultimately it is God who prevails (Proverbs 19:21).

Lord, we abandon ourselves to You, surrendering our lives to the very One who created us. We pray Your will be known, lived out, and done in and through our lives, Lord, that we would be pleasing to You in thought, word, and deed. Thank You, Jesus! Amen.

MARCH 5TH

For all have sinned and fall short of the glory of God, and all are justified freely by His Grace through redemption that came by Christ Jesus.

ROMANS 3:23-24

Good morning! What's on our inside? A.W. Tozer wrote, "That which is on the inside will eventually come out on the outside."[7] We all have a sinful nature that, left unchecked, will challenge our treatment of others and our walk with the Lord. All sin makes us sinners and cuts us off from our holy God. All sin, therefore, leads to death, regardless of how small or insignificant it may seem, because it separates us from God. Our inside condition matters! What is left in the darkness makes its way into the light. Sin does and will impact our lives and those around us. But God! He makes a way for repentance and forgiveness: His name is Jesus! He sets the captives free!

God, in His grace, freely makes us right in His sight. He did this through Christ Jesus when He freed us from the penalty for our sins. But we have to be willing to do the work of seeking God, allowing Him to reveal our sins. We must repent and be cleansed of all unrighteousness. The sins we harbor will make their way into our thinking, behaviors, and actions. *Have mercy on me, O God, according to Your unfailing love; according to Your great compassion blot out my transgressions. Wash away all my iniquity and cleanse me from my sin* (Psalm 51:1-2).

Lord, what a perfect expression of our deeply felt need for Your mercy and forgiveness. Lord, cleanse us, that we would be white as snow. Lord, we want to be pleasing to You, and effective in ministry to others. Remove the stumbling blocks within us that we might be of service to the work needed to be done in this broken world. Thank You, Jesus! Amen.

---

7. A.W. Tozer, *My Daily Pursuit* (Grand Rapids: Bethany House, 2014), 75.

MARCH 6TH

Praise be to the God and the Father of our Lord Jesus Christ,
who has blessed us in the heavenly realms with every spiritual blessing in
Christ. For He chose us in Him before the creation of the world to be holy and
blameless in His sight. In love, He predestined us for adoption to sonship
through Jesus Christ, in accordance with His pleasure and will—to the praise
of His glorious grace, which He has freely given us in the One He loves.

EPHESIANS 3:3-6

Good morning! We may never receive an earthly inheritance, but what we have in Christ Jesus far surpasses anything this world can give! In Christ Jesus, we have all the benefits of knowing God— being chosen for salvation, being adopted as His children, forgiveness, insight, the gifts of the Spirit, power to do God's will, the hope of living forever with Christ. And what's more—as if we needed more—because we have an intimate relationship with Christ, we can enjoy these blessings now. These blessings are eternal— heavenly realms, not limited by earthly bounds!

We are "chosen in Him"—our salvation is fully dependent on God, not because we deserve it, but because God is gracious and has freely gifted us salvation. And because of Jesus, we are holy and blameless in God's sight. God graciously accepts us, undeserving as we are, through His Son Jesus. There is no inheritance on earth that can come anywhere close to the one promised and given through Christ Jesus!

Lord, thank You for adopting us into Your kingdom, an inheritance unearned and undeserved. We praise You for who You are, Lord of all, and are humbled by Your grace, love, and mercy toward us, that we are called Your sons and daughters. Thank You, Jesus! Amen.

MARCH 7TH

Praise be to the God and Father of our Lord Jesus Christ! In His great mercy He has given us new birth into a living hope through the resurrection of Jesus Christ from the dead, and into an inheritance that can never perish, spoil or fade. This inheritance is kept in heaven for you, who through faith are shielded by God's power until the coming of the salvation that is ready to be revealed in the last time. In all this you greatly rejoice, though now for a little while you may have had to suffer grief in all kinds of trials. These have come so that the proven genuineness of your faith—greater than gold, which perishes even though refined by the fire—may result in praise, glory and honor when Jesus Christ is revealed.

1 PETER 1:3-7

Good morning! So many people are experiencing trials and overwhelming circumstances that seem humanly impossible to endure. This is not a new phenomenon to mankind, and God's Word has much to say about how we are to respond. We have hope in times of trouble because of the confidence we have from what God has done for us in Christ Jesus. Our hope is not just for the future of eternal life but begins with trusting Christ and joining God's family.

God will help us remain true to our faith through whatever difficult times we face. Our faith must be firmly grounded in Christ Jesus. It is promised that in this world we will face troubles. But God will use them to refine and strengthen our faith and increase our capacity to love and share the gospel.

Lord, we pray our response to difficulties moves from questioning "why me" to confidence in Your plans and wisdom, to perseverance in facing what's set before us and courage from knowing You are with us and we are Yours. Lord, all things are possible through You. Thank You, Jesus! Amen.

MARCH 8TH

For you were once darkness, but now you are light in the Lord.
Live as children of light (for the fruit of light consists in all goodness,
righteousness and truth) and find out what pleases the Lord.

EPHESIANS 5:8-10

Good morning! We are to be as a "light in darkness," not "covered by a bushel." This is not because of ourselves but the result of Christ in us. We cannot boast or take any credit! Left to our own devices, we are but sinners, messed up and broken. Our words and our actions should reflect Jesus living in and through us and exhibiting our faith.

Are we reflecting God's goodness to those around us? Jesus stressed this truth: *"You are the light of the world. A town built on a hill cannot be hidden. Neither do people light a lamp and put it under a bowl. Instead they put it on its stand, and it gives light to everyone in the house. In the same way, let your light shine before others, so that they may see your good deeds and glorify your Father in heaven"* (Matthew 5:14-16).

When we live for Jesus, we will illuminate the darkness (shine like lights), showing others what Christ is like. Are we shining brightly, or are we satisfied to live with our lights dimmed, hidden, or fully burned out? *Wake up, sleeper, rise from the dead, and Christ will shine on you"* (Ephesians 5:14).

Lord, may we live boldly for You with our lights shining brightly in and through us. Let us not be quiet when we should be speaking out. Lord, let us share our light with others and not ignore the needs You set before us. We stand firm in Your truth and stand for what is right. Thank You, Jesus! Amen.

MARCH 9TH

And over all these virtues [compassion, kindness, humility, gentleness, patience, forgiveness] put on love, which binds them all together in perfect unity. Let the peace of Christ rule in your hearts, since as members of one body you were called to peace. And be thankful.

COLOSSIANS 3:14-15

Good morning! Love, peace, and thankfulness. To live in love leads to peace between people. Others will challenge our capacity to love and reveal the weaknesses in us. We are called to *love others as ourselves* and *to love as God first loved us*. This extends beyond those who live in agreement with us in our beliefs and lifestyle. Where or whom are we struggling to love? We must ask God to examine our hearts and reveal our weaknesses and sin.

We all want peace in our lives, and peace is a byproduct of love. Our hearts are the center of conflict where our feelings and desires battle. We need God to rule in our hearts and choose to be obedient to His commands. Use the rule of loving others and allow the peace of Christ to reign in your life today. To live in love leads to peace.

Lord, we thank You for Your Word and for saints gone before us who shared the gospel and Your teaching. Thank You for leading and guiding us through this life that we might one day experience the glory of Your presence face to face. Lord, help us to love others and have Your peace in our lives. Thank You, Jesus! Amen.

MARCH 10TH

For it is by grace you have been saved, through faith—and this is not from yourselves, it is the gift of God—not by works, so that no one can boast. For we are God's handiwork, created in Christ Jesus to do good works, which God prepared in advance for us to do.

EPHESIANS 2:8-10

Good morning! There is nothing we have or could do to earn our salvation or even our faith. These are gifts from God. It is God's unmerited grace, not our efforts, abilities, choices, or acts of service that bring us to Christ. So then, how should we respond? Out of gratitude for God's free gift, we ought to seek to help and serve others with the same kindness, love, and gentleness God has shown us. We must think more of others and much less of pleasing ourselves and our own comfort. *Each of you should use whatever gift you have received to serve others, as faithful stewards of God's grace in its various forms* (1 Timothy 4:10).

While it is not our works that can save us, God intends our salvation to result in acts of service. We are not saved only for our own benefit but to serve Christ and build up His kingdom and the church. We are saved to be restored into a loving, intimate, and eternal relationship with God, out of which we glorify Him and are transformed into the image of Jesus, His Son.

Lord, we thank You for Your gift of salvation that cost You everything and gained us gifts we could never earn or deserve. May our hearts respond in humility and gratitude and with a willingness to do the good works You prepared in advance for us to do. Lord, our desire is to serve You and others with the same passion You demonstrated. We love You and want to be pleasing to You. Thank You, Jesus! Amen.

MARCH 11TH

If you declare with your mouth, "Jesus is Lord," and believe in your heart
that God raised him from the dead, you will be saved. For it is with your
heart that you believe and are justified, and it is with your mouth
that you profess your faith and are saved.

ROMANS 10:9-10

Good morning! We all believe in something but there is only One sure thing! Smith Wigglesworth emphatically shared, "Believe! Oh, believe! It is the Word of God."[8] This world is filled with questions, difficulties and struggles. People are searching for their lifelines and for answers. The ONLY answer with eternal meaning is found in the Word of God—His name is Jesus! *But these are written that you may believe that Jesus is the Christ, the Son of God, and that by believing you may have life in His name* (John 20:31).

Our salvation comes when we confess with our mouth that Jesus is Lord and believe in our heart that God raised Him from the dead. We must have faith and believe in the One who makes a way for us. *Jesus said to him, "I am the way, and the truth, and the life. No one comes to the Father except through Me"* (John 14:6). The words, actions, and miracles of Jesus should give us confidence to believe in His Word and in His Promises. He is the One the Father sent, His one and only Son. Following Jesus and accepting Him as Lord and Savior is the only path to salvation and eternal life. "Oh, believe!"

Lord, we thank You that Your Word is Truth. You are the only Way to Life—to the Father and eternal life! We confess with our mouths that You are Lord and believe in our hearts that You were raised from the dead that we might be saved. You are the only One, and You are all we need. Thank You, Jesus! Amen.

---

8. Smith Wigglesworth, *Smith Wigglesworth Devotional*, 124.

MARCH 12TH

*For this reason I kneel before the Father, whom every family
in heaven and on earth derives its name.*

EPHESIANS 3:14

G ood morning! So many times, we find ourselves struggling with
feeling lonely or unlovable, but those feelings are simply not
true. As believers in Christ Jesus, we are made to be a part of the
family of God. There is no other family that compares. God is our
Father and a parent to all of humanity. Paul goes on, *I pray that out of
His glorious riches He may strengthen you with power through His Spirit
in your inner being, so that Christ may dwell in your hearts through faith.
And I pray that you, being rooted and established in love, may have
power, together with all the Lord's holy people, to grasp how wide and
long and high and deep is the love of Christ, and to know this love that
surpasses knowledge—that you may be filled to the measure of all the
fullness of God* (Ephesians 3:15-19).

The challenge we have is accepting and understanding just how
much God loves us and the huge impact that makes on all areas of our
lives. It's a lie that we are alone and not loved. The enemy (the devil)
uses lies to deceive us and separate us from God's truth. God promises
His love, that we will be filled up to overflowing with the infinite
presence, power, love, and glory of Jesus Christ. God is the source of all
creation, the rightful owner of everything. Stay connected to Him, His
power and love, and the family of God.

*Lord, we are never alone in the body of Christ, and we are always loved.
Penetrate our hearts with Your truth. Fill us with Your power to stand firm in
faith and to share Your love in unity with our brothers and sisters and all
whom we meet. Thank You, Jesus! Amen.*

MARCH 13TH

*"Seek first His kingdom and His righteousness,
and all these things will be given to you as well."*

MATTHEW 6:33

Good morning! Everything we need is found in Jesus. We can so easily get ahead of ourselves and find our priorities are way out of order. The results we experience are disappointment, frustration and a lack of peace and fulfillment. The solution is spelled out for us throughout Scripture: Seek God first. Turn to Him for help, to fill our thoughts with His desires, to take His character for our pattern, and serve and obey Him in everything. We must actively choose to give God first place in our lives and take our needs to Him.

You do not have because you do not ask God. When you ask, you do not receive, because you ask with the wrong motives (James 4:2-3). God gives us good gifts that He wants us to enjoy, but we are called to seek Him, to obey Him, to follow Him. When we pray, we should pray for God's wisdom, not from a worldly perspective but His.

Every good and perfect gift is from above, coming down from the Father of the heavenly lights, who does not change like shifting shadows (James 1:17). Worldly desires distract us from the one true need we must all have as our priority: Jesus as Lord. Our prayers become powerful when we allow God to change our desires so they perfectly align with His will for our lives.

Lord, may we continually seek after You and the good gifts You have planned for us! You are the only thing we need, and everything good comes from You. May our faith be strengthened and our hearts be set on You. Thank You, Jesus! Amen.

MARCH 14TH

"Do not be afraid, Abram. I am your shield, your very great reward."

GENESIS 15:1

Good morning! We are living in frightening times. This world is a scary mess! But God! We must grab ahold of His Word for ourselves. The words God spoke to Abram and others throughout Scripture are words intended for and spoken to us as well. We must know and claim His Word as our own! We must be lifted up as we read with our hearts and minds fully embracing God's promises: *"Why are you troubled, and why do doubts rise in your minds?"* (Luke 24:36); *"I will never leave you nor forsake you"* (Hebrews 13:5 NKJV); *"And even the very hairs of your head are all numbered"* (Matthew 10:30). Your name is *written in the Lamb's book of life* (Revelation 21:27), and He has *engraved you on the palms of His hands* (Isaiah 49:16).

Allow God's Word and His love be a balm over you, encouraging and strengthening you. His Word is personal and speaks into your faith. Imagine Jesus' hands on you as He says, *"I have prayed for you that your faith may not fail"* (Luke 22:32).

Whatever happens in this world and in our lives, God is in control of ALL things! And He knows exactly what we need. *Even to your old age and gray hairs I am He, I am He who will sustain you. I have made you and I will carry you; I will sustain you and I will rescue you* (Isaiah 46:4). Our God created us and cares for us, and His love endures for all of time.

Lord, thank You that You remain the same, yesterday, today, and always. What You spoke to Abram, You speak to us. Lord, we claim Your Word as our own and will seek You first that we would live accordingly. Thank You, Jesus! Amen.

MARCH 15TH

It is for freedom that Christ has set us free. Stand firm, then,
and do not let yourselves be burdened again by a yoke of slavery.

GALATIANS 5:1

Good morning! If we are still experiencing the bondage of sin and shame, let us look to Jesus. Because it isn't that He didn't do the work He was sent to do. The problem lies within us. What are the burdens we are still carrying? Call out to the Lord and give it all over to Him. *When hard pressed, I cried to the Lord; He brought me into a spacious place* (Psalm 118:5).

Jesus came to set us free, that we would live as overcomers, not hanging on by a thread or the skin of our teeth. Freedom in Christ Jesus is the most powerful thing we can have, because with it, we have the promise of eternal life. *For God so loved the world that He gave His one and only Son, that whoever believes in Him shall not perish but have eternal life* (John 3:16).

Finding freedom in Christ starts with seeking and living out God's plan for our lives. We are no longer slaves to sin and the riches of the world, but rather have found our freedom in Christ Jesus. *If we confess our sins, He is faithful and just and will forgive us our sins and purify us from all unrighteousness* (1 John 1:9). Confession eases our conscience and lightens our load so we can enjoy fellowship with the Lord. Through Christ's sacrifice, we are forgiven and reconciled to God.

Lord, forgive us for our sins and strengthen us, Lord, that we would not wander from You. Our lives are Yours to do as You will. Lead and guide us as we seek to remain near to You and stand firm in our faith. Our freedom and victory are found in You alone. Thank You, Jesus! Amen.

MARCH 16TH

"Father, the hour has come. Glorify Your Son, that Your Son may glorify You. For You granted Him authority over all people that He might give eternal life to all those You have given Him."

JOHN 17:1-2

Good morning! We can't even come close to fully understanding the sacrifice Christ made to bring us the privilege to choose a life with and for Him. Within John 17, we find three powerful prayers spoken by Jesus: for Himself (1-5), for His disciples (6-19), and for future believers (20-26). Jesus acknowledged His time on earth was ending and prayed not for His mission to be lifted from Him, but that God would protect and keep safe His chosen believers from Satan's power, setting them apart, and making them pure and holy, united in truth.

"Now this is eternal life: that they know You, the only true God, and Jesus Christ, whom You have sent" (John 17:3). By knowing God the Father Himself through the Son, Jesus Christ, we are offered eternal life. We must enter into a personal relationship with God in Jesus. We admit our sin and turn away from it, and Christ's love lives in us by the Holy Spirit. This is why Jesus came, suffered, died, and rose. *"I have brought You glory on earth by finishing the work You gave Me to do"* (John 17:4).

Lord, You left Your throne, seated with Your Father in heaven, to save us from Satan's grasp and to offer us new life in You. We can never fully comprehend Your sacrifice. May we recognize our need for You and seek You first. Lord, thank You for loving us so much that You sacrificed it all, Your very life. We love You, we believe in You, and we thank You, Jesus! Amen.

MARCH 17TH

I waited patiently for the Lord; He turned to me and heard my cry. He lifted me out of the slimy pit, out of the mud and mire; He set my feet on a rock and gave me a firm place to stand. He put a new song in my mouth, a hymn of praise to God. Many will see and fear the Lord and put their trust in Him. Blessed is the one who trusts in the Lord ... Nothing can compare with You.

PSALM 40:1-4, 5

Good morning! Nothing on the outside compares to God's presence on the inside! Live in the world, become worldly; live in God's Word, become holy. We are in desperate need of experiencing the awesomeness of God's presence in our lives, and afterward, we will never again be impressed or bothered by things external. God has not moved. He waits patiently for us to turn away from our external focus to find Him. He is the only One who transforms lives into something worthwhile and eternal.

Do we know Him? Do our lives still feel like a tangled mess, overwhelming and stressful? To know God is to know peace. "No God, no peace. Know God, know peace." We will never solve the external mess of this world, but God is the answer for our internal peace. He alone will fill us up to overflowing that we might delight in the conscious presence of Him! Smith Wigglesworth said, "The more of God's Word you hide in your heart, the easier it is to live a holy life."[9]

Lord, You came that we would have abundant life, life to the full. You gave us Your Word that we would be filled, that we would know You and live in Your power and presence. Lord, may we turn away from the things of this world that distract and destroy, and turn to You—our hope and life. Thank You, Jesus! Amen.

---

9. Smith Wigglesworth, *Smith Wigglesworth Devotional*, 132.

MARCH 18TH

*"Who am I that I should go to Pharaoh
and bring the Israelites out of Egypt?"*

EXODUS 3:11

Good morning! We might be startled by, possibly even chuckle at Moses' response to God's calling, and his reluctance didn't end there. He questioned God's appointment, even his own ability to speak! *Moses said to the Lord, "Pardon Your servant, Lord. I have never been eloquent, neither in the past nor since You have spoken to Your servant. I am slow of speech and tongue"* (Exodus 4:10). Moses went so far as to even say to God, *"Pardon your servant, Lord. Please send someone else"* (Exodus 4:13)!

Before we laugh out loud or judge Moses too harshly, what about us? What is God desiring to do in and through our lives that we're hesitating to do? Feeling unworthy or incapable of? God addressed Moses' reluctance and made a way for him, and He will address ours as well.

When we respond to God's call, we're saying yes to the plans and purposes He has for us. We're acknowledging that we trust Him enough to lead us into the unknown and surrender our plans and desires in exchange for His will. Too many times, we limit God's presence and power in our lives by our self-imposed limitations. If God is in it, He will make a way for us to do it. Our God is with us and for us! His call may look different for each one of us, but I assure you that He always has a purpose and a plan. And we can always trust it is for our good and His glory.

Lord, forgive us when we hesitate or question what You are calling us to do or to go where You are asking us to go. Give us ears to hear Your calling and hearts obedient to Your will for our lives. Who are we that we would question You? You made us for Your purpose and plans. Lord, we surrender all to You in hopes that our lives would be pleasing to You, glorifying and honoring You. Thank You, Jesus! Amen.

MARCH 19TH

*"But seek first His kingdom and His righteousness,
and all these things will be given to you as well."*

MATTHEW 6:33

Good morning! The world of entertainment and desire for ease has encroached, possibly even overtaken, our lives. Everything centers on pleasure, delight, and levity. Books, shows, hobbies, and pastimes. They may be a method of escape from the seriousness and troubles of our world, but they reek of temporary relief with no long-lasting benefits. But God! What if we chased after Him with the same consistency, fervor, and excitement? What if we filled ourselves with His Word, His purposes?

God is our answer to every question, problem, concern, trouble, and trial! In and through Him, we find our joy and delight! We are seeking after the wrong things. We have it backward. We're stepping on shadows of temporary pleasures rather than chasing after the Son, the One who gave us His all and is the gateway to eternity.

God provides everything we need. He knows how to provide good things to and for His children. He has made everything beautiful in its time. *He has also set eternity in the human heart, yet no one can fathom what God has done from beginning to end (Ecclesiastes 3:11). And my God shall supply all your needs according to His riches in glory by Christ Jesus* (Philippians 4:19 NKJV). When we have faith in Jesus and live righteously, God will provide us a glorious life in His name.

Lord, we fix our eyes and hearts on You. Your Word and Your promises are true, they never change. We can live in confidence that You will provide for all our needs, that You hear and answer our prayers, and that You will be with us always—even unto eternity with You in paradise. Thank You, Jesus! Amen.

MARCH 20TH

Therefore, if anyone is in Christ, the new creation has come.
The old has gone, the new is here!

2 CORINTHIANS 5:17

Good morning! My husband and I live in the Midwest (Ohio) and enjoy the changing of seasons, each one having its own unique aspects to enjoy. Ah, but spring is most likely my favorite as it heralds new birth, freshness, and the warmer temperatures soon to come! And I love that Easter falls in the spring with the story of Jesus' death and resurrection—believe in Him and find new life!

We are brand new people on the inside. The Holy Spirit gives us new life, and we are not the same anymore. We are not reformed, rehabilitated, or re-educated. We are recreated, new creations, living in vital union with Christ. Just as spring transforms the dead from winter to new buds of life, Jesus transforms lost sinners to life in Him. We have a new hope and confidence.

You were taught, with regard to your former way of life, to put off your old self, which is being corrupted by its deceitful desires; to be made new in the attitude of your minds; and to put on the new self, created to be like God in true righteousness and holiness (Ephesians 4:22-24). We put our old selves behind us just like the dead of winter is gone. Jesus is a once-and-for-all decision and a daily conscious decision for living life to the full in Him.

Lord, thank You for the dawning of each new day and for offering us a way to new life in You. We choose You, to become new creations and to walk in tandem with You. In Your Spirit, we have a new way of thinking and living. Thank You, Jesus! Amen.

MARCH 21ST

If My people, who are called by My name, will humble themselves and pray and seek My face and turn from their wicked ways, then I will hear from heaven, and I will forgive their sin and heal their land.

2 CHRONICLES 7:14

Good morning! Three blessings before I even stepped foot out of bed—I opened my two eyes and woke to a new day! *God said ... and there was ... and it was good* (Genesis creation story).

Nothing has changed. What God says, is, and it is good! The sin of man altered God's perfect plan, and still in His goodness He makes a way for us! Believe in who He is, what He says He can and will do, and be saved. God's Word tells us everything we need to know in order to live lives pleasing to God, dedicated to His good purposes. Are we spending time with Him? Do we know His Word?

God gave Solomon conditions for forgiveness: humble yourself by admitting your sins, pray to God for forgiveness, seek God continually, and turn away from sinful behavior. Why do we continue to do the very things God has told us not to do and then get angry with or blame Him for the results? And yet, God STILL loves us! *But God demonstrates His own love for us in this: While we were still sinners, Christ died for us. Since we have now been justified by His blood, how much more shall we be saved from God's wrath through Him!* (Romans 5:8-9).

We are given and shown daily evidence of God's Sovereignty, and also His grace, mercy, love and forgiveness. What will be our response to God's goodness and His faithfulness?

Lord, You are so good. Even when we don't see or recognize You moving and working in our lives, You are. You never leave or abandon us. You are who You say You are, and You do what You promise. And You have made a Way for us to be united with You as one. Thank You, Jesus! Amen.

MARCH 22ND

How good it is to sing praises to our God,
how pleasant and fitting to praise him!

PSALM 147:1

Good morning! We have so many reasons to praise God, and yet so often we choose to live and act as if He doesn't even exist. Why is that? I challenge each one of you reading this today to stop and consider how great our God is. Think of the good things He's done and all that we have in and from Him.

Shout for joy to the Lord, all the earth. Worship the Lord with gladness; come before Him with joyful songs. Know that the Lord is God. It is He who made us, and we are His; we are His people, the sheep of His pasture. Enter His gates with thanksgiving and His courts with praise; give thanks to Him and praise His name. For the Lord is good and His love endures forever; His faithfulness continues through all generations (Psalm 100:1-5).

Stop blaming God for the results of man's sin and acknowledge Him for who He really is and all He has done. He has made a way for us to live! *But God, who is rich in mercy, out of the great love with which He loved us, even when we were dead through our trespasses, made us alive together with Christ—by grace you have been saved* (Ephesians 2:4-5).

God is bigger than we'll ever be able to comprehend within the limitations of our humanity. He is divine: Father, Son, and Holy Spirit. He is the One True, Triune God. Choose today to live in a way that is honoring to our God—worship Him, spend time with Him, and share the gospel with someone who needs His love and salvation.

Lord, You alone are worthy of all praise, glory, and honor. Forgive us when we fall short, when we are so consumed with earthly concerns that we neglect and even ignore who You are, that You exist. You have given us abundant life in You! More than we can comprehend! Thank You, Jesus!

MARCH 23RD

Oh, the depth of the riches of the wisdom and knowledge of God! How unsearchable His judgements, and His paths beyond tracing out! "Who has known the mind of the Lord? Or who has been His counselor? Who has ever given to God, that God should repay them?" For from Him and through Him and for Him are all things. To Him be the glory forever! Amen.

ROMANS 11:33-36

Good morning! If we are only willing to splash about in the safe shallows of faith and the things of God, we miss the immersing depth of freedom and the full experience of all God has intended for us. God's means and methods are far surpassing our comprehension, but God IS in control! He governs the universe and our lives in perfect wisdom, justice, and love. We are not meant to understand the mind of God, and He owes us nothing. But God! In all His absolute power and absolute wisdom is the source of all things— including us!

We are absolutely dependent on God! So jump into the depths of who He is! He is the power that sustains us and rules the world we live in. God works all things to bring glory to Himself. He deserves our fullest measure of attention, devotion, pursuit, love, and praise. Do you know Him? Are you seeking after Him daily?

Lord, we immerse ourselves in You, surrendering our all to the One who knows all! In You we find all that we need. You are our All in all—a great God, a great King above all others. You hold the depths of the earth and the mightiest mountains in Your hands. The seas are Yours, and the dry land. And we were formed by You, created by Your hands in our mother's womb. You are greatly to be praised. Thank You, Jesus! Amen.

MARCH 24TH

*Search me, God, and know my heart; test me and know my anxious
thoughts. See if there is any offensive way in me,
and lead me in the way everlasting.*

PSALM 139:23-24

Good morning! They greeted Him with palm branches and shouts of "Hosanna!" One week later their shouts were the merciless demand to "Crucify Him!" We know the whole story, and yet do our behavior and words not sometimes take on a similar display? We say that we love the Lord and serve Him but see someone in need only to ignore or walk away with the need unmet. Or we grumble and complain in the midst of serving, as if we should be getting extra kudos for being thoughtful and kind.

David despised the wicked who spoke against God, as we are appalled by the shouts against Jesus. We, just as David did, must recognize that we are not perfect—that sin might be lurking in our hearts and minds. We invite God to search our hearts and our thoughts, to protect us from Satan's lies and deception that poison our spirits. Let everything we think, do, or say be pleasing to the Lord. *Do not let any unwholesome talk come out of your mouths, but only what is helpful for building others up according to their needs, that it may benefit those who listen* (Ephesians 4:29). May the words we choose be glorifying to God.

Lord, we praise Your holy name. You and You alone are worthy. Lord, protect us from the devil's snare that all we think, do and say would be acceptable and pleasing to You. Guard us Lord in all our ways! Thank You, Jesus! Amen.

MARCH 25TH

He heals the brokenhearted and binds up their wounds.

PSALM 147:3

Good morning! Out of desperation comes our faith and freedom! We have to come to the end of ourselves in order for God to have His way with us. When we realize that on our own we cannot take one more step, when we cry out to Him, He will be there. As long as we think we have all the answers, or worse yet, that we are the answer, we are living on the edge of disaster. WE ALL NEED JESUS!

Then you will call, and the Lord will answer; you will cry for help, and He will say: "Here am I" (Isaiah 58:9). God's promise to save us from spiritual death and into abundant life is the foundation and beginning of His saving relationship with us. But we have to recognize our need for Him and surrender ourselves to Him. *For everyone who calls on the name of the Lord will be saved* (Romans 10:13, Joel 2:32).

The truth is that closeness with God is a direct result of calling out to Him in our desperation—calling out to Him in prayer, bringing Him our deepest and most transparent thoughts and feelings often and always. *The Lord is close to all who call on Him* (Psalm 145:18a). God is waiting, and He will transform us from our desperation to His holiness. *And we all, who with unveiled faces contemplate the Lord's glory, are being transformed into His image with ever-increasing glory, which comes from the Lord, who is the Spirit* (2 Corinthians 3:18). He takes our mess and turns it into His message!

Lord, we surrender all to You. We so desperately need You! And You came for that very reason—to save us from our sin and turmoil, our mess—to make us to be Your sons and daughters that we would have abundant life, life eternal with You! Thank You, Jesus! Amen.

MARCH 26TH

"My son, do not make light of the Lord's discipline, and do not lose heart
when He rebukes you, because the Lord disciplines the one He loves,
and He chastens everyone He accepts as His son."
Endure hardship as discipline; God is treating you as His children.
For what children are not disciplined by their father?

HEBREWS 12:5-7

Good morning! One of the many challenges of parenting comes from having to discipline our children. The goal is to correct a damaging behavior or redirect a poor choice in order that they would not be hurt or suffer further consequences. And so it is with God! Discipline is necessary to correct, train, and even at times punish a child to help them learn what is right. It may not be pleasant to be disciplined or corrected by God, but it is a sign of His deep love for us and a means of teaching, guiding or redirecting us.

But God disciplines us for our good, in order that we may share in His holiness. No discipline is pleasant at the time, but painful. Later on, however, it produces a harvest of righteousness and peace for those who have been trained by it (Hebrews 12:10-11). May we accept God's discipline with gratitude for His being our loving Father.

Lord, we thank You for loving us so much that You discipline us as Your sons and daughters to train us in the way You would have us to go. You never give up on us but continue to correct, teach, and guide us, blessing us with Your presence and leading us to a place of righteousness and peace. Thank You, Jesus! Amen.

MARCH 27TH

*By faith Abraham, when called to go to a place
he would later receive as his inheritance, obeyed and went,
even though he did not know where he was going.*

HEBREWS 11:6

Good morning! It is much easier to have faith and confidence when life appears to be going the way we've hoped for and have planned. But what about when the unknown and undesirable creeps in, when we're asked to do or go through uncharted, unknown territory? We balk, holler, and complain when life doesn't go our way or throws us a foul ball, or some kind of unexpected or unwanted zingers present themselves.

Abraham acted in faith! God called him to go, and he went! He didn't ask questions like "why me?" or "where am I going?" or "what's happening?" Abraham acted in faith on the knowledge of God as he knew Him.

Believing God exists is only the beginning of our journey; *even the demons believe* that much (James 2:19-20). God wants our faith to lead us to a deep personal and dynamic relationship with Him that trusts and acts upon His Word, no questions asked. God wants our trust and faith. So let me ask you—what is God asking of you? Where is He leading you? Do you trust Him? Is your faith only in things that are seen? *For we walk [live] by faith, not by sight* (2 Corinthians 5:7). Faith allows room for the unexplainable works of God and trusts His promises.

Lord, we love You. Increase in us a faith that goes beyond lip service into obedience and action, even when it involves the unknown. Lord, may we always be willing to say "yes" to You. Where You lead, we will follow; where You send us, we will go. May our trust in You never waver as we stand firm in our faith in You. You are who and all that You say You are—Lord God Almighty! Thank You, Jesus! Amen.

MARCH 28TH

Praise be to the God and Father of our Lord Jesus Christ, the Father of compassion and the God of all comfort, who comforts us in all our troubles, so that we can comfort those in any trouble with the comfort we ourselves receive from God. For just as we share abundantly in the sufferings of Christ, so also our comfort abounds through Christ.

2 CORINTHIANS 1:3–5

Good morning! We must learn to welcome every pressure and trouble, as well as we do the blessings, from God's Hand. Our circumstances are not just for our benefit to experience, go through, and learn from, but also that we might share them for someone else's benefit. Just as God comforts those who experience suffering, He wants every trial we endure to help us comfort and encourage others who are suffering similar troubles. Our suffering can make us more sensitive servants to God and empathetic to others who are suffering. *If one part suffers, every part suffers with it; if one part is honored, every part rejoices with it* (1 Corinthians 12:26). Then, how much more are we able to come alongside and be an encouragement to others?

The more we suffer, the more comfort God gives us, for He is the source of all mercy and comfort for those who are hurting. Then we are able to share the comfort He gave us with others who walk down similar paths.

Lord, thank You for preparing us to care for others through the mercy and comfort You extend to us. May our hearts be sensitive to those hurting and in need of comfort and encouragement. Thank You that You make a way for our sufferings to lead to opportunities for Your ministry in and through us. Lord, teach us how to love unconditionally those You put in our lives to serve. Thank You, Jesus! Amen.

MARCH 29TH

Do not be anxious about anything, but in everything by prayer and supplication with thanksgiving let your requests be made known to God. And the peace of God, which surpasses all understanding, will guard your hearts and your minds in Christ Jesus.

PHILIPPIANS 4:6-7

Good morning! Abandon all and let God have His way! We are not to hold on to the troubles and cares of this world. God desires so much more for us and has made a way. The phrase "fear not" or "do not be afraid" appears in the Bible over 365 times, and the phrase "do not be anxious" appears over 100 times. Are we willing to surrender all to Him? God invites us to cast our burdens onto Him because He cares and He provides. *Cast your cares on the Lord, and He will sustain you; He will never permit the righteous be shaken* (Psalm 55:22).

Strength, power and victory are ours in and through the Lord Jesus Christ! What is holding us back? God intends for our lives to hold His abundance, full of His mercy, grace, and forgiveness. When we choose to hold onto the weight of our past, the burdens of our sin and our troubles, we are denying the blessings God intends in and for our lives. Jesus bore the weight of it all that we might live. *"The thief comes only to steal and kill and destroy. I came that they may have life and have it abundantly"* (John 10:10). Whatever is weighing you down, give it to the Lord. He is willing and able to take away our burdens and give us His peace.

Lord, we thank You for making a way for us to live in peace and in Your abundance. May we choose to surrender all our cares and all our anxieties to You. Thank You for Your invitation to live an abundant life in You. Thank You, Jesus! Amen.

MARCH 30TH

I pray that out of his glorious riches he may strengthen you with power through his Spirit in your inner being, so that Christ may dwell in your hearts through faith. And I pray that you, being rooted and established in love, may have power, together with all the Lord's holy people, to grasp how wide and long and high and deep is the love of Christ, and to know this love that surpasses knowledge—that you may be filled to the measure of all the fullness of God.

EPHESIANS 3:16–19

Good morning! As you start this day, sit for a moment and experience the fullness of God in your very being. God's love reaches every corner of every experience we can and will ever have. His love is wide enough to cover each one of us and the entire world. His love is long enough to cover everyone's entire life. His love is high enough to reach every elation and celebration. His love is deep enough to reach the depths of discouragement, despair, isolation, and yes, even death. We can never be lost to God's love.

Are you experiencing the fullness of God? It is not lost! It is expressed only in Christ Jesus. In union with Christ and through His empowering Holy Spirit, we are complete. We have all the fullness of God available to us. His love is beyond our comprehension and His fullness fills every aspect of our lives. *I can do all this through him who gives me strength* (Philippians 4:13). Everything we do and everything we are is made possible through Christ Jesus. Don't miss out on the love and fullness of God.

Lord, teach us and guide us, that we would experience and remain grounded in Your immeasurable and inexhaustible love. In union with You, we are complete and have Your fullness to appropriate through faith and prayer as we live our lives for You. Thank You, Jesus! Amen.

MARCH 31ST

"Who has done this and carried it through,
calling forth the generations from the beginning?
I, the Lord—with the first of them and with the last—
I am he."

ISAIAH 41:4

Good morning! When we're stuck, overwhelmed, or just plain fed up, we are most likely focused on the wrong thing or looking for answers where they don't exist. Throughout the ages, each generation has and continues to get caught up in its own problems. But God! He has a plan for all generations: He works personally in the lives of His people. *Jesus Christ is the same yesterday, and today, and forever* (Hebrews 13:8). Jesus Christ is unchangeable. He has been and will be the same forever. We can safely put our hope and our trust in Him. We are His. We belong to Him. *"I took you from the ends of the earth, from its farthest corners I called you. I said, 'You are My servant'; I have chosen you and have not rejected you. So do not fear, for I am with you; do not be dismayed, for I am your God. I will strengthen you and help you; I will uphold you with my righteous right hand"* (Isaiah 41:8-10).

God is with us, He established a relationship with us, and He gives us the assurance of His strength, hope, and victory over all, even sin and death. So whatever you are facing, you are not facing it alone. Remain in Him! Focus on the One who makes all things new and righteous.

Lord, You are faithful and good. May we remain in You, our hearts and minds set on You. You are the author and finisher of our faith. You are the Lord, there is no other. You speak the truth and declare what is right. There is no God apart from You, our righteous God and Savior—none but You. In You, Lord alone, are deliverance and strength. Thank You, Jesus! Amen.

April

APRIL 1ST

This is what the Lord says to you: "Do not be afraid or discouraged because of this vast army. For the battle is not yours, but God's."

2 CHRONICLES 20:15

Good morning! What battle are you facing today? Temptations, fears, pressures? We do not fight our battles alone. As believers in Christ Jesus, we have God's Spirit within us! *"Take up your positions; stand firm and see the deliverance the Lord will give you, Judah and Jerusalem. Do not be afraid; do not be discouraged. Go out to face them tomorrow, and the Lord will be with you"* (2 Chronicles 20:17). We first must realize, believe, and trust that the battle is not ours, and the victory has already been won. We have human limitations, but we stand firm in His strength and His promises to rescue faithful people from challenges.

Jehoshaphat *bowed down with his face to the ground, and all the people of Judah and Jerusalem fell down in worship before the Lord ... Jehoshaphat stood and said ... "Have faith in the Lord your God and you will be upheld"* (2 Chronicles 20:18, 20). We must never waiver in our faith, but reverently seek God, honoring Him, pursuing His interests and not our own selfish desires. Bow down and worship the Lord and be obedient to His Word. *Jehoshaphat appointed men to sing to the Lord and to praise Him for the splendor of His holiness ... "Give thanks to the Lord, for His love endures forever"* (2 Chronicles 20:21). We seek God first and always for help to fight our battles and praise Him for who He is and all He does.

Lord, how we need You every day, in all circumstances. Let us not be fearful and discouraged, not wavering in faith but standing firm on Your Word. May the things that interest You be those that we pursue, seeking You first and always. Our battles are Yours, and we will find victory when we follow You. Thank You, Jesus! Amen.

APRIL 2ND

Praise be to the God and Father of our Lord Jesus Christ! In His great mercy, He has given us new birth into a living hope through the resurrection of Jesus Christ from the dead, and into an inheritance that can never perish, spoil, or fade. This inheritance is kept in heaven for you, who through faith are shielded by God's power until the coming of the salvation that is ready to be revealed in the last time.

1 PETER 1:3-5

Good morning! The intensity of Easter morning celebrations should have an impact on our lives that motivates us to a newfound boldness to proclaim the gospel to others in need. Jesus' resurrection is more than just a story. It begs for a response. We are either compelled to embrace the gospel and share it, or we disregard it. Peter's words offer joy and hope in times of trouble, and he bases his confidence on what God has done for us in Christ Jesus. This is a message worth sharing! Whom do you know that needs to hear of the living hope found in Jesus?

No matter what trials or persecutions we may face, our souls cannot be harmed if we have accepted Christ's gift of salvation. We will receive the promised rewards. *If you declare with your mouth, "Jesus is Lord," and believe in your hearts that God raised Him from the dead, you will be saved* (Romans 10:9). We should want this for everyone we know! Share the good news of Jesus to others so they too can respond.

Lord, we surrender our lives in obedience to You. We know we are not worthy, that it is by Your grace, mercy, and forgiveness alone that we are made right in You. Give us a renewed boldness and a fervor for sharing the gospel with all those You put before us. Thank You, Jesus! Amen.

APRIL 3RD

But they that wait upon the Lord shall renew their strength; they shall mount
up with wings as eagles; they shall run, and not be weary;
and they shall walk, and not faint.

ISAIAH 40:31

Good morning! What happens to us when we are waiting can be an
indicator of our level of trust and faith in the One who is in
control of all things. God uses our times of waiting to build our
character. We are not to be focused so much on what it is we are
waiting for because the details don't really matter. Whether test
results, a promotion, answers to prayers, replies to questions, or
whatever comes next, our focus must be on the One who is our
Provider and who knows.

Our time of waiting is an opportunity for spiritual growth presented
to us as we lean into trusting God and putting our hope in Him. *I wait for*
the LORD, my whole being waits, and in His Word I put my hope (Psalm
130:5).

We are not waiting for "the" answer. We are waiting on God's reply!
We may tire of the battle and the waiting, but God's power and strength
never wain. He is never too tired to listen, nor is He neglectful in
responding. Let us not tire too easily or give up but instead seek the Lord
through prayer, being still, and studying His Word. The great promise to
those who wait on and seek after the Lord is that He will be found by
them! *He rewards those who earnestly seek Him* (Hebrews 11:6). Trust and
have faith, for when He is found, there is great reward.

Lord, we wait on You, for there is no greater reward to be found! Thank You,
Lord, for Your perfect timing and Your provision that is always the best for us!
We put our trust and hope in You, the One who is faithful and true. Thank You,
Jesus! Amen.

APRIL 4TH

Dear friends, let us love one another, for love comes from God. Everyone who loves has been born of God and knows God. Whoever does not love does not know God, because God is love.

1 JOHN 4:7-8

Good morning! Have you ever really thought about God's love and how it should propel us to love—really sat down and meditated on it? Love is more than a feeling; it is a choice and an action. God's love for us propelled Him enough to sacrifice His Son, Jesus. *This is how God showed His love among us: He sent His one and only Son into the world that we might live through Him. This is love: not that we loved God, but that He loved us and sent His Son as an atoning sacrifice for our sins* (1 John 4:9-10).

God's love is our example and should be the pattern for our love to Him and others. God demonstrated a love that moves a person to self-sacrifice that is grounded in truth. God's love is sacrificial, self-giving, and merciful. *We love because He first loved us ... Anyone who loves God must also love their brother and sister* (1 John 4:19, 21). Our love is a response to God loving us first, and the response must mirror the love He demonstrated. When we love like God, we show others what God is like and make them want that kind of love in their lives too.

Lord, let us be people that love others the way You have loved us, not just in words but in deeds. Help us, Lord, to see people as You see them, to recognize their needs, and share Your love with them. Thank You for Your Holy Spirit in and through us, whose presence in our lives testifies we belong to You and gives us the power to love. Thank You, Jesus! Amen.

APRIL 5TH

But because of His great love for us, God, who is rich in mercy, made us alive with Christ even when we were dead in transgressions—
it is by grace you have been saved.

EPHESIANS 2:4

Good morning! God's mercy and grace paves the way for all who repent, turn away, and believe that they would be made new in Christ Jesus! Look around. Whom do we know that needs to hear the message of God's mercy and grace—of God's invitation to a new life? Maybe it's even you as you read this. *Therefore, if anyone is in Christ, the new creation has come. The old has gone, the new is here! All this is from God* (2 Corinthians 5:17-18). We must make the choice to turn away from sinful living and turn toward the new life God offers us. *In the same way, count yourselves dead to sin but alive to God in Christ Jesus. Therefore, do not let sin reign in your mortal body so that you obey its evil desires* (Romans 6:11).

We consider our old sinful nature as dead and unresponsive to sinful living. We live in union and identification with Christ Jesus. *You were taught, with regards to your former way of life, to put off your old self, which is being corrupted by its deceitful desires; to be made new in the attitude of your minds; and to put on the new self, created to be like God in true righteousness and holiness* (Ephesians 4:22-24).

We are alive in Christ Jesus, united to Him, and a part of His purpose. We join in a lifetime pursuit of who He is, who we are in Him, and trusting in the One who is in control, full of mercy, grace, and forgiveness.

Lord, we are new creations when we decide to accept Your free gift of salvation! We choose to make a daily commitment to seek and follow You, to put on the new and rebuke the old, to head in a new direction toward You, with a new way of thinking that Your Holy Spirit gives. Thank You, Jesus! Amen.

APRIL 6TH

Anyone who lives on milk, being still an infant, is not acquainted with the teaching about righteousness. But solid food is for the mature, who by constant use have trained themselves to distinguish good from evil.

HEBREWS 5:13-14

G ood morning! The more we seek after God, the more He reveals to us. Just as a baby doesn't remain on its mother's milk, so it is with us and the Word of God. In order to flourish in our Christian faith, we need to mature and grow. *Then we will no longer be infants ... we will grow to become in every respect the mature body of Him who is the head, that is Christ* (Ephesians 4:14a,15). Spiritual maturity is growing to become more like Christ through an ongoing, daily relationship with the Lord. It is not instantaneous; there is no shortcut. It takes discipline. Our spiritual journey should be transforming us to become more like Jesus. *But grow in the grace and knowledge of our Lord and Savior Jesus Christ* (2 Peter 3:18).

No matter where we are in our spiritual maturity, this world will always challenge our faith. We need to continually seek after knowing Christ more, to be equipped in His Word and His Ways, drawing closer to Him. *Be diligent in these matters; give yourself wholly to them, so that everyone may see your progress* (1 Timothy 4:15). Our lives should be so focused on becoming more like Jesus and serving Christ that it is obvious to everyone that our lives reflect His teachings.

Lord, may we not be content with infants' milk but hunger after the solid food of Your Word. Teach us and show us. Reveal Yourself to us. May we seek after and pursue spiritual maturity with persistence and consistency, yearning to know You more. Thank You, Jesus! Amen.

APRIL 7TH

So God created mankind in His own image, in the image of God
He created them; male and female He created them.

GENESIS 1:27

Good morning! Many of us have children in our lives whom we pray for and desire to have meaningful relationships with. When they are young, that means snuggling them, loving and nurturing them, hearing their first words and sweet little giggles. As they grow, it's experiencing milestones and connecting in moments of special conversations. It's also teaching, guiding, and disciplining them. Our Father in Heaven has these same desires for a relationship with us. He doesn't need us; He wants us. When was the last time we curled up onto God's lap, snuggled close to Him, sat quietly with Him, or had an endless conversation with Him?

We aren't meant to live apart from God! God created us for one reason: to know Him, love Him, and have fellowship with Him. Sin separated man from God. But God! He still loves us and yearns for us to be in a relationship with Him. He made a way for us to live in concert with Him for all eternity by sending His Son Jesus into this broken world to save us, God *who wants all people to be saved and to come to a knowledge of the Truth* (1 Timothy 2:4). We need to prioritize spending time with our Father God each and every day.

Lord, thank You for this day and time set aside to rest in You. May we seek to be in constant fellowship with You, an intimate relationship that grows in knowledge, love, and understanding. Teach us to be who You created us to be, that we would fulfill our purpose in this world for Your glory. Thank You, Jesus! Amen.

APRIL 8TH

You have searched me, Lord, and You know me.
Before a word is on my tongue You, Lord, know it completely.
You hem me in behind and before, and You lay Your hand upon me.
Such knowledge is too wonderful for me, too lofty for me to attain.

PSALM 139:1,4-6

Good morning! God knows. What strength, comfort, and peace this should bring to us. There are so many things we don't understand, but God! We know the One who *knows everything* (1 John 3:20). God knows our hearts; He knows our fears and our concerns; He knows our motives and our actions. When doubts and uncertainty creep in, when we feel lost or confused and simply don't understand, we can take heart—God knows and He is in the midst of whatever it is.

Where can I go from Your Spirit? Where can I flee from Your presence? If I go up to the heavens, You are there; if I make my bed in the depths, you are there. If I rise on the wings of the dawn, if I settle on the far side of the sea, even there Your hand will guide me, Your right hand will hold me fast (Psalm 139:7-12).

God is able to be everywhere at once. We have no cause for anxiety or worry, for doubt or concern, for confusion or lack of clarity, for what's happening or what's next. Because God knows. *The Lord will watch over your coming and going both now and forevermore* (Psalm 121:8). Throughout all the activities of every day, we can be confident of the Lord's presence and protection. God knows.

Lord, thank You that we don't need to know. We will never have all the answers on this side of heaven, and we aren't supposed to. We put our trust and hope in You, the One who knows. Thank You, Lord, for Your presence and protection, for being with us and watching over us. Thank You, Jesus! Amen.

APRIL 9TH

"Give us this day our daily bread."

MATTHEW 6:11

G ood morning! In the Lord's Prayer, the "daily bread" we pray for is not just the physical bread that provides our physical nourishment or sustains physical life. We are asking for spiritual nourishment and acknowledging that God is our sustainer and provider. The daily bread we need is Jesus, the bread of life. *"It is My Father who gives you the true bread from heaven. For the bread of God is the bread that comes down from heaven and gives life to the world. I am the bread of life. Whoever comes to Me will never go hungry, and whoever believes in Me will never be thirsty"* (John 6:32-33, 35).

Our spiritual hunger can only be satisfied, and our spiritual life sustained, by a right relationship with Jesus. He must be the foundation of our daily walk, as Jesus alone brings life and sustains us.

"I am the living bread that came down from heaven. Whoever eats this bread will live forever" (John 6:51). As manna came down from heaven to physically nourish the Israelites in the desert, Jesus came down from heaven for our spiritual nourishment. The ministry of Jesus is spiritual, not physical. When we eat of the living bread, we accept Christ into our lives and become united with Him. God sent the "true bread from heaven," in the form of the person Jesus, that whoever believes in Him will have eternal life.

Lord, we thank You for Your gift of daily bread, the bread of life. Lord, let us not miss Your invitation to daily intimacy with You: a life-giving relationship of faith in You that leads to one day being physically resurrected to eternal life! Thank You, Jesus! Amen.

APRIL 10TH

And let us consider how we may spur one another on toward love and good deeds, not giving up meeting together, as some are in the habit of doing, but encouraging one another—and all the more as you see the Day approaching.

HEBREWS 10:24-25

Good morning! It is vital that we surround ourselves with other believers who encourage and speak truth into our lives. Do we have a core group of people we share life with? If we want to know the Lord and become more like Him, we must surround ourselves with friends who desire the same things. Having a family of believers to regularly gather together in fellowship, prayer, and worship, provides an opportunity to share faith and strengthen each other in Christ. *As iron sharpens iron, so one person sharpens another* (Proverbs 27:17). To neglect Christian fellowship is to give up the encouragement and help of other believers. Our difficulties and busy schedules should never be excuses for missing out on gathering together but instead should propel us toward each other and Christ.

Two are better than one, because they have a good return for their labor: if either of them falls down, one can help the other up. But pity anyone who falls and has no one to help them up. Also, if two lie down together, they will keep warm. But how can one keep warm alone? Though one may be overpowered, two can defend themselves. A cord of three strands is not quickly broken (Ecclesiastes 4:9-12). Christian life is designed for community. We are not here for isolation and serving ourselves but to serve God and each other.

Lord, thank You for the family of believers You have chosen to surround us with. Let us not fall short in serving or neglect one another but instead be a support and encouragement to each other. Thank You, Jesus, for modeling Christian service and community for us to learn and to grow in spiritual maturity. Amen.

APRIL 11TH

"My sheep listen to my voice; I know them, and they follow me.
I give them eternal life, and they shall never perish;
no one will snatch them out of my hand."

JOHN 20:27-28

Good morning! What voice do we listen to? When those "conversations" happen in our minds, their content should readily reveal their source! Every single believer should recognize the voice of God, listen to, and obey what He says. God desires a relationship with us. And just as earthly relationships grow and deepen in understanding with time invested and commitments made, so it is with God.

Don't be satisfied with a Sunday-only acquaintance! Spend time with God, get to know His heart, and move into friendship with Him. *"I no longer call you servants, because a servant does not know his master's business. Instead, I have called you friends, for everything that I learned from My Father I have made known to you"* (John 15:15). What comfort and reassurance there is to know we are called friends of Jesus! But it doesn't end with friends. No, we are invited into an intimate relationship. We spend time with Him, studying in His Word, in worship, in prayer, and in silence, waiting for and expecting Him to speak.

Don't mistake the rhetoric of this world or the deceptive lies from Satan as having any merit or truth in our lives. Half of communication is listening! It is the most important half—we have two ears but only one mouth for good reason! Listen to the voice of Jesus and follow Him.

Lord, thank You for Your voice. May we be still and know it is You. Teach us through Your Word and guide us by Your Holy Spirit. Help us, Lord, to be still, to listen, and to recognize Your voice. Thank You, Jesus! Amen.

APRIL 12TH

"Enter through the narrow gate. For wide is the gate and broad is the road that leads to destruction, and many enter through it. But small is the gate and narrow the road that leads to life, and only a few find it."

MATTHEW 7:13-14

G ood morning! We told our children as they were growing up, "The choices you make today will impact the rest of your lives." A quote from the CS Lewis Institute says, "God takes sin very seriously—far more seriously than we do. We either obey God or disobey Him, there is no other option, and He holds us accountable for our choices. We make our choices, and then our choices make us."

Life boils down to two choices: the "narrow gate" that leads to eternal life, and the "wide" that's worldly and brings permanent death and suffering. Believing in Jesus is the only way to heaven, to the Father and eternal life. *"I am the only way, and the truth, and the life. No one comes to the Father except through Me"* (John 14:6).

Jesus died for our sins and made us right before God. We will be faced with temptations and trials. We will choose wrongly and sin. But God made a way for us through Jesus—the "narrow gate" which opens onto a difficult road, from a worldly perspective, but leads to eternal life. The choice for the "wide gate" appears easier with more choices, and most will prefer it, but the implication is an eternal fate of destruction. Living the way of Jesus may not be the most popular way, but it is the only way, and it is true and right.

Lord, thank You for making a way for us, One way. Thank You for showing us, leading us, and guiding us to the narrow path—the one that leads to eternal life with You. Thank You, Jesus! Amen.

APRIL 13TH

*So Christ Himself gave the apostles, the prophets, the evangelists, the pastors
and teachers, to equip His people for works of service,
so that the body of Christ may be built up until we reach unity in the faith
and in the knowledge of the Son of God and become mature,
attaining to the whole measure of the fullness of Christ.*

EPHESIANS 4:11-13

Good morning! God has equipped us to serve, each out of the
capacity of his or her own gifts or talents that were given, but to
serve, nevertheless. This is not the mentality of the self-centered
"me-first" culture we are living in. We have been given gifts to be
used to grow God's church, and it is crucial that we use them and
that we look for opportunities to be of service. We are God's church,
and as such, we were given the responsibility and calling to *"make
disciples in every nation"* (Matthew 28:18-20).

There are many tasks involved in fulfilling His command
individually and collectively. *"And you, my son Solomon, acknowledge the
God of your father, and serve Him with wholehearted devotion and with a
willing mind, for the Lord searches every heart and understands every desire
and every thought"* (1 Chronicles 28:9).

God sees and understands everything in our hearts and minds. Do we
have a servant's heart that desires to please God and fulfill the purpose
He's given us? Or are we reserved, hesitant or even resentful of what
we're being called to do? The Scripture says, *"do all things as unto the
Lord"* (Colossians 3:23).

*Thank You, Lord, for the gifts and the talents You have blessed each one of us
with. You created us with purpose and supplied us with what we need to
accomplish what You've set before us to do. May we serve You and others
unreservedly, with sincere hearts and dedicated minds. Thank You, Jesus!
Amen.*

APRIL 14TH

*"No one can serve two masters. Either you will hate the one and love the
other, or you will be devoted to the one and despise the other. You cannot
serve both God and money [possessions, fame, status,
or whatever is valued more than the Lord]."*

MATTHEW 6:24

Good morning! If we are trying to live in this world and get along
with it or simply accept it as it is, we are living in opposition
with our Lord Jesus Christ. When we accept Jesus as Lord in our life,
we cannot waiver in our belief and commitment to God and spiritual
matters. Whatever we store up, spend time and energy on, is what we
value most. Is God, not the things of this world, our master? Does He
occupy more of our thoughts, time, and efforts?

God knows what we need, and He comes alongside us to strengthen
us in carrying our burdens. *"Take My yoke upon you and learn from Me, for
I am gentle and humble in heart, and you will find rest for your souls. For My
yoke is easy and My burden is light"* (Matthew 11:29-30).

The burdens of this world are difficult and weigh us down. But God!
Come to know His strength. Take up the yoke of Jesus and learn of Him.
There is nothing to gain in this world that will ever compare. *"But as for
me and my household, we will serve the LORD"* (Joshua 24:15). There is
peace and light and joy in God. We are never weak in God's strength. He
shares our burdens and uses them for our growth and betterment and
His glory.

*Lord, may we be a people who choose to live for You. Thank You for bringing
us into a place where we have communion with You. Thank You for the
pressure of Your Hand and the strength found in Your yoke of shared burdens.
There is no other but You, Lord, our strength and redeemer God. Thank You,
Jesus! Amen.*

APRIL 15TH

*You were taught, with regard to your former way of life, to put off your old
self, which is being corrupted by its deceitful desires; to be made new
in the attitude of your minds and to put on the new self,
created to be like God in true righteousness and holiness.*

EPHESIANS 4:22-24

G ood morning! Have we accepted the extended Hand of God's
grace, mercy, and forgiveness—Christ's gift of salvation? If so, a
change should begin in our hearts, minds, and actions reflective of
Christ in our lives. We head in a new direction, turning away from
wickedness and sin, and we have a new way of thinking, that the
fruits of the Spirit would begin to manifest themselves within us.

*Get rid of all bitterness, rage and anger, brawling and slander, along with
every form of malice. Be kind and compassionate to one another, forgiving
each other, just as in Christ God forgave you. Follow God's example, therefore,
as dearly loved children, and walk in the way of love* (Ephesians 4:31-5:2).

Just as little children imitate their parents, we should imitate
Christ's love and live in sacrificial service to God and others. *Therefore, as
God's chosen people, holy and dearly loved, clothe yourselves with
compassion, kindness, humility, gentleness and patience. Bear with each
other and forgive one another if any of you has a grievance against someone.
Forgive as the Lord forgave you. And over all these virtues put on love, which
binds them all together in perfect unity* (Colossians 3:12-14). In God's
forgiveness our sins have been removed, and restoration has taken
place. We must live out of our place of restoration in the new life God
gives through Christ Jesus.

*Lord, let Your light shine in and through us, that our new life would be seen
and draw others to a saving knowledge of who You are. May we love others as
You have loved us. Thank You, Jesus! Amen.*

APRIL 16TH

*By faith Abraham, when called to go to a place
he would later receive as his inheritance, obeyed and went,
even though he did not know where he was going.*

HEBREWS 11:6

Good morning! It is much easier to have faith and confidence when life appears to be going the way we've hoped for and have planned. But what about when the unknown and undesirable creeps in, when we're asked to do or go through uncharted, unknown territory? We balk, holler, and complain when life doesn't go our way or throws us a foul ball, or some kind of unexpected or unwanted zingers present themselves.

Abraham acted in faith! God called him to go, and he went! He didn't ask questions like "why me?" or "where am I going?" or "what's happening?" Abraham acted in faith on the knowledge of God as he knew Him.

Believing God exists is only the beginning of our journey; *even the demons believe* that much (James 2:19-20). God wants our faith to lead us to a deep personal and dynamic relationship with Him that trusts and acts upon His Word, no questions asked. God wants our trust and faith. So let me ask you—what is God asking of you? Where is He leading you? Do you trust Him? Is your faith only in things that are seen? *For we walk (live) by faith, not by sight* (2 Corinthians 5:7). Faith allows room for the unexplainable works of God and trusts His promises.

Lord, we love You. Increase in us a faith that goes beyond lip service into obedience and action, even when it involves the unknown. Lord, may we always be willing to say "yes" to You. Where You lead, we will follow; where You send us, we will go. May our trust in You never waver as we stand firm in our faith in You. You are who and all that You say You are—Lord God Almighty! Thank You, Jesus! Amen.

APRIL 17TH

The Lord Jesus, on the night he was betrayed, took bread,
and when he had given thanks, he broke it and said,
"This is my body, which is for you; do this in remembrance of me."

1 CORINTHIANS 11:23–24

G ood morning! There are so many hidden lessons to be discovered in the words that Jesus spoke. Jesus "gave thanks" for His broken body and His shed blood. We can easily miss this profound message that reveals the depth of Christ's heart and His love for us. We are to pattern our lives after His, sacrificially loving, being thankful for opportunities to give of ourselves and to serve others.

When evening came, Jesus was reclining at the table with the Twelve. And while they were eating, he said, "Truly I tell you, one of you will betray me." They were very sad and began to say to him one after the other, "Surely you don't mean me, Lord?" (Matthew 26:20-22).

Jesus told His disciples that there was a betrayer amongst them, that one them eating from the common bowl together would betray Him. Jesus knew it would be Judas, but He kept that to Himself.

There are things we know about people, individuals, that should remain with us. This is the time for intercessory prayer and sharing God's Word to encourage, correct, and love them, not to gossip or slander them. We need to take time to study the recorded words of Jesus, asking Him to reveal the deeper meanings and allowing them to impact our lives and extend out into the lives of others. Love God, love others.

Lord, Your words are rich, filled with deep meaning for the betterment of our lives and those You put before us. May we not be content with skimming over the words that are written, but seek the depth and richness of what is written, the hidden meaning of what Your Word says. Lord, we long to fully know and aptly love You. Thank You, Jesus! Amen.

APRIL 18TH

Do not be anxious about anything, but in everything by prayer and supplication with thanksgiving let your requests be made known to God. And the peace of God, which surpasses all understanding, will guard your hearts and your minds in Christ Jesus.

PHILIPPIANS 4:6-7

Good morning! Abandon all and let God have His way! We are not to hold on to the troubles and cares of this world. God desires so much more for us and has made a way. The phrase "fear not" or "do not be afraid" appears in the Bible over 365 times, and the phrase "do not be anxious" appears over 100 times. Are we willing to surrender all to Him? God invites us to cast our burdens onto Him because He cares and He provides. *Cast your cares on the Lord, and He will sustain you; He will never permit the righteous be shaken* (Psalm 55:22).

Strength, power and victory are ours in and through the Lord Jesus Christ! What is holding us back? God intends for our lives to hold His abundance, full of His mercy, grace, and forgiveness. When we choose to hold onto the weight of our past, the burdens of our sin and our troubles, we are denying the blessings God intends in and for our lives. Jesus bore the weight of it all that we might live. *"The thief comes only to steal and kill and destroy. I came that they may have life and have it abundantly"* (John 10:10). Whatever is weighing you down, give it to the Lord. He is willing and able to take away our burdens and give us His peace.

Lord, we thank You for making a way for us to live in peace and in Your abundance. May we choose to surrender all our cares and all our anxieties to You. Thank You for Your invitation to live an abundant life in You. Thank You, Jesus! Amen.

APRIL 19TH

I pray that out of His glorious riches He may strengthen you with power
through His Spirit in your inner being, so that Christ may dwell in your
hearts through faith. And I pray that you,
being rooted and established in love,
may have power, together with all the Lord's holy people, to grasp how wide
and long and high and deep is the love of Christ, and to know this love
that surpasses knowledge—that you may be filled
to the measure of all the fullness of God.

EPHESIANS 3:16–19

Good morning! As you start this day, sit for a moment and experience the fullness of God in your very being. God's love reaches every corner of every experience we can and will ever have. His love is wide enough to cover each one of us and the entire world. His love is long enough to cover everyone's entire life. His love is high enough to reach every elation and celebration. His love is deep enough to reach the depths of discouragement, despair, isolation, and yes, even death. We can never be lost to God's love.

Are you experiencing the fullness of God? It is not lost! It is expressed only in Christ Jesus. In union with Christ and through His empowering Holy Spirit, we are complete. We have all the fullness of God available to us. His love is beyond our comprehension and His fullness fills every aspect of our lives. *I can do all this through him who gives me strength* (Philippians 4:13). Everything we do and everything we are is made possible through Christ Jesus. Don't miss out on the love and fullness of God.

Lord, teach us and guide us, that we would experience and remain grounded in Your immeasurable and inexhaustible love. In union with You, we are complete and have Your fullness to appropriate through faith and prayer as we live our lives for You. Thank You, Jesus! Amen.

APRIL 20TH

"Who has done this and carried it through,
calling forth the generations from the beginning?
I, the Lord—with the first of them and with the last—
I am He."

ISAIAH 41:4

Good morning! When we're stuck, overwhelmed, or just plain fed up, we are most likely focused on the wrong thing or looking for answers where they don't exist. Throughout the ages, each generation has and continues to get caught up in its own problems. But God! He has a plan for all generations: He works personally in the lives of His people. *Jesus Christ is the same yesterday, and today, and forever* (Hebrews 13:8). Jesus Christ is unchangeable. He has been and will be the same forever. We can safely put our hope and our trust in Him. We are His. We belong to Him. *"I took you from the ends of the earth, from its farthest corners I called you. I said, 'You are My servant'; I have chosen you and have not rejected you. So do not fear, for I am with you; do not be dismayed, for I am your God. I will strengthen you and help you; I will uphold you with my righteous right hand"* (Isaiah 41:8-10).

God is with us, He established a relationship with us, and He gives us the assurance of His strength, hope, and victory over all, even sin and death. So whatever you are facing, you are not facing it alone. Remain in Him! Focus on the One who makes all things new and righteous.

Lord, You are faithful and good. May we remain in You, our hearts and minds set on You. You are the author and finisher of our faith. You are the Lord, there is no other. You speak the truth and declare what is right. There is no God apart from You, our righteous God and Savior—none but You. In You, Lord alone, are deliverance and strength. Thank You, Jesus! Amen.

APRIL 21ST

*Now to Him who is able to do immeasurably (exceedingly abundantly) more
than all we can ask or imagine, according to His power at work within us,
to Him be glory in the church and in Christ Jesus throughout all generations,
for ever and ever! Amen!*

EPHESIANS 3:20–21

Good morning! We serve a limitless God, rich in glory, and
abundant in grace, mercy, and forgiveness. We put the limits on
what God can do by not believing that He *is able to do all things*, by
offering up weak prayers that lack faith, by not trusting in His
sufficiency, and by ignoring His promises. We think too small, with
expectations too low.

*Abraham in hope believed ... being fully persuaded that God had power to
do what He had promised* (Romans 4:18a, 21). Abraham never doubted
that God would fulfill His promise. He made mistakes, sinned, and had
failures, but Abraham consistently trusted God.

What about us? What limits have we put on what God can do in our
lives? A. B. Simpson said, "There is no limit to what we may ask and
expect of our glorious El Shaddai—our Almighty God. And there is no
way for us to measure His blessings."[10]

*Jesus looked at them [the disciples] and said, "With man this is
impossible, but with God all things are possible"* (Matthew 19:26). Believe
that God IS able and let His power work in and through us. *I can do all
things through Christ who strengthens me* (Philippians 4:13).

*Lord, there is no other like You. You are not confined by material space, and
You are timeless. You are not limited in Your knowledge of everything. You
have the power to do all things according to Your will. Thank You, Lord, for
loving us, for calling us unto Yourself, for giving us abundant life and purpose.
Thank You, Jesus! Amen.*

---

10. L. B. Cowman, *Streams in the Desert* (Nashville: Zondervan, 1997), 165.

APRIL 22ND

It is the Lord your God you must follow, and Him you must revere.
Keep His commands and obey Him; serve Him and hold fast to Him.

DEUTERONOMY 13:4

Good morning! Is God first in our lives? Does all that we say and do demonstrate He is first? Purpose in life begins with who we know, not what we know or how good we are. It is impossible to fulfill our God-given purpose unless we revere God and give Him first place in our lives.

Who, then, are those who fear the Lord? He will instruct them in the ways they should choose. ... The Lord confides in those who fear Him; He makes His covenant known to them. My eyes are ever on the Lord, for only He will release my feet from the snare (Psalm 25:12, 14-15).

To "fear" God is to respect and stand in awe of Him because of Who He is. There is none other like Him. He is holy, righteous, and good. He is the Almighty One. *"I am the Lord, and there is no other, apart from Me there is no other. I will strengthen you though you have not acknowledged Me. So that from the rising of the sun to the place of its setting, men may know there is none besides Me. I am the Lord and there is no other"* (Isaiah 45:5-6).

When we recognize who God is and who we are in comparison, we will humbly fall at His feet. There is no other relationship that could ever compare to the one we have with our Lord, God Almighty! He shows us His way and offers us an intimate relationship with Him. Choose God first and always.

Lord, You are our All in all, the One Who has no beginning or end, Alpha-Omega. There is no other like You. You are first and last; You go before and behind. You never leave us or forsake us. You are all we will ever need. Thank You, Jesus! Amen.

APRIL 23RD

*Be very careful, then, how you live—not as unwise but wise,
making the most of every opportunity, because the days are evil.
Therefore do not be foolish, but understand what the Lord's will is.*

EPHESIANS 5:15-17

Good morning! We are being challenged every moment of every day to *make the most of every opportunity* (Colossians 4:5), but not by our own ways, words, and thinking. We need to live with a sense of urgency, because our days are difficult and they are numbered. It is important that we keep our focus on what God's will is and not be distracted by the evil surrounding us.

Through Christ's death and resurrection, God equips us, working in and through us, to make us the kind of people and to do the kind of work that is pleasing to Him. *Now may the God of peace, who through the blood of the eternal covenant brought back from the dead our Lord Jesus Christ, that great Shepherd of the sheep, equip you with everything good for doing His will, and may He work in us what is pleasing to Him, through Jesus Christ, to whom be glory for ever and ever* (Hebrews 13:20-21).

On our own, we will fail. We need to surrender to God and let Him work in and through us. He changes us from within to make the most of us, to use us to help others.

Lord, change us from within. Use us as You will to make the most of every opportunity You set before us. Lord, may we be surrendered and obedient to Your calling in our lives, that we would be pleasing to You. Thank You, Jesus! Amen.

APRIL 24TH

One of those days Jesus went out to a mountainside to pray,
and spent the night praying to God.

LUKE 6:12

Good morning! Before every important event in Jesus' life, He took the time to go off by Himself and pray—to spend time alone with God. Jesus prioritized time with His Father. Our private devotional time with God has a direct impact on and will influence the effectiveness of our personal lives and our public ministry.

Be still and know that I am God (Psalm 46:10). Do we want to sit secure, to know our purpose and plan in this life? Get alone with God! It is during our moments alone with God that we will be connected with Him in the deepest areas of our hearts. He will open our ears to hear His voice and our minds to receive understanding of His Word. Our knowledge of and faith in Him will be strengthened. *Truly my soul finds rest in God; my salvation comes from Him. Truly He is my rock and my salvation; He is my fortress, I will never be shaken* (Proverbs 62:1-2).

When we spend time alone with God, we are able to experience a deep personal connection and intimacy with Him. Solitude with God helps us to find peace, strength, and renewal. Smith Wigglesworth shared, "Oh, how we need to get alone with God, to be broken, to be changed, to be transformed! And when we do meet with Him, He interposes, and all care and strife are brought to an end."[11]

Lord, we come before You today, each one in our own situation and set of circumstances. In the quiet of this moment, we are alone with You. May we listen as You speak to us. Reveal Yourself to us, Your purpose and plans. We long for a deeper relationship with You and are wholly Yours. May we remain surrendered and obedient to Your Word, Your will, and Your ways. Thank You, Jesus! Amen.

---

11. Smith Wigglesworth, *Smith Wigglesworth Devotional*, 195.

APRIL 25TH

In all this you greatly rejoice, though now for a little while you may have to suffer grief in all kinds of trials. These have come so that the proven genuineness of your faith—of greater worth than gold, which perishes even though refined by fire—may result in praise, glory and honor when Jesus Christ is revealed.

1 PETER 1:6–7

Good morning! Whatever the trials and pain (they are promised to come), there is purpose and victory in Christ Jesus. God does not leave us alone or abandon us in the midst of them. He will provide all that we need to see it through, and His result will be glorious. The trials are part of the refining process that burns away our impurities and prepares us to meet Jesus. Just as gold is heated to bring the impurities to the top to be skimmed away, our trials, struggles, and persecutions refine and strengthen our faith, making us useful to God.

We may find ourselves consumed in frustration as a result of the negative circumstances that surround us. But the reality of our eternal circumstances and our faith in Christ Jesus give us cause to rejoice. *For our light and momentary troubles are achieving for us an eternal glory that far outweighs them all* (2 Corinthians 4:17).

Our human problems and limitations have purpose and should not diminish our faith. Our trials are temporary, and the eternal glory of heaven will far exceed our earthly difficulties.

Lord, thank You for Your sustaining power in and through Your Holy Spirit. In the midst of our trials, may we find ourselves holding on to our faith and the truth of the eternal glory promised us through Christ Jesus. Thank You, Jesus! Amen.

APRIL 26TH

Then King David went in and sat before the Lord and said, "Who am I, oh Lord God, and what is my house that you have brought me thus far?"

1 CHRONICLES 17:16

Good morning! I know who I am, and I know what I deserve—but God! We deserve nothing, but God gives everything! Sit for a moment and think about what King David is saying here. He is receiving the promises from God, the blessings from God, and his question is, "Who am I?"

We should consider this same question—who are we that we have received God's promises and blessings? That we know Who He is and Whose we are! It is not on our own merit. We've done nothing to deserve to be in a relationship with or to have eternal life in Him. *For it is by grace you have been saved, through faith—and this is not from yourselves, it is the gift of God—not by works, so that no one can boast* (Ephesians 2:8-9).

So let me ask you, what are you doing with the gifts God has given you? There are over three billion people who need the gospel who have not heard the good news of God's grace in Jesus, so why us? Why haven't they heard? And why have we? Why have we heard, believed, and know we are saved, redeemed children of the Most High King, the Lord God Almighty through the death and resurrection of His Son Jesus Christ?!

We have been given the gospel for a reason, and it is not solely for us! It's for the spreading of the Good News to every person, everywhere.

Lord, none of us deserve to be in Your presence. We thank You and praise You that we are Yours. We pray for the unsaved, for those who don't know You, for those who have never heard of You, for those who have rejected You. Lord, may we be Your Light in the darkness. Renew us, empower us, and embolden us with Your Holy Spirit that we would truly be on fire with and for You. Thank You, Jesus! Amen.

APRIL 27TH

The Lord is near to all who call on Him,
to all who call on Him in prayer [truth].

PSALM 145:18

Good morning! What does our prayer life consist of? Are we in a hurry? Are we just going through the motions, repeating memorized prayers or crying out our needs and wants? Prayer is one of God's greatest gifts and such a privilege—an invitation to spend time with Him. To call on God in prayer is like a visit with a close friend, where you knock on the door and are invited in for a conversation. *Pray without ceasing [continually]* (1 Thessalonians 5:17). This is a command and means that we should pray always, all the time, a lot!

Do not be anxious about anything, but in everything by prayer and supplication with thanksgiving let your requests be made known to God (Philippians 4:7). God knows what we need before we ask (Matthew 6:8), yet He invites us to pray for our needs with gratitude. Jesus encouraged persistent prayer and modeled it throughout His earthly ministry.

From beginning to end, the Bible is filled with invitations to approach God—to be with Him, to draw close to Him, to receive guidance and comfort, to praise and worship Him, and to simply share what's on our hearts with Him. The more time we spend with God, our Heavenly Father, the more intimate our relationship, the more we'll know Him and recognize His voice.

Lord, teach us how to pray! Let our hearts be sincere and filled with the desire to know You, increasing with each moment spent with You. Thank You for Your open invitation to pray and to come near to You, our God. Thank You, Jesus! Amen.

APRIL 28TH

Blessed is the one who perseveres under trial because,
having stood the test, that person will receive the crown of life
that the Lord has promised to those who love Him.

JAMES 1:12

Good morning! Oh, how we fight against our trials, praying for them to be lifted and blessings to come. "Every highway of life descends into the valley now and then. And everyone must go through the tunnel of tribulation before they can travel on the high road of triumph."[12]

There is great purpose in the trials we endure. *The testing of your faith produces perseverance. Let perseverance finish its work in you that you may be mature and complete, not lacking anything* (James 1:3-4). We will never know the depth of our character through smooth sailing but by seeing how we respond under pressure. It is easy to be kind, loving and compassionate to those who agree with us. But what about when we are unduly accused or in the midst of struggles? Is our response that of the character of Christ? Thank God for His promise of tough times.

There is great purpose in each tribulation we face. Instead of praying for them to be removed quickly, ask for help in solving the problem or the strength to endure them. God's crown of life is not glory and honor on earth, but the reward of eternal life—living with God forever. The way to be in God's winners' circle is by loving Him and staying faithful even under pressure.

Lord, may we learn to rejoice whenever we face trials, having a response worthy of You and in keeping with what trials can produce in our lives. May we turn our hardships into times of learning, trusting in You, growing in and deepening our faith. Thank You, Jesus! Amen.

---

12. L. B. Cowman, *Streams in the Desert* (Nashville: Zondervan, 1997), 174.

APRIL 29TH

In You, Lord, my God, I put my trust. I trust in You ...

PSALM 25:1-2

Good morning! Life is full of surprises. We never know what's next! The One we can be certain of is God! David addressed his prayer to the One and only true God, Yahweh, the covenant-keeping God. Prayer is an opportunity to wholeheartedly focus on God, earnestly sharing our hearts and minds. It is an exercise of faith, of certainty in God, leaving everything to Him.

"Even to your old age and gray hairs I am He, I am He who will sustain you. I have made you and I will carry you; I will sustain you and I will rescue you" (Isaiah 46:4). God created us, and He cares for us, not just for a moment in time, but throughout our lifetime and even through death. In every uncertain time, we have the certainty of God's promises, confirmed with an oath (Hebrews 6:17).

Oswald Chambers said, "To be certain of God means that we are uncertain in all our ways, we do not know what a day may bring forth."[13] But God! We are uncertain of the next step, but we are certain of God. We abandon all to Him and He packs our lives full of surprises. Those who leave everything in God's Hands will eventually see God's Hands in everything.

Lord, life is full of ups and downs, constant uncertainties. There is only One certainty, and that is You. With You, Lord, we can face whatever may come with a full assurance of Your presence. May we seek You first and always. "But seek first His kingdom and His righteousness, and all these things will be given you as well" (Matthew 6:33). Thank You, Jesus! Amen.

---

13. *Oswald Chambers, My Utmost for His Highest, February 17th. 2017 by Discovery House*

APRIL 30TH

Is there anything too hard for the Lord?

GENESIS 18:14

Good morning! There is no work too much for God! *Nothing is too hard for You [the Lord]!* (Jeremiah 32:17). What is your circumstance? Disobedient children? Struggling relationship or failing marriage? Financial distress? The list is endless! Stop trying to "fix life" yourself. There is one answer, and it is not us! God's power is limitless, His promises secure. His love is endless, and His mercy endures forever. *"I am the Lord, the God of all mankind. Is anything too hard for Me?"* (Jeremiah 32:27).

Surrender all to Him! There is no greater action we can choose or take. There is no situation or person too hard or too difficult for God to change. It is our unwilling hearts and spirits, our ungodly attitudes, that bind the very able, willing Hands that want to bless us.

For You are great and do marvelous deeds; You alone are God. Teach me Your way, Lord, that I may rely on Your faithfulness; give me an undivided heart, that I may fear Your Name. I will praise You, Lord my God, with all my heart; I will glorify Your Name forever. For great is Your love toward me; You have delivered me from the depths, from the realm of the dead (Psalm 86:10-13).

There is only one answer to our dilemmas: that One is God. He is alive and able to do mighty things for those who love Him, who believe and follow Him. Only He is worthy of our praise.

Lord, we surrender all to You. Humbly we come before You, Lord. Teach us Your ways and give us undivided hearts! Increase our awareness of You and improve our obedience to You! More of You, less of us. You are the One, the only answer we will ever and always need. Thank You, Jesus! Amen.

May

MAY 1ST

His divine power has given us everything we need for a godly life through our knowledge of Him who called us by His own glory and goodness. Through these He has given us His very great and precious promises, so that through them you may participate in the divine nature, having escaped the corruption in the world caused by evil desires.

2 PETER 1:3–4

Good morning! God's promises are certain! And the only way to know the promises of God is to study His Word, to know Him, and to know what they are. When we are born again in His promises, God by His Spirit empowers us with His own moral goodness, *in the hope of eternal life, which God, who does not lie, promised before the beginning of time* (Titus 1:2). Are we growing in Christ Jesus? Do we know and are we participating in, and receiving, the promises of God?

Grace and peace be yours in abundance through the knowledge of God and of Jesus our Lord (2 Peter 1:2). We all, as believers, want an abundance of God's grace and peace, but are we willing to put forth the effort to get to know Him better through Bible study and prayer? To partake in and enjoy the privileges God offers us freely (His promises), we must have *the knowledge of God and Jesus our Lord* that comes from the Spirit of God. The eternal life that God has promised will be ours, because He keeps His promises. We must build our faith on the foundation of a trustworthy God, *who does not lie.*

Lord, thank You for giving us everything we need to live in abundance in and through You. May we fervently seek after You, to grow in our knowledge and understanding of Your Word and who You are. Thank You for Your promise of eternal life to those who believe. Thank You, Jesus! Amen.

MAY 2ND

*Now to Him who is able to do immeasurably [exceedingly, abundantly]
more than we ask or imagine, according to His power that is at work
within us, to Him be glory in the church and in Christ Jesus
throughout all generations, for ever and ever! Amen!*

EPHESIANS 3:20-21

Good morning! God is able! We cannot fathom His power, His
love, or His desire for us. We approach Him with such limited
faith and belief in what He can and will do. I'm not talking about our
material requests or our "please fix it" prayers. Do we believe He can
change us, transform us from weak, broken sinners to strong,
restored disciples for Him?

*My flesh and my heart may fail, but God is the strength of my heart and
my portion forever* (Psalm 73:26). Our strength is found in God. He is the
One who can do for us what we could never do alone, without Him.

*We are glad whenever we are weak but you are strong; and our prayer is
that you may be fully restored* (2 Corinthians 13:9). Paul was encouraging
the Corinthians to grow into mature believers. The power of Christ
dwells and is at work within us. He is able to keep His people from falling
prey to deception and lies when we fully trust and are grounded in Him.
*To Him who is able to keep you from stumbling and to present you before His
glorious presence without fault and with great joy—to the only God our
Savior be glory, majesty, power and authority, through Jesus Christ our Lord,
before all ages, now and forevermore! Amen!* (Jude 24-25.) Yes, our God IS
able! He is God, and we are not!

*Lord, we live in treacherous times, closer than ever to Your return. We need not
fear or throw up our hands in despair. You are able to do ALL things! You keep
us from falling, and You promise that if we remain faithful, You will bring us
into Your presence, fully restored and redeemed, giving us everlasting joy and
peace. Thank You, Jesus! Amen.*

MAY 3RD

"I will give you a new heart and put a new spirit in you;
I will remove from you your heart of stone and give you a heart of flesh."

EZEKIEL 36:26

Good morning! Any of us can change our mind, but only God can change hearts! God gives us a new heart for following Him, and He puts His Spirit in us. We are new creations in Christ Jesus, transformed and empowered to do God's will and to love as He loves us. No matter what we've done or where we've come from, God offers a new and a fresh start. We can have our sins washed away, receive a cleansed heart, and have His Spirit dwell within us.

Create in me a pure heart, O God, and renew a steadfast spirit within me (Psalm 51:10). David wrote these words after having stolen another man's wife. He sought God's forgiveness and asked Him to cleanse him from the inside. Our sin nature drives us to wrong thinking and behaviors perpetuated out of our self-centeredness. But God! He is able to wash us clean, cleanse our hearts from the guilt of sin, and fill us with God's love and His Holy Spirit.

For God, who said, "Let light shine out of darkness," made His Light shine in our hearts to give us the light of the knowledge of God's glory displayed in the face of Christ (2 Corinthians 4:6). It is God who gives us a new heart for following Him and puts His Spirit in us. God's light and glory can only come out of a clean heart and spirit.

Lord, thank You for the fresh start we can have through accepting You. Cleanse our hearts for Your glory! Make us pure of heart, that our thoughts and desires would be pleasing to You. Fill us with Your Light and Your Love, with hearts made new. Thank You Lord! Amen.

MAY 4TH

Abraham believed God, and it was credited to him as righteousness.

GENESIS 15:6

Good morning! Are we living out a faith in whom we believe and not what we believe? Abraham demonstrated his faith through his actions, but it was his belief in the Lord, not his actions, that made him right with God. A right relationship is based on faith—the heartfelt inner confidence that God is who He says He is and does what He says He will do.

Right actions are natural by-products of believing in God. All the "right" outward actions—church attendance, prayer, good deeds—will not of themselves make us right with God. We must know in whom we believe! Real faith depends upon the character of God and looks nowhere else. *I know whom I have believed, and am convinced that He is able to guard what I have entrusted to Him until that day* (2 Timothy 1:12).

Our trust is in the One so powerful that even our weak faith is sufficient. Like Paul, we must base our confidence in Christ on an intimate relationship with Him, with personal knowledge of God. *And without faith it is impossible to please God, because anyone who comes to Him must believe that He exists and that He rewards those who earnestly seek Him* (Hebrews 11:6). Stop looking for outside answers to an inside solution—but God! He is all we need! "Know God, know peace. No God, no peace."

Lord, may our faith be rooted deep in who You are. Our faith is not about what we believe, but in whom we believe. And we believe in You—the author and finisher of our faith, our All in all, Alpha-Omega, beginning and end. Thank You, Jesus! Amen.

MAY 5TH

As for God, His ways are perfect; The Lord's Word is flawless;
He shields all who take refuge in Him. For who is God besides the Lord?
And who is the Rock except our God? It is God who arms me with strength
and keeps my way secure.

PSALM 18:30-32

Good morning! The weak are made strong by the power of God. Our dependence should be in God alone. God is our shield when we are too weak to face certain trials by ourselves. But He also strengthens, protects, and guides us in order to face this world triumphantly in and for Him. *My soul finds rest in God alone; my salvation comes from Him. He alone is my rock and my salvation; He is my fortress, I will never be shaken* (Psalm 62:6).

Trusting God to be our rock, salvation, and fortress changes our entire outlook on life. When we are resting in God's strength, nothing can shake us. *My salvation and my honor depend on God; He is my mighty rock, my refuge. Trust in Him at all times, you people; pour out your hearts to Him, for God is our refuge* (Psalm 62:7-8).

There is no other like our God. He is Mighty to save. Even in the midst of our trials, troubles, and sufferings, we can rely on God by trusting that He is in control. We are invited to bring everything to Him: *pour out your hearts to Him.* He is our refuge and hiding place from the storms of life, and He gives us strength and keeps us secure.

Lord, we can't begin to comprehend Your ways, but we can and will put our trust and hope in You. You alone are God! You are our Protector and Provider, our Redeemer and Savior. Our strength is found in You! Thank You, Jesus! Amen.

MAY 6TH

When Jesus spoke again to the people, He said, "I am the Light of the world. Whoever follows Me will never walk in darkness, but will have the Light of life."

JOHN 8:12

Good morning! We cannot hide from God. He sees all we do, whether we choose to remain in the darkness or come into His Light. There is nothing we say or do in our lives that can be kept hidden from God. When we try to hide in darkness from Him, we are only delaying or preventing the changes needed to live lives according to God's plan and purpose.

Jesus brings Light to mankind. In His Light, we see who we really are—sinners in need of a Savior. When we say "yes" to Jesus, believe in, and follow Him, His Light fills us so we no longer have to walk blindly in the darkness. The true Light of Christ and His Word light our way. *Your word is a lamp for my feet, a light on my path* (Psalm 119:105).

When we walk in darkness, we are prone to stumble and fall into sin and evil. God's Word reveals the things that trip us up, false values, and wrong priorities. As we walk in His Light, Jesus shows us the Way in which we are to go. He points us onto the right path. *"In the same way, let your Light shine before others, that they may see your good deeds and glorify your Father in heaven"* (Matthew 5:16). In turn, we have the opportunity to shine brightly for Christ, pointing others to Him and sharing His love.

Lord, may we choose to live in the Light of Your Word, and share Your brightness with those around us. You have rescued us from the dangers of darkness, setting us on a safe path with You leading and guiding us. May we shine brightly in the dark world, that others may see who You are and come to know You. Thank You, Jesus! Amen.

MAY 7TH

Now all has been heard; here is the conclusion of the matter: Fear God and keep His commandments, for this is the duty of all mankind.

ECCLESIASTES 12:13

Good morning! It is not up to us where God will put us or how God will use us. It is only for us to surrender all in obedience to His calling and find our hope and purpose for His glory. Our lives are for the purpose of knowing God! Our purpose and meaning are not found in the things of this world or in our human endeavors. Our efforts apart from God are futile. God comes first—now and always. Everything and anything good is a gift from God Himself.

In Him we were also chosen, having been predestined according to the plan of Him who works out everything in conformity with the purpose of His will, in order that we, who were the first to put our hope in Christ, might be for the praise of His glory (Ephesians 1:11). God's purpose is to offer salvation to the world, just as He planned. God is Sovereign, and He is in control. Nothing happens that He doesn't know. When life seems crazy and out of control, when we don't know what to do next, God knows. Rest in His Truth: Jesus is Lord. God's purpose for our lives cannot be blocked or defeated. No matter what this world or Satan may bring, God's victory is won.

Lord, thank You for the Presence of Your Holy Spirit and the Power of Your work in us, transforming us for Your good purposes, and the Promise of life eternal with You. We are wholly and dutifully Yours. Thank You, Jesus! Amen.

MAY 8TH

... because God has said, "Never will I leave you; never will I forsake you."

HEBREWS 13:5

Good morning! Why do we choose to walk alone when we have an open invitation from the greatest companion of all? God is always with us! Do you believe this? Are you experiencing His presence in the midst of your days? Throughout God's Word He promises to walk with us in and through our lives if we seek Him. *"If you seek Him, He will be found by you"* (1 Chronicles 28:9). King David told his son Solomon, *"Acknowledge the God of your father, and serve Him with wholehearted devotion and a willing mind, for the Lord searches every heart and understands every desire and every thought"* (1 Chronicles 28:9).

God assuredly is with us always, but do we choose to be with Him and serve Him with wholehearted devotion? What priorities in our lives take precedence? *Keep your lives free from the love of money and be content with what you have, because God has said, "Never will I leave you; never will I forsake you." So we say with confidence, "The Lord is my helper; I will not be afraid. What can mere mortals do to me?"* (Hebrews 13:5-6). Yes, God is our constant companion, but experiencing His presence rests in our acknowledging Him as Lord.

Lord, may we look to You today and every day. Show us, Lord, what it means to "serve You with wholehearted devotion." Our contentment is found in realizing and trusting in Your sufficiency to meet all our needs and knowing You are always with us. "You hem us in behind and before; and You lay Your Hand upon us" (Psalm 139:5). You know us and love us completely. We praise You, worship You, and magnify Your Name, our Lord and constant companion. Thank You, Jesus! Amen.

MAY 9TH

Sing to the Lord a new song; sing to the Lord, all the earth. Sing to the Lord, praise His name; proclaim His salvation day after day. Declare His glory among the nations, His marvelous deeds among all peoples. For great is the Lord and most worthy of praise; He is to be feared above all gods.

PSALM 96:1-4

Good morning! Are we overwhelmed by all that the Lord has done for us? His marvelous works are too much to contain and should lead us to ceaseless praise and worship. It is impossible to refrain from sharing who He is and all He's done. So worthy is the Lord that His praise overflows from our hearts into songs and acts of worship.

Many, Lord my God, are the wonders You have done, the things You planned for us. None can compare with You; were I to speak and tell of Your deeds, they would be too many to declare (Psalm 40:5). God's wonderful works are too numerous to fully recount or describe. The magnitude of His power is beyond our comprehension. All that God does and who He is should compel us to share about Him with others.

How precious to me are Your thoughts, God! How vast is the sum of them! Were I to count them, they would outnumber the grains of sand—when I awake, I am still with You (Psalm 139:17-18). We can't do anything for God until we understand the depth of the knowledge of His love for us. God thinks of us all the time, and we get to be with Him any time we want. He is worthy of all honor and praise.

Lord, we thank You and praise You for who You are and all that You have done, are doing, and will continue to do in our lives. We cannot grasp the magnitude of Your works or Your love that compels us to respond in endless praise and worship. Thank You, Jesus! Amen.

MAY 10TH

What does the Lord your God ask of you but to fear the Lord your God, to walk in obedience to Him, to love Him, to serve the Lord your God with all your heart and with all your soul, to observe the Lord's commands and decrees that I am giving you today for your own good?

DEUTERONOMY 10:12-13

Good morning! Many are bristled by this, and some walk away—there are rules to kingdom living. We don't get to enjoy all the benefits without following the rules. "What?" you might be asking. We have been saved by grace, but that doesn't excuse us from living in obedience to God's Word, which is both necessary and beneficial. David Jeremiah wrote, "God has given us rules for our own good, and when we obey them, we're healthier, happier, and holier."[14]

Obedience not only glorifies God, it also blesses our lives and others. Ephesians 4:32 commands us to *be kind and compassionate to one another, forgiving each other, just as in Christ God forgave you.* Being kind and compassionate means taking on characteristics of God for the benefit of ourselves and others.

The command of forgiveness is given throughout the gospels and within the Lord's Prayer. God does not forgive us because we deserve it or because we are willing to forgive others, but solely because of His mercy. When we come to understand His mercy, we desire to become more like Him and extend that to others. Yes, God gives us rules because He is so good, and He wants what is good for us.

Lord, may we choose to follow You and follow Your rules of kingdom living. You are our Creator and know how we are intended best to function. You are an expert on the care of souls. O Lord, that our lives will glorify and magnify You! Thank You for loving us enough to bless us with Your commands. Thank

---

14. David Jeremiah, *Turning Points with God* (Carol Stream: Tyndale House Publishers, 2014), 137.

MAY 11TH

*"Come to me, all you who are weary and burdened, and I will give you rest.
Take My yoke upon you and learn from Me, for I am gentle
and humble in heart, and you will find rest for your souls."*

MATTHEW 11:28-30

Good morning! It is a rainy morning, and our house is quiet except for the soft snoring of our dog Raleigh. I am fully aware this is a different stage of life from many who might be reading this. Your time will come too. What struck me as I studied this morning are the words of this hymn: "My goal is God Himself, not joy, nor peace, Nor even blessing, but Himself, my God; 'Tis His to lead me there—not mine, but His—At any cost, dear Lord, by any road."[15]

For many years, my prayers were centered on escaping where I was in my life—the self-inflicted chaos, challenging circumstances, difficulties, any discomfort life presented to me. But God! He knows best! He can and will use whatever is necessary to draw us to Himself. He desires us to know Him, to be in fellowship with Him. Man's solutions are temporary and fleeting and ultimately lead to death. God is the only real and lasting answer in and to life, and He repeatedly, constantly invites us into relationship with Him. *But seek first His kingdom and His righteousness, and all these things will be given to you as well* (Matthew 6:33). Stop trying to navigate life alone, carrying heavy burdens you are not intended to bear on your own efforts. Jesus took them all upon Himself on the cross to set us free to live abundant lives in and through Him. I don't know your burden, but I do know without any doubt that God is your answer!

Lord, we don't deserve Your grace, mercy and forgiveness, but You freely offer it to us. Whatever we're facing, we give it all to You. We exchange it for knowing You! Do what You must to break the chains that bind us from being wholly Yours, for You, Lord, are all we need! Thank You, Jesus! Amen.

---

15. Frances Brook, "My Goal Is God Himself," public domain.

MAY 12TH

So then, just as you received Christ Jesus as Lord, continue to live your lives in Him, rooted and built up in Him, strengthened in the faith as you were taught and overflowing with thankfulness. See to it that no one takes you captive through hollow and deceptive philosophy, which depends on human tradition and the elemental spiritual forces of this world rather than on Christ.

COLOSSIANS 2:6–8

Good morning! Are we living lives grounded in Christ? Receiving Christ as Lord of our lives is just the beginning of life with Him. Like a tree planted by water receives nourishment from the soil and stream, we must be planted deep in life-giving strength from Christ Jesus. Our faith is a result of being rooted in Christ, not ourselves, as we walk with and draw our strength from Him.

"*I am the vine; you are the branches. If you remain in Me and I in you, you will bear much fruit; apart from Me you can do nothing*" (John 15:5). Jesus likens himself to a vine and His disciples (us) to branches. We are nourished by staying close to Jesus, like a branch attached to the vine. Jesus is the gardener who nourishes our spirits, and if we remain faithful to Him, we will bear much fruit. Apart from Him, we wither like a branch separated and thrown away.

God is glorified when we are in the right relationship with Him. It is then that we begin to "bear much fruit" for building His kingdom.

Lord, thank You for making a way for us to remain rooted in You. Without You, we are not able to live truly good lives. We need to be and stay close to You. Thank You for loving us, nurturing us, and growing the fruits of Your Spirit in us, the qualities of Your character. Thank You, Jesus! Amen.

But in fact God has placed the parts in the body, every one of them, just as He wanted them to be. If they were all one part, where would the body be? As it is, there are many parts, but one body.

1 CORINTHIANS 12:18-20

Good morning! We each have a part to play in the work of God. Not one is greater or lesser—all are needed. We are not in competition with each other but intended to be the unified body of Christ. The church is composed of many types of people from a variety of backgrounds, with a myriad of gifts and abilities. These differences are not intended to divide but to unite us in accomplishing what God sets before us to do. Believers are united by their faith in Christ and baptized by one Holy Spirit into one body of believers. We maintain our individual identities, but we have an overriding oneness and purpose in Christ Jesus. No one is superior or inferior in the body of Christ.

Therefore encourage one another and build each other up, just as in fact you are doing. Now, we ask you, brothers and sisters, to acknowledge those who work hard among you, who care for you in the Lord and who admonish you. Hold them in the highest regard in love because of their work. Live in peace with each other (1 Thessalonians 5:11-13).

Believers are called to be an encouragement to one another, to band together in sharing life—work and play, joy and sorrow, united in purpose and love.

Lord, sometimes we fail miserably at being Your body. Help us to be united in purpose and plan. Teach us and show us our part, refine us to be effective, loving and doing what You have created and called us to do. Lord, may we learn to encourage each other in love, without jealousy, malice, and pride, that we would grow in You and increase in numbers for the purpose of making Your gospel known. Thank You, Jesus! Amen.

MAY 14TH

But we have this treasure in jars of clay to show that this all-surpassing
power is from God and not from us. We are pressed on every side,
but not crushed; perplexed, but not in despair; persecuted,
but not abandoned; struck down, but not destroyed. We always carry around
in our body the death of Jesus, so that the life of Jesus may also be revealed in
our body. For we who are alive are always being given over to death for
Jesus' sake, so that His life may also be revealed In our mortal bodies.

2 CORINTHIANS 4:7–11

Good morning! What is the disposition of our response when we feel like *we are pressed on every side* from the disagreeable things in life? Do we reveal Jesus, or do we display our irritation and frustration? Paul reminds us that we may feel at the end of our rope, beyond our capacity, but we are never without hope. Our perishable bodies are subject to sin and suffering, but God never abandons us. We press into Him, that the Christ in us will be what shines through and out of us.

But thanks be to God! He gives us the victory through our Lord Jesus Christ! (1 Corinthians 15:57). Christ has won the victory, and we who are in Christ Jesus share in His victory. We are able to claim and live the victorious life Christ has set before us. All our risks, humiliations, and trials are opportunities for Christ to demonstrate His power and presence in and through us.

Lord, thank You for Your all-surpassing power and the victory we have been given through You. We pray that when opposition, slander, or disappointment threaten to rob us of our victory, we stand firm in our faith and in what You have accomplished in and through our lives. May we represent You well. Thank You, Jesus! Amen.

MAY 15TH

Do not merely listen to the word, and so deceive yourselves. Do what it says ...
But whoever looks intently into the perfect law that gives freedom,
and continues in it—not forgetting what they have heard, but doing it—
they will be blessed in what they do.

JAMES 1:22, 25

Good morning! It is important that we study and listen to what God's Word says, but it is even more important that we obey it, to do what it says. Hearing the Word without action is self-deceptive. *Be doers of the Word, and not hearers only* (James 1:22 NKJV). Hearers only listen to and know God's Word but never live it out. Doers, on the other hand, listen, know, and obey.

We are not here to dictate to God. We are here to submit to His will so He can work through us what He wants. If we are still stuck in the "me" and the "I," we are not living surrendered lives to Him. We must stop telling God what we want Him to do and live in surrendered obedience to what His Word says and what he is calling us to do.

We are saved by God's grace, and salvation frees us from sin's control. We are free to live as God created us to live, but that does not mean we are free to do as we please. Our obedience is an effective measure of our surrender and the maturity of our faith.

Lord, thank You for Your Word. May we be obedient doers, not just hearers, that we would do whatever You put before us to do. Transform us, Lord, into vessels for Your work and glory. It is You we desire to serve and please. Thank You Lord for saving us and for the hope of eternity before us. Thank You, Jesus! Amen.

MAY 16TH

And this is the testimony: God has given us eternal life,
and this life is in His Son. Whoever has the Son has life;
whoever does not have the Son of God does not have life.

1 JOHN 5:11-12

Good morning! Sun-filled mornings seem to make everything just a little bit better. But a Son-filled life—there is definitely nothing better than that! Whoever believes in God's Son has eternal life, that is freely given, a gift from God Himself—guaranteed! Jesus is all we need. He is the giver of life! But there is another who, in contrast, steals life away. *"The thief comes only to steal and kill and destroy. I came that they may have life and have it abundantly"* (John 10:10). The thief intends only to wreak havoc, causing destruction and suffering.

Jesus' purpose is life, and the life He gives right now is abundantly richer and fuller. It is eternal, yet it begins immediately. The abundant life Jesus offers is more than material wealth and prosperity. It is the promised life of fullness, joy, and strength for our spirits, souls, and bodies. It's a life not built on outside circumstances but on a relationship with God. *"I give them eternal life, and they shall never perish; no one will snatch them out of My hand"* (John 10:28).

Life in the Son, Jesus Christ, is an abundant life because of who He is and all He does. There is no one like Jesus! Accept God's Son and live in abundance and eternity.

Lord, You give us eternal life. We will not perish, and no one can snatch us out of Your Hand. You are the Way, the Truth, and the Life. No one comes to the Father except through You. Lord, illuminate our lives with Your Presence! May we choose to be surrendered and obedient to Your calling that we would experience abundant life and share Your gospel with all whom You put in our paths. Thank You, Jesus! Amen.

MAY 17TH

Then Jesus said to his disciples, "Whoever wants to be my disciple must deny themselves and take up their cross and follow me. For whoever wants to save their life will lose it, but whoever loses their life for me will find it.

MATTHEW 16:24-25

Good morning! There is no decision, nothing we could ever do, that has more impact than surrendering our lives to Jesus. And yet, we hesitate because we know that means surrendering ourselves—our self-centeredness and selfish desires. We want the good stuff that comes from following Jesus—the fruits of the Spirit: *"love, joy, peace, patience, kindness, goodness, faithfulness, gentleness, and self-control"* (Galatians 5:22). But we don't want to give up ourselves and the things of this world. But what benefit do they produce?

What good will it be for someone to gain the whole world, yet forfeit their soul? Or what can anyone give in exchange for their soul? For the Son of Man is going to come in His Father's glory with His angels, and then He will reward each person according to what they have done (Matthew 16:26-27).

We make choices as if this world were all there is and all we have. If we know Jesus Christ as our Lord and Savior, our choices must be different, honoring and obedient to Him. This life is but an introduction to eternity, and what we accumulate here has no bearing in the eternal life set before us. Each one of us—believers and non-believers—will face a final judgment. How are we handling the gifts, opportunities, and responsibilities God's given us? Will we hear our Savior's precious words, *"Well done, good and faithful servant!"* (Matthew 25:23)?

Lord, we commit our lives to following You. May we look to You each and every day, with a deep desire to know You and please You. There is nothing in this world of any value but You and the people You put before us to love. May we love You, and love others well. Thank You, Jesus! Amen.

MAY 18TH

"But blessed is the one who trusts in the Lord, whose confidence is in Him."

JEREMIAH 17:7

Good morning! It is easy to remain faithful when life is smooth, and our road is level. But what happens when adversity strikes, when the news is not good, when the unforeseen comes out of nowhere and totally disrupts the rhythm of our lives? In times of trouble, those who trust in human beings will come up short, without strength or resolve. But those who trust in the Lord will have abundant strength, not just for themselves but even for those around them. *Cast your cares on the LORD and He will sustain you; He will never let the righteous be shaken* (Psalm 55:22). God invites us to bring everything to Him, to share all our burdens with Him. He is waiting for us to surrender them to Him. There is nothing that is too much or too big for our God!

Is worry and anxiety wearing you down? Did an unforeseen tragedy or illness strike? *Do not be anxious about anything, but in every situation, by prayer and petition, with thanksgiving, present your requests to God* (Philippians 4:6). The same God who saves us from our sin, who sets our feet upon the rock of salvation, is trustworthy to save us from whatever trial or circumstance we currently face. It seems impossible that we would never be anxious or worried in the midst of life's challenges, but Paul's advice is to turn everything over to God in prayer. Pray more, worry less.

Lord, thank You for being just a prayer away. May our trust increase and our faith be strengthened in the midst of life's challenges. Thank You that there is nothing we can't share with You and be strengthened by Your presence. Thank You, Jesus! Amen.

MAY 19TH

And the peace of God, which surpasses all understanding,
will guard your hearts and minds in Christ Jesus.

PHILIPPIANS 4:7

Good morning! The secret to living a more peaceful life can be found in the pages of God's Word. First, don't look back! In the story of the destruction of Sodom and Gomorrah, God sends two angels to warn Abraham's nephew Lot to *"Flee for your lives! Don't look back, and don't stop anywhere in the plain! Flee to the mountains or you will be swept away!"* (Genesis 19:17). But Lot's wife disobeys. She stops to look back at the life behind her and is turned into a pillar of salt. Looking back can harden us, and we get stuck where we're not meant to remain.

Second, don't worry about tomorrow! *"Therefore do not worry about tomorrow, for tomorrow will worry about itself. Each day has enough trouble of its own"* (Matthew 6:34). This verse tells us not to take on the anxiety of what's not here, the what ifs and the worldly things we have no control over. Corrie Ten Boom said it well: "Worry does not empty tomorrow of its sorrow; it empties today of its strength." The secret is to live in today, in this precious moment God has given us. For each day is a gift, and a grateful heart and disposition make all the difference. *This is the day the Lord has made; We will rejoice and be glad in it* (Psalm 118:24). We must trust in God enough to know that He will and does take care of us. He has a plan we know nothing about, and His desire is that we faithfully live grounded in Him.

Lord, thank You for Your Word. You love us so much that You've set before us Your guidebook to living successful, productive, and peaceful lives in You. Help us, Lord, to follow Your Word, to not look back or ahead, but to trust You in this moment, knowing You are with us in the midst of whatever we're facing. Thank You, Jesus! Amen.

MAY 20TH

"This, then, is how you should pray: 'Our Father in heaven,
hallowed be Your name, Your kingdom come, Your will be done,
on earth as it is in heaven. Give us today our daily bread.
And forgive us our debts, as we also have forgiven our debtors.
And lead us not into temptation, but deliver us from the evil one.'"

MATTHEW 6:9-13

Good morning! Prayer is a powerful tool, a privilege and a gift from God, that is oftentimes left unused. Why is that? We can't use the excuse "I don't know how to pray" because Jesus, when asked, told His disciples how to pray. And we can't say we don't know what we are to pray because we're told in Romans 8:26-28, *For we do not know what we should pray for as we ought, but the Spirit Himself makes intercession for us with groanings which cannot be uttered.*

Not praying is like not talking to someone you love—your spouse, children, family, friends. Prayer is a lifeline to God. Pray His promises, pray in faith, pray in need, pray in rejoicing and celebration. *And pray in the Spirit on all occasions with all kinds of prayers and requests. With this in mind, be alert and always keep on praying for all the Lord's people* (Ephesians 6:18).

Prayer should be our natural response to every situation. Our very lives become a prayer when we prioritize everything around God's desires and teachings.

Lord, may our lives be a prayer in a world that needs Your powerful presence and influence. May our first response always be to bring whatever it is to You in prayer. Thank You for the privilege and gift of prayer. Thank You, Jesus! Amen.

MAY 21ST

*Do not conform to the pattern of this world, but be transformed
by the renewing of your mind. Then you will be able to test
and approve what God's will is—His good, pleasing, and perfect will.*

ROMANS 12:2

Good morning! I heard a teaching the other night about not conforming to this world and our sinful desires, but to live transformed lives in Jesus Christ. God's plans for us, His children, are "good, pleasing, and perfect." He wants us to be transformed people with renewed minds, living to honor and obey Him. God wants what is best for us, and because He gave His Son Jesus to make our new lives possible, we should joyfully give ourselves as living sacrifices for His service. A "living sacrifice" is described as being willing to offer oneself to God and live according to His purposes. This means being fully at God's disposal, available, and willing to obey Him in whatever He asks or commands.

Therefore, with minds that are alert and fully sober, set your hope on the grace to be brought to you when Jesus Christ is revealed at His coming. As obedient children, do not conform to the evil desires you had when you lived in ignorance. But just as He who called you is holy, so be holy in all you do; for it is written: "Be holy, because I am holy" (1 Peter 1:13-16).

As new creations, we are set apart to be totally devoted and dedicated to God, different from the world. Our focus and priorities are His.

Lord, thank You for Your mercy and justice, for caring for us, and for new life in You. May we live disciplined lives devoted to You, becoming more like You through the power of Your Holy Spirit in and through us. Thank You, Jesus! Amen.

MAY 22ND

"Now this is eternal life: that they know You, the only true God, and Jesus Christ, whom You have sent."

JOHN 17:3

Good morning! There is a difference between "knowing about" God and actually "knowing Him"! Jesus tells us clearly that the result of knowing God the Father Himself through Jesus Christ is eternal life. Eternal life requires entering into a personal relationship with God in Jesus Christ—to know Him. When we admit our sin and turn away from it, Christ's love lives in us by the Holy Spirit. There is only One way to enter the Kingdom of God and eternal life. Only by knowing God do the doors to the Kingdom of Heaven and eternal life open.

"That all of them may be one, Father, just as You are in Me and I am in You. May they also be in us so that the world may believe that You have sent Me"(John 17:21). Jesus prayed that we would be one with the Father as He is. He prayed this for you, for me, and for future believers. As disciples of Christ, we cannot live independently from Him. Jesus prayed for nothing less for us than absolute oneness with Himself as He was one with the Father. God will not leave us alone until we are one with Him, because Jesus has prayed that for us.

Lord, we want to know You more, to be fully Yours. Make us one with You, Lord. Reveal the stumbling blocks and the things of this world that keep us from You. We pray, as Jesus did for us, for unity, for protection from evil, and for holiness. Lord, help us to be unified as a powerful witness to the reality of Your love. Thank You, Jesus! Amen.

MAY 23RD

"He must increase, but I must decrease."

JOHN 3:30

Good morning! We do not need more self-love, as the world prescribes. We need more love of and for Jesus in our lives! How are we to be a living testimony for Christ Jesus if we are consumed with ourselves? To be viable vessels for sharing the gospel, Christ must grow in importance in our hearts, minds, and everyday lives. More of Him, less of us. Yes, we have a story to tell, but not just through our words. We are all called to show and live a life that will invite others to find the love of God through the Lord Jesus Christ in us. The way we love and serve is the most impactful, compelling way of telling our story, the story of what God has done and continues to do in and through our lives.

I have been crucified with Christ and I no longer live, but Christ lives in me. The life I now live in the body, I live by faith in the Son of God, who loved me and gave Himself for me (Galatians 2:20). Our Christian lives begin when, in unity with Christ, we die to our old selves. In our daily lives we must choose Christ over our sinful, fleshly thoughts and desires that keep us from following Him. Our focus is on living for Christ and letting His Holy Spirit lead and guide our lives. We are no longer alone—Christ lives in us! He is our power for living and our hope for the future. Out of the life of Christ Jesus in us, we have a story to tell!

Lord, fill us so full with Your holy presence that no trace of our old selves remains! More of You, Lord, and less of us. We pray that You alone become the Lord of our lives. Remove from us anything that is not of You. We surrender all to You. Thank You, Jesus! Amen.

MAY 24TH

"'For in Him we live and move and have our being.'
As some of your own poets have said, 'We are His offspring.'"

Good morning! A day is not a day without God leading, guiding, and directing our way! Everything in all creation is upheld by God's mighty hand, including our very existence. We would not be able to live and move and have our being apart from Him. God is Sovereign and yet He is close and personal. God is our Creator, and we owe everything to Him. *"I am the vine; you are the branches. If you remain in Me and I in you, you will bear much fruit; apart from Me you can do nothing"* (John 15:5). Jesus is the true source of life for us. Connected to Him, we draw everything we need to survive and flourish. Apart from Christ, our efforts are useless.

I have been crucified with Christ and I no longer live, but Christ lives in me. The life I now live in the body, I live by faith in the Son of God, who loved me and gave Himself for me (Galatians 2:20). Our lives are intertwined with Christ, so much so that we die with Him and He begins to live in us. His death paid for our sin, and in that way we are crucified with Him. We have become one with Christ. We are no longer alone, for Christ lives in us—*the hope of glory* (Colossians 1:27). Christ is our power for living and our hope for the future.

Lord, thank You for who You are in our lives, for creating us in Your image to live in Your presence. May we remain connected to You, Lord, because it is only in You that we find life—the abundant life that only comes from and through You. Thank You, Jesus! Amen.

MAY 25TH

And we all, with unveiled faces, beholding the glory of the Lord, are being changed into his likeness, from one degree of glory to another; for this comes from the Lord who is the Spirit.

2 CORINTHIANS 3:18

Good morning! What is God trying to teach us today? If we believe that God is in the process of transforming us into the likeness of Christ, it will come with lessons. In part, as we grow in relationship with God, we are transformed into the image of Christ through the work of the Holy Spirit. The Apostle Paul summarizes Christlikeness in nine words: love, joy, peace, patience, kindness, goodness, faithfulness, gentleness, and self-control. God uses our life circumstances, good and bad, to refine and grow our character into the very definition of Christlikeness Paul describes. Our part is to be surrendered and obedient to God, to trust Him and be willing to be disciplined and refined. Discipline is not intended to punish but to teach. And our refining is a means to purify us.

Don't ignore God's lessons. Don't be stubborn and foolish, thinking there's an easier, better way. There is only One way, and it's found through Jesus Christ. Be there for each other in life's lessons—to encourage, to grieve or mourn, to celebrate, or to just sit quietly alongside. Sometimes the lesson is to simply *Be still, and know that I am God* (Psalm 46:10). Don't be in such a hurry to move on and get through or simply have it to be over and done. We need to take the time necessary to learn our lessons well.

Lord, I pray for each person reading this, that they would experience Your calling on and presence in their life. That they may come to know Your voice, surrender to Your teaching, and grow more in love with You each day. Teach us, mold us, guide us, Lord, that "we shall also bear the image of the man of heaven [Jesus]" (1 Corinthians 15:49). Thank You, Jesus! Amen.

MAY 26TH

Jesus Christ is the same yesterday, and today, and forever.

HEBREWS 13:8

Good morning! There is no one like the Lord God Almighty! And nothing about Him has or will ever change. *"The Son of Man has come to seek and to save that which was lost"* (Luke 19:10). The mission of Jesus Christ is still being lived out today in and through believers just like us. Jesus paid the debt for our sin, the sin of all mankind, that the lost might be saved and have everlasting life. There has been no change in the mission or the message. We too must bring the lost to Jesus. He is the only way to the Father (John 14:6), and we need to be bold witnesses of this truth. Just as the four friends of the paralyzed man found a way to get him to Jesus by dropping him through a thatched roof (Mark 2:1-12), we need to let nothing stop us from getting others to Jesus. *When Jesus saw their faith, He said to the paralyzed man, "Son, your sins are forgiven"* (Mark 2:5).

Jesus not only healed the man, He also recognized the faith of the four men. There is a lesson here for us that is not to be missed. We are to be moved by the needs of others—*that which was lost.* There are many people with spiritual and physical needs, people who need Jesus. Are we bold enough in our faith and do we have enough compassion to take action?

Lord, give us a boldness to press on in faith to bring many people to know You. There is no greater privilege than to speak Your Name and share Your gospel with everyone You place before us. Thank You, Jesus! Amen.

MAY 27TH

"My command is this: Love each other as I have loved you.
Greater love has no one than this: to lay down one's life for one's friend."

JOHN 15:12-13

Good morning! We have freedom in this country that many may never experience. A freedom that comes with sacrifice. Take time today to consider and pray for those who have, are, and will sacrifice their time and lives for this freedom, and for their families. Not all of us will choose the path of military service as the means of "laying down our life." But we are called to love each other as Jesus loved us, and He loved us enough to give His life for us. What are we willing to do for others?

"By this everyone will know that you are my disciples, if you love one another" (John 13:35). We may not ever be called to die for someone else, but there are other ways to practice sacrificial love. Be present with people. Be attentive, loving, compassionate, and kind. Listen, help, encourage, give. Today, be intentional toward someone in need by offering the love of Jesus. Give all you are able and then go a little further to give a little bit more.

Lord, we thank You for the hearts of men and women who willingly sacrifice for others—those in military service and civilians who give toward the needs of others. Thank You, Lord, for Your ultimate sacrifice that has made a way for those who believe and follow You. You have set the ultimate example for our lives, and we choose to follow You. Thank You, Jesus! Amen.

MAY 28TH

For it is by grace you have been saved, through faith—and this is not from yourselves, it is the gift of God—not by works, so that no one can boast.

EPHESIANS 2:8-9

Good morning! We cannot earn our salvation. But there is a manner of living that reflects a follower of Jesus Christ, standards of thinking and behavior. *Therefore, if anyone is in Christ, the new creation has come: The old has gone, the new is here!* (2 Corinthians 5:17). We are brand new people on the inside. The Holy Spirit gives us new life, and we are not the same anymore. We are re-created in Christ Jesus. Our new life should be visible in our thoughts, words, and deeds.

Since then, you have been raised with Christ, set your hearts on things above, where Christ is, seated at the right hand of God. Set your minds on things above, not on earthly things. For you died, and your life is now hidden with Christ in God. Therefore, as God's chosen people, holy and dearly loved, clothe yourselves with compassion, kindness, humility, gentleness, and patience. Bear with each other and forgive one another ... And over all these virtues put on love, which binds them together in perfect unity (Colossians 3:1-3, 12-13a, 14).

We are to bring honor to Christ in every aspect of daily living. We are representatives of Christ Jesus at all times. *Therefore, we are ambassadors for Christ, God making His appeal through us. We implore you on behalf of Christ, be reconciled to God* (2 Corinthians 5:20). What impression do people have of Christ after seeing, speaking with, or spending time with us?

Lord, cleanse our hearts and fill them with Your unconditional love. Give us Your eyes to see people as You see them. Give us Your ears to hear and compassion to respond as You would have us to. May our lives be a living testimony to Your mercy, grace, love, and forgiveness. Thank You, Jesus! Amen.

MAY 29TH

"If we are thrown into the blazing furnace, the God we serve is able to deliver us from it, and He will deliver us from Your Majesty's hand. But even if He does not, we want you to know, Your Majesty, that we will not serve your gods or worship the image of gold you have set up."

DANIEL 3:17–18

Good morning! How far will you go? Facing what appeared to be certain death—to be thrown into a blazing furnace bound alive—the faith of Shadrach, Meshach, and Abednego did not waver one bit! No matter what, they trusted God to deliver them! *"The God we serve is able."* Do we believe that to the depths of our souls? To the point where we would stand firm in our faith no matter what? *"But even if He doesn't ... we will not serve your gods."* These men of God were determined to be faithful regardless of the consequences.

God IS able, but if God always rescued those who were true to Him, would we need faith? We must be faithful to serve God in the midst of every situation and circumstance. *"The LORD your God is with you, He is mighty to save. He will take great delight in you, He will quiet you with His love, He will rejoice over you with singing"* (Zephaniah 3:17). Don't pursue the easy way out. Pursue deep fellowship with God with a faith that shouts out, "My God is able, but even if not, I will serve Him and only Him."

Our faith has the power to move others to belief. *Then Nebuchadnezzar said, "Praise be to the God of Shadrach, Meshach and Abednego, who has sent His angel and rescued His servants! ... No other god can save in this way"* (Daniel 3:28, 29).

Lord, You alone are able! May our lives glorify and magnify You, that we would display relentless faith so others might come to believe in who You are, the Lord God Almighty! The Holy One! Thank You, Jesus! Amen.

MAY 30TH

For this very reason, make every effort to add to your faith goodness;
and to goodness, knowledge; and to knowledge, self-control; and to self-
control, perseverance; and to perseverance, godliness; and to godliness,
mutual affection; and to mutual affection, love. For if you possess these
qualities in increasing measure, they will keep you from being ineffective
and unproductive in your knowledge of our Lord Jesus Christ.

2 PETER 1:5–8

Good morning! Faith must be more than belief in certain facts. It must result in action, growth in Christian character, and the practice of moral discipline, or it will die away. Peter shared the actions of faith that require hard work but must be a continual part of our Christian life. We work on them all together, and God empowers and enables us, but not without giving us the responsibility to learn and to grow.

Therefore, since we are surrounded by such a great cloud of witnesses, let us throw off everything that hinders and the sin that so easily entangles. And let us run with perseverance the race marked out for us (Hebrews 12:1). The Christian life involves hard work and requires us to give up whatever endangers our relationship with God. We all share a common enemy, Satan—the devil, the father of lies, deceitful and ruthless, cunning and baffling. By faith, we enter a lifelong spiritual course with the Holy Spirit leading, guiding, and encouraging us as He whispers ways that aid and carry us to certain victory. He tells us to keep our eyes on Jesus, because He alone is our pacesetter and victorious example.

Lord, may we not fall prey to the devil's schemes and lies, but instead live receptive to the teaching of Your Holy Spirit, that we would cast off everything not of You that would hinder us from growth in and obedience to Your will. Thank You, Jesus! Amen.

MAY 31ST

"My sheep listen to my voice; I know them, and they follow me."

JOHN 10:27

Good morning! The noise of this world can be so distracting and misleading! The question becomes whose voice are we listening to? God's voice brings peace, comfort, and stillness—it doesn't rush and worry. God's voice leads and encourages—it doesn't push and discourage. Are we listening to His voice?

Just as a shepherd protects his flock of sheep, feeding and guiding them, so it is with Jesus. *The Lord is my shepherd; I shall not want [lack nothing]. He makes me lie down in green pastures, He leads me beside the still waters. He restores my soul; He leads me in the paths of righteousness for His name's sake* (Psalm 23:1-3). Sheep are completely dependent on the shepherd for everything. We are the Lord's flock, and He is the Good Shepherd. He protects us—His flock, His people—from eternal harm.

Even though I walk through the valley of the shadow of death, I will fear no evil, for You are with me; Your rod and Your staff they comfort me. You prepare a table before me in the presence of my enemies. You anoint my head with oil; my cup overflows. Surely Your goodness and mercy shall follow me all the days of my life, and I will dwell in the house of the Lord forever (Psalm 23:4-6).

We are safe in the Shepherd's presence and listening to His voice. Yet, there are many who ignore God's voice with hearts of stone, set on worldly advice and direction. *As has just been said: "Today, if you hear His voice, do not harden your hearts as you did in the rebellion"* (Hebrews 3:15). Ignoring God's voice and lacking trust in Him will always prevent us from receiving the best—what God offers and provides.

Thank You, Lord, for being the Good Shepherd. Help us to listen for and to obey Your voice. May we not be deceived by the devil's lies or have hearts that are hardened to Your truth. It is only through You that the way is made clear to eternal life with You. Thank You, Jesus. Amen.

June

JUNE 1ST

For as in Adam all die, so in Christ all will be made alive.

1 CORINTHIANS 15:22

Good morning! We are set free and made clean through Christ Jesus. There is no other way! Only when we surrender to the truth that we are all sinners saved by grace can we fully realize the depth of God's love and the magnitude of Christ's sacrifice. *For it is by grace you have been saved, through faith—and this is not from yourselves, it is the gift of God—not by works, so that no one can boast. For we are God's handiwork, created in Christ Jesus to do good works, which God prepared in advance for us to do* (Ephesians 2:8-10).

So then, what is our response? Do we ignore this truth and continue on in ourselves? Or do we live as new creations from God? *For Christ's love compels us, because we are convinced that one died for all, and therefore all died. And He died for all, that those who live should no longer live for themselves but for Him who died for them and was raised again* (2 Corinthians 5:14-15).

Everything we do is to honor God, and Christ's love compels our actions. Out of His great love for us, Jesus gave up His life that we might live. Jesus did not act out of self-interest, selfishly holding on to the glory of heaven already His. No! He left all to die for us, that we might die to our old lives and be made new in His resurrection. We no longer live to please ourselves: we should spend our lives pleasing Christ and doing the work God's planned for us to do.

Lord, You are full of mercy and grace. Our lives were in ruins, wrecked by sin, but You made a way for us. Your grace has set us free! We surrender our lives in obedience to and with the hope of honoring You. Thank You, Jesus! Amen.

JUNE 2ND

"'For in Him we live and move and have our being.'
As some of your own poets have said, 'We are His offspring.'"

Good morning! God is Sovereign and in control, yet He is close and personal. Let our Creator, the Creator of the universe, rule in our lives. God is not a distant God, separated from us. He lives in and through us, for those who believe in Him. *Those who know Your Name trust in You, for You Lord, have never forsaken those who love You* (Psalm 9:10). If we are honestly seeking and following God, we will find Him. *Submit yourselves, then, to God. Resist the devil, and he will flee from you. Come near to God and He will come near to you* (James 4:7-8). Yield to God's authority and commit your life to Him—the One who loves us more than we can fathom!

And I pray that you, being rooted and established in love, may have power, together with all the Lord's holy people, to grasp how wide and long and high and deep is the love of Christ, and to know this love that surpasses knowledge—that you may be filled to the measure of all the fullness of God (Ephesians 3:17-19).

God's love covers every corner of our experiences. It reaches out to the whole world and continues through our entire lives—from heights of celebrations to depths of despair and disappointments. We have the fullness of God available to us through faith and prayer. Ask the Holy Spirit to fill every aspect of your life to the fullest.

Lord, there is none like You! Your love knows no bounds and Your fullness is beyond measure. Thank You for who You are in our lives and all that You do! Thank You, Jesus! Amen.

JUNE 3RD

*"I am the Good Shepherd; I know My sheep and my sheep know Me—just as
the Father knows me and I know the Father—
and I lay down my life for the sheep."*

JOHN 10:14-15

Good morning! Are we listening for and hearing the voice of the
Good Shepherd? God is able to revive His people, bringing us
back to spiritual life. He pours out His love on us. He renews us and
our love for Him. He knows us, hears us, and knows our voices. But
we must turn from our sinful ways, from worldly desires, and return
to Him. *I will listen to what God the Lord says; He promises peace to His
people, His faithful servants—but let them not turn to folly. Surely His
salvation is near those who fear Him, that His glory may dwell in our
land* (Psalm 85:8-9).

Do not be deceived by the loud voices of this world. Listen for the
voice of God. Surrender and submit yourselves to the Good Shepherd
who loves and cares for you. This world is temporal and is not our home
as God intended. *For this world is not our home; we are looking forward to
our everlasting home in heaven* (Hebrews 13:14 TLB). But God is with us,
leading and guiding us, using this world and this time to transform us to
be more like Him. One day, He will call us home to Himself. Will we hear
Him say the precious words, *"Well done My good and faithful servants"*
(Matthew 25:21)?

*Lord, it is Your voice we long to hear and listen to, that we would follow You all
the days of our lives. Thank You for loving and caring for us, for leading and
guiding us. We are Your humble servants, surrendered to You. Thank You,
Jesus! Amen.*

JUNE 4TH

What, then, shall we say in response to these things?
If God is for us, who can be against us?

ROMANS 8:31

Good morning! When we are faced with overwhelming circumstances, challenges that test us, where is our focus? If our focus is on the difficulty, we will feel defeated. But God! Our hope and strength are found in God. Jesus is the answer to everything in our lives.

He who did not spare His own Son, but gave Him up for us all—how will He not also, along with Him, graciously give us all things? Who will bring any charge against those whom God has chosen? It is God who justifies. Who then is the one who condemns? No one. Christ Jesus who died—more than that, who was raised to life—is at the right hand of God and is also interceding for us. Who shall separate us from the love of Christ? Shall trouble or hardship or persecution or famine or nakedness or danger or sword? No, in all these things we are more than conquerors through Him who loved us (Romans 8:32-35, 37).

Christ gave His life for us. We must choose to surrender our lives to Him. No matter what happens to us, no matter where we are, we can never be lost to His love. Any suffering we experience will draw us closer to Him, make us identify with Him further, and allow His love to penetrate our hearts and lives to reach us and bring healing. All we need is found in Him, for He truly is our Rock and Strong Tower.

Lord, thank You for saving us. While we were yet sinners, You came; You loved and died for us. You are our hope and our strength, the only One we need. Help us, Lord, to surrender ourselves to You and find the freedom knowing You brings. Thank You, Jesus! Amen.

JUNE 5TH

Put on the full armor of God, so that you can
take your stand against the devil's schemes.

EPHESIANS 6:11

Good morning! What are we inviting into our lives? If we ignore or worse yet, rebel against God's Word in our lives, we are opening ourselves to the enemy. We are in a battle. *For our struggle is not against flesh and blood, but against the rulers, against the authorities, against powers of this dark world, and against the spiritual forces of evil in the heavenly realms* (Ephesians 6:12). In order to withstand the attacks of our enemies, we must depend on God's strength and use every piece of His armor. Satan is constantly battling against all who are on the Lord's side and will go after every weakness and unguarded foe.

Therefore put on the full armor of God, so that when the day of evil comes, you may be able to stand your ground, and after you have done everything, to stand. Stand firm then, with the belt of truth buckled around your waist, with the breastplate of righteousness in place, and with your feet fitted with the readiness that comes from the gospel of peace. In addition to all this, take up the shield of faith, with which you can extinguish all the flaming arrows of the evil one. Take the helmet of salvation and the sword of the Spirit, which is the word of God (Ephesians 6:13-17).

We must depend on God's strength and use every piece of His armor to fight the battles of this world.

Lord, thank You that You never leave or forsake us. You have armed us in Your strength and the power of Your Holy Spirit. With You on our side, we will have Your victory. Thank You, Jesus! Amen.

JUNE 6TH

*"Watch and pray so that you will not fall into temptation.
The spirit is willing, but the flesh is weak."*

MATTHEW 26:41

Good morning! When we don't take time to *"watch and pray,"* our alertness is compromised, and we will suffer as a result. Temptations are waiting to confront us, and we are unprepared to withstand them. Jesus, the omnipotent Son of God, felt it necessary to rise early each morning before dawn to pour out His heart to His Father in prayer. How much more should we be compelled to seek and pray to the Father?

No temptation has overtaken you except what is common to mankind. And God is faithful; He will not let you be tempted beyond what you can bear. But when you are tempted, He will also provide a way out so that you can endure it (1 Corinthians 10:13).

God will give us strength to endure the inevitable temptations we will face and show us a way out. The way to overcome temptation is to keep watch and pray. Watching means being aware of the possibilities of temptation, sensitive to the subtleties, and spiritually equipped to fight. Temptation strikes where we are most weak, and we can't resist it alone. Prayer is essential because it is in the Lord's strength that we are made strong in defense against Satan's power.

A life without prayer is a powerless life—a life filled with noise and activity, but far removed from God and Jesus, who day and night prayed to His Father.

Lord, morning and night we are protected and strengthened by time taken to "watch and pray." May we not give in to the laziness that robs us of the rich freshness and strength that come from time with and wisdom imparted during moments with You. We need You, Lord. Fill us with Your Word, that our lives would be living testimonies to You. Thank You, Jesus! Amen.

JUNE 7TH

"Abide in Me, as I also abide in you. No branch can bear fruit by itself; it must remain in the vine. Neither can you bear fruit unless you abide in Me."

JOHN 15:4

Good morning! To Abide in Christ is to have faith in Him alone, and to live in a way that is directed by His Word, allowing it to fill our minds, direct our wills, and transform our affections. Abiding in Christ is the place where God comes to live within us. It's a relationship with God that brings new life through His Holy Spirit. God's intent for our lives is to move from barrenness to fruitfulness, to live in spiritual abundance.

As we abide in Christ, we "bear fruit"—from a Christ-like character and actions that are the spontaneous work of the Holy Spirit in us. *But the fruit of the Spirit is love, joy, peace, patience, kindness, goodness, faithfulness, gentleness, and self-control* (Galatians 5:22). These "fruits" are by-products of lives joined in Christ—remaining and abiding in Him. They are by-products of the condition of our hearts. *"This is to My Father's glory, that you bear much fruit, showing yourselves to be My disciples"* (John 15:8).

We must know Him, remember Him, and imitate Him. If our lives are lacking, we are not abiding. Love God, love others, and abide in Him.

Lord, the only way to live a truly good life is to stay close to You, abiding in You, like a branch attached to the vine. Apart from You, our efforts are fruitless—we can do nothing. Thank You for the nourishment and richness of life that comes from abiding in You. Thank You, Jesus! Amen.

JUNE 8TH

"Now that I, your Lord and Teacher, have washed your feet,
you also should wash one another's feet. I have set you an example
that you should do as I have done for you."

JOHN 13:14-15

G ood morning! Stop a minute and consider the verses you just
read. The Son of God, the Lord Jesus Christ, took the position of
the lowest of servants and washed the disciples' feet—filthy, smelly
from walking the dusty, animal-trodden roads wearing sandals. And
then Jesus goes on to tell them to follow His example! What? But
why, Lord? *"Very truly I tell you, no servant is greater than his master,*
nor is a messenger greater than the one who sent him" (John 13:16).
Jesus used this powerfully humbling act to demonstrate how far we
should be willing to go in serving God and others. We are to walk in
humility, with compassion and loving kindness, serving those whom
we are called to share the gospel.

"My command is this: Love each other as I have loved you. Greater love
has no one than this: to lay down one's life for one's friend" (John 15:12-13).
Jesus shared the message to love and serve others throughout His
earthly ministry, in what He said and what He did, even until death on
the cross. We are to follow His sacrificial example of taking a servant's
role. *"Now that you know these things, you will be blessed if you do them"*
(John 13:17). We glorify God through our loving service to others.

Lord, You set an example for us of how we are to serve others in Your Name.
Humble us, Lord, that we would honor You through our servant's heart and
acts of compassion and kindness. May we be surrendered to You in obedience
to Your teaching and example. Thank You, Jesus! Amen.

JUNE 9TH

Truly my soul finds rest in God; my salvation comes from Him. Truly He is my rock and my salvation; He is my fortress. I will never be shaken.

PSALM 62:1-2

Good morning! The true resolution of trials comes from an enduring hope in God's ultimate salvation. There is no greater source of confidence than that which is found in trusting God. We find our hope and power in Him, knowing we can safely rely on His strength. Through Christ we find our deliverance.

My salvation and my honor depend on God; He is my mighty rock, my refuge. Trust in Him at all times, you people; pour out your hearts to Him, for God is our refuge (Psalm 62:7-8). We can experience rest or calm in the midst of our trials when we rest in God because He is our "mighty rock" who keeps us safe from harm. And we can trust that God will guide us, no matter what is happening around us or in our lives. Are we anchored and trusting in Him?

One thing God has spoken, two things I have heard: "Power belongs to You, God, and with You, Lord, is unfailing love"; and, "You reward everyone according to what they have done" (Psalm 62:11-12).

Placing all hope in God, knowing that He is in control, allows us relief from earthly troubles and lets God have His way with us. Jesus went about doing good, for He knew and trusted God was with Him. And God is with us, too, empowering us to live righteous lives worthy of Him.

Thank You, Lord, for the hope that comes from knowing and trusting in You. You are our Rock of Salvation and we are Your people. Lord, may we "walk in a manner worthy of You, fully pleasing to You, bearing fruit in every good work, and increasing in the knowledge of You" (Colossians 1:10). Thank You, Jesus! Amen.

JUNE 10TH

*"No one can serve two masters. Either you will hate the one
and love the other, or you will be devoted to the one and despise the other.
You cannot serve both God and Mammon."*

MATTHEW 6:24

Good morning! Have we humbled ourselves enough to know how much we need Jesus to rule over our lives? We cannot have this world as our focus and live for Jesus. Don't miss what this verse is telling us: We can't—it is impossible to—*serve two masters.* It doesn't matter what or who the other master is.

"Mammon" is a term that essentially personifies wealth as a competing master to God, meaning we cannot fully serve both God and the pursuit of material wealth. Anything that is a powerful, demanding force can easily consume our lives when prioritized over our faith in God. Anything that takes us away from God in mind, body or spirit is potentially a second master. God alone deserves to be our master! Our first loyalty is to Him, not those things that fade, can be stolen, used up, or worn out. We must not be consumed with our possessions and things of earthly value.

"But store up for yourselves treasures in heaven, where moths and vermin do not destroy, and where thieves do not break in and steal. For where your treasure is, there your heart will be also" (Matthew 6:20-21). The more concerned we are with ourselves and our own things, the less we will seek God and do what is right—what God has called us to do. *"Seek first His kingdom and His righteousness, and all these things will be given to you as well"* (Matthew 6:33). Seek God with all you are and all you have, and you will find Him.

Lord, forgive us when we live lukewarm lives, torn away from You by this world and our own selfishness. You desire all of us! May we choose You first and You only, living lives fully dedicated to You and Your calling. Thank You, Jesus! Amen.

JUNE 11TH

Shout for joy to the Lord, all the earth. Worship the Lord with gladness; come before Him with joyful songs. Know that the Lord is God. It is He who made us, and we are His; we are His people, the sheep of His pasture. Enter His gates with thanksgiving and His courts with praise; give thanks to Him and praise His name. For the Lord is good and His love endures forever; His faithfulness continues through all generations.

PSALM 100

Good morning! We serve a benevolent God who deserves our constant praise and adoration. Did you know that God is present and actively engaged when we praise Him? *But You are holy, enthroned in [inhabiting] the praises of Israel* (Psalm 22:3). Even in our darkest times, we are told to praise God and that His presence brings with it His character of love and peace. And honestly, it should be irresistible to praise God when we consider who He is, all He has done, continues to do, and promises He will do!

God is our Creator and gives us all we have. God is worthy of being worshiped and joyfully praised. Remember His goodness, His faithfulness, always dependable, loving, and kind. Our praise is a pleasing act of worship to God. *Through Jesus, therefore, let us continually offer to God a sacrifice of praise—the fruit of lips that openly profess His name* (Hebrews 13:15).

How many times do we praise God in a day? He is deserving of anthems of praise, endless songs of adoration. *Let everything that has breath praise the Lord. Praise the Lord* (Psalm 150:6). Our praise is a celebration of our gratitude and representative of our thankfulness to our God and King.

We thank and praise You, Lord, for who You are and all that You do in our lives. Thank You for Your Holy Spirit who fills every aspect of our lives to the fullest. May our lives be reflective of Your love as we worship, love, and serve You. Thank You, Jesus! Amen.

JUNE 12TH

Though you have not seen Him, you love Him;
and even though you do not see Him now, you believe in Him
and are filled with an inexpressible and glorious joy.

1 PETER 1:8

Good morning! Are we living out of "an inexpressible and glorious joy"? If not, why not? Peter is sharing about faith—believing in Jesus, that He is who He said He is—the faith of salvation and the promises it holds. Our joy comes from pursuing and having a consistent relationship with Jesus—from knowing who He is and all He's done for us. We have been washed clean. Our sins are forgiven. We are new creations promised a day when all pain will end and perfect justice will begin. We are promised a day when we will see Jesus face to face. Why would we choose to not live in the abundance of His love, mercy, and grace? And why would we not respond in abundant joy?

May the God of hope fill you with all joy and peace as you trust in Him, so that you may overflow with hope by the power of the Holy Spirit (Romans 15:13). People should see in us a joy so complete they can't help but constantly come to us asking, "What is the source of your joy and delight?" *Always be prepared to give an answer to everyone who asks you to give the reasons for the hope that you have* (1 Peter 3:15). We are redeemed by the blood of the Lamb! Forgiven and set free! Believe and be filled.

Lord, may our lives shout out the testimony of what You have done so many will ask and come to know You—to believe and be saved into Your abundant life, hope, and a future! Thank You, Jesus! Amen.

JUNE 13TH

"Get behind me, Satan! You are a stumbling block to Me;
you do not have in mind the concerns of God, but merely human concerns."

MATTHEW 16:23

Good morning! Jesus called it like it was! Peter, after hearing Jesus tell of His suffering and death soon to come, took Jesus aside, *"Never, Lord!"* he said. *"This shall never happen to You!"* (Matthew 16:22). Peter's response countered God's perspective and plan. His attitude was limited to his earthly understanding. We, too, must beware of setting our minds on earthly things and outcomes instead of setting ourselves on the things of God.

Satan's temptations of Jesus in the wilderness were all worldly in nature, and Jesus countered with the power of God's Word and Truth (Luke 4:1-13). *Jesus answered, "It is said, 'Do not put the Lord your God to the test'"* (Luke 4:12).

We will face temptations and if we aren't standing firm in Christ, if we don't know who He is and understand what He's done for us—the truth and completeness of our redemption, salvation, and promise of eternity—we will fall prey to Satan's lies. Satan *"is a liar, and the father of lies"* (John 8:44), and he is our enemy. He wants to destroy believers and neutralize us through sin, shame, guilt, and separation. But God! He made a Way for us to reign victorious in Christ Jesus! Rely on the Word of God and stand firm in commitment to worship God alone, above all else. Know who you are and whose you are in Christ Jesus!

Thank You, Lord, for making a way for us. We are and we have nothing without You. You give us life, hope, and a future. You are the Way, the Truth, and the Life—the only Way to the Father! Satan is a powerless, defeated foe, and You are the victorious One. Thank You, Jesus! Amen.

JUNE 14TH

"Everything is possible for one who believes."

MARK 9:23

Good morning! Are we standing firm in our faith, or is our faith failing? Jesus did not mean that we can automatically obtain anything we want by simply thinking positively, but that nothing is too difficult for God. We cannot have everything we pray for as if by magic. God is not a three-wish genie. But with faith, we can have everything we need to serve Him.

Now faith is being sure of what we hope for and certain of what we do not see (Hebrews 11:1). Godly faith means relying on God even when we don't fully understand or know what's next. We trust in Him, that He is who He says He is and that He will do what He says He will do. Our pride will interfere and tell us we need something more than an obscure faith. But real faith is acting in full confidence that God will do as He promised and is based on that fact and our experiences.

"If we are thrown into the blazing furnace, the God we serve is able to deliver us from it, and He will deliver us from Your Majesty's hand. But even if He does not, we want you to know, Your Majesty, that we will not serve your gods or worship the image of gold you have set up" (Daniel 3:17-18).

Faith that trusts produces obedience, resulting in God's blessings. Our faith should compel us into action. We are saved only through faith in Christ, believing and trusting in Him. Just because we don't understand how God will act does not mean He can't or won't.

Lord, may we demonstrate a faith that is built on an unwavering trust in You, that we would respond in obedience to You. We thank You, Lord, that You are with us; You never leave us; You lead and guide us. We are saved by faith in You alone. Thank You, Jesus! Amen.

JUNE 15TH

"I have loved you with an everlasting love;
I have drawn you with unfailing kindness."

JEREMIAH 31:3

Good morning and Father's Day blessings to all who are dads to children, their own and bonus ones! We have a heavenly Father who loves each of us with an everlasting, unconditional love. God reaches out to us with kindness motivated by a deep and everlasting love. He is eager to do what is best for us, His children, if we let Him.

The parable of the prodigal son in Luke 15 is a depiction of the Father's love that is unconditional, extravagant, and freely given. The Father's love is also undeserved and unearned and extends even to gifts and celebration of the son's return.

God desires a relationship with us, His children. The apostle John says it so well: *See what great love the Father has lavished on us, that we should be called children of God! And that is what [who] we are!* (1 John 3:1).

If you do not know the love of the Father, if you have fled from Him and are running away, choose today to return home to Him. He is waiting with open arms. He wants for none to live without Him. The Father is benevolent, full of grace, mercy, and love.

Lord, we thank You for loving us, for calling us Your children. May we be encouraged as Your children to live as Jesus our brother did, as co-heirs, growing in character and knowledge of You, as we are led by the Spirit. Lord, may we surrender to You, with hearts set on obedience and pleasing You. Thank You, Jesus! Amen.

JUNE 16TH

Many are the plans in a person's heart,
but it is the Lord's purpose that prevails.

PROVERBS 19:21

Good morning! Life can be full of the ordinary and mundane, days or weeks that seem to be driven by the same dull routine without anything striking or remarkable. Or our lives can feel hectic and chaotic, without a moment to breathe, racing from one crisis to the next. Have we taken God out of the equation? God has a purpose for our lives and directs our way. *In their hearts humans plan their course, but the Lord establishes their steps* (Proverbs 16:9).

Where has God placed us, and what has He put in front of us to do? God is Sovereign and He is in control. The things we consider mundane or chaotic may be the very things He is using to direct us to the people and places He has planned. *In Him we were also chosen, having been predestined according to the plan of Him who works out everything in conformity with the purpose of His will* (Ephesians 1:11).

There are no accidents in God's plans, events or people. Our response to our lives, whatever they appear to be to us, is to recognize God is in control. Believe that God has His Hand in and on our lives. Spend time in prayer, seeking His will and listening for His voice. Surrender and obey; then wait and see what the Lord will do!

Lord, Your mercies are new every morning! There is nothing that happens without Your knowledge. Lord, may we choose to surrender ourselves to You, to seek You first and always. Your ways are higher, and we will trust in You alone, no matter how our lives appear to us. You are in control of all things! Thank You, Jesus! Amen.

JUNE 17TH

"For I know the plans I have for you," declares the Lord, "plans to prosper you and not to harm you, plans to give you hope and a future."

JEREMIAH 29:11

Good morning! Our problems and life's troubles are magnified through the lens of our selfishness and constant need to control. We are not God; He is. Let Him be! We can be assured that God has plans for us that He knows. When we take God out of the equation, when we think we know more than He does or that we don't need Him, our lives become a confusing mess, chaotic and dark. *"Then you will call on Me and come and pray to me, and I will listen to you. You will seek Me and find Me when you seek Me with all your heart"* (Jeremiah 29:12-13).

God knows everything about us, and His desire is that we follow His plans for our lives and let Him lead us to fulfill the mission He intends. We can live in boundless hope because He will see us through to a glorious conclusion. *"Even to your old age and gray hairs I am He, I am He who will sustain you. I have made you and I will carry you; I will sustain you and I will rescue you. I am God, and there is no other; I am God, and there is no other like Me. I have made known the end from the beginning, from ancient times, what is still to come. I say, 'My purpose will stand, and I will do all that I please'"* (Isaiah 46:4,9-10).

God created us and cares for us. His love is so enduring that He will care for us throughout our lifetime and even through death. He is Almighty God, unique in His knowledge and in His control of the future. His consistent purpose is to carry out what He has planned.

Lord, forgive us for pursuing anything that separates us from You, for the times that we think we know more than You and live in rebellion against Your Word. You alone are God: apart from You we can do nothing. Thank You, Jesus! Amen.

JUNE 18TH

Then Peter got down out of the boat, walked on the water and came toward Jesus. But when he saw the wind, he was afraid and, beginning to sink, cried out, "Lord, save me!"

MATTHEW 14:29-30

Good morning! We are far too easily distracted by the things of this life. We know Jesus is "the Way, the Truth, and the Life," but we shift our focus off Him and onto our circumstances and troubles. The wind, water, and waves were there the entire time, as was Jesus. The moment Peter took his eyes, his focus, off of Jesus, his fear—the circumstances surrounding him—overtook him. How often in our own lives do we choose fear over faith—those times when we're not trusting in God's Word but instead dreading and rehashing where we are and what's happening? *Immediately Jesus reached out His Hand and caught him. "You of little faith," He said, "why did you doubt?"* (Matthew 14:31).

The instant—"immediately"—Peter cried out, Jesus rescued him. When our faith falters like Peter's, we reach out to Jesus because He is the only answer—the only One we need. When we are apprehensive about or overwhelmed by our troubles and doubt Jesus' presence, power, and ability to help, we sink into and under the pressure of them. Jesus is the only One who is able to really help. He is the only answer we ever need. We must learn to always abandon ourselves to Him!

Lord, may our life's circumstances not distract us from who You are and all You are able to do. May we keep our eyes fixed on You, trusting You are in control. We know that nothing is impossible with and for You. Reveal our weaknesses, that we would repent and fully trust in You. Thank You, Jesus! Amen.

JUNE 19TH

"Blessed are those who hunger and thirst for righteousness,
for they shall be satisfied [will be filled]."

MATTHEW 5:6

Good morning! There is a natural longing inside each one of us for something more, to be satisfied. We try to fill the void with earthly treasures, advancement, awards, and recognition, busyness, and activity. But all those things are not the "more" that satisfies the longing we have. In Jesus' Sermon on the Mount, we read in the Beatitudes about the blessings promised to those who are in God's kingdom. To "be satisfied," Jesus said we are to "hunger and thirst for righteousness." We are to conform to the will of God, sincerely seeking to be saved by trusting in Jesus for the forgiveness of our sins, living in obedience to God and in a right relationship with Him and others.

Psalm 107:9 says, *He satisfies the longing soul.* The longing for satisfaction is a desire and yearning from our heart. God created us with desires, longings, yearnings, wants. Sin corrupted our desires, directing them toward the wrong things. We have forsaken God for ourselves and our selfish desires (Jeremiah 2:13). But God! Our satisfaction is perfectly filled by Him who loves us. He rescued us from sin by sending Jesus. He is all-satisfying. *"I am the bread of life; whoever comes to Me shall not hunger, and whoever believes in Me shall never thirst"* (John 6:35).

Our quest is over when we find Jesus. The desire of our hearts is filled. Sin will rear its ugly head, but we know the One who fills us with living water, *a well of water springing up to eternal life* (John 4:14). Our true satisfaction is found in Jesus.

Lord, You are the only One who truly satisfies. We thank You for who You are in our lives. Continue, Lord, to teach us, show us, and guide us in the way everlasting. Thank You, Jesus! Amen.

JUNE 20TH

"Do not judge, and you will not be judged. Do not condemn,
and you will not be condemned. Forgive, and you will be forgiven."

LUKE 6:37

Good morning! We miss out on so much of God's peace and purpose when we hold onto old hurts and experiences from our past, reliving scenarios meant to be prayed over, forgiven, and left for God's dealings. By reliving our past, choosing to dwell on someone else's behavior toward or against us, we are giving them authority in our life that doesn't belong to them, and we are judging their actions, condemning them as lost and unforgivable.

Bear with each other and forgive one another if any of you has a grievance against someone. Forgive as the Lord forgave you (Colossians 3:13). Pray for those who have hurt you. Follow the example of Jesus. *But God demonstrates His own love for us in this: While we were still sinners, Christ died for us* (Romans 5:8). God sent Jesus to die for us—not because we deserved it, or because we were good enough, but because He loved us. It is not our job to deal with the sin of this world. Christ came, and He died for that. We are to love as Christ loves, forgive as Christ forgives, and trust that in due time He will judge when He returns (2 Timothy 4:1, Matthew 25:31–46).

God knows our hurts and all we've gone through. The real evidence of our faith is the way we act and respond. What we do in response to others demonstrates what we really believe about Jesus and His words to us.

Lord, may we be a people separated from unbelievers by the way we think, speak, and act. Cleanse our hearts from all unrighteousness, that we would love and serve others in a manner that glorifies You. Thank You, Jesus! Amen.

JUNE 21ST

*Then the word of the Lord came to Jeremiah: "I am the Lord,
the God of all mankind. Is anything too hard for Me?"*

JEREMIAH 32:26-27

Good morning! Smith Wigglesworth said, "Unless God brings us
into a place of brokenness of spirit, unless God remolds us in the
great plan of His will for us, the best of us will utterly fail. But when
we are absolutely taken in hand by the Almighty God, God turns even
our weakness into strength."[16] We all need Jesus. Since the first sin of
mankind in the garden, we live in a corrupted world that is not as it
was intended to be. But God! *Jesus looked at them and said, "With man
this is impossible, but with God all things are possible"* (Matthew 19:26).
Stop living life for yourself without God being first to lead and direct
your way. Don't listen to the lies of a broken world overrun with "me
first" and "my way."

Out of brokenness, God is able to restore and bring new life, life as
He intended. *Therefore, if anyone is in Christ, the new creation has come:
The old has gone, the new is here!* (2 Corinthians 5:17). Only God can give
new life—a life set apart, forgiving and forgetting our past, giving us a
new way of thinking and looking at things and people. We surrender our
brokenness to Him and He will restore! *And He who was seated on the
throne said, "Behold, I am making all things new"* (Revelation 21:5). God is
our Creator. His Word begins with the majestic story of His creation of
the universe, and it concludes with His creation of a new heaven and a
new earth. When we are with God, our sins are forgiven and our future
secure. One day we will be made perfect like Christ.

*Lord, You make all things new! We look forward to the day we see You face to
face—when there will be no more death or mourning or crying or pain. In this
life, Lord, we will surrender ourselves to Your will and Your ways. Thank You,
Jesus! Amen.*

---

16. Smith Wigglesworth, *Smith Wigglesworth Devotional*, 281.

JUNE 22ND

*But whatever were gains to me I now consider loss for the sake of Christ.
What is more, I consider everything a loss because of the surpassing worth of
knowing Christ Jesus, my Lord, for whose sake I have lost all things.
I consider them garbage, that I may gain Christ.*

PHILIPPIANS 3:7–8

Good morning! We are not nearly as smart as we think we are. But God! When I think I am "finished," that God's done with me, that I've arrived and have nothing more to gain, I am quickly reminded of how selfish, prideful, and arrogant I can be. It is not about our credentials, credits, or successes. Our achievements and knowledge are nothing compared to our relationship and what we have in Christ Jesus. Paul considered everything he had accomplished in his life *garbage* in comparison to Christ Jesus.

What about us? Do we value our relationship with Jesus more than anything else? *Jesus replied, "'Love the Lord Your God with all your heart and with all your soul and with all your mind.' This is the first and greatest commandment"* (Matthew 22:37–38).

We need the revival touch of God in our hearts and over our lives. God must change us in His way to emulate Him. Oh, how humbling it is when God shows us what our thinking, our attitude, and our behavior looks like to Him. We are works in progress who need our Savior!

Lord, forgive us when our sinful nature takes over and we leave You out of our lives. Thank You for touching us with Your tenderness, for softening our hearts toward wanting more of You, for forgiving us and loving us in spite of ourselves. We want to be who You want and created us to be. Transform us as only You can! Thank You, Jesus! Amen.

JUNE 23RD

"Peace I leave with you; My peace I give to you. I do not give to you as the world gives. Do not let your hearts be troubled and do not be afraid."

JOHN 14:27

Good morning! Many days, we miss out on the promised peace of God in exchange for the certain intensity of our anxiety, fear, and madness. We pray for opportunities to serve Him and complain of the package they appear in—the complexity and difficulty, or how unreasonable or painful. The question is, are we relying on God or ourselves?

Jesus promised the disciples that the Holy Spirit would help them remember what He had been teaching them. This promise of the Holy Spirit is also ours. As we seek and follow Jesus and study God's Word, we can trust Him to plant truth in our minds, lead us in God's will, and show us when we stray. The end result of the Holy Spirit's work in our lives is deep and lasting peace. *And the peace of God, which transcends all understanding, will guard your hearts and your minds in Christ Jesus* (Philippians 4:7).

His peace is not of this world, absent of conflict, but a peace that is confident assurance in any and all circumstances. With Christ's peace, we have no need to fear the present or dread the future. The peace of God moves into our hearts and lives to restrain such hostile forces, to knock out fear and anxiety, and offer comfort in their place.

Lord, thank You for sending Jesus and Your Holy Spirit, for giving us a way of peace not of this world but of You. Show us, Lord, when we stray from Your Word and Your Ways. May we pray for Your will to be done in our lives every day. Thank You, Jesus! Amen.

JUNE 24TH

"Truly I tell you, if anyone says to this mountain, 'Go, throw yourself into the sea,' and does not doubt in their heart but believes that what they say will happen, it will be done for them. Therefore I tell you, whatever you ask for in prayer, believe that you have received it, and it will be yours."

MARK 11:23-24

Good morning! Challenge your mountain to move. The constant repetition and uncertainty of our prayers of unbelief have caused them to be ineffective. The kind of prayer that moves mountains is prayer for the fruitfulness of God's kingdom. It would seem impossible to move a mountain into the sea, so that is the very picture Jesus used to say that God can do anything.

God will answer our prayers, but not because of a positive mental attitude. We must believe in Him. We must not hold a grudge or grievance against another person. We must not pray with selfish motives. Our request must be for the good of God's kingdom. Effective prayer comes out of faith in God, not faith in the object of our request.

Jesus prayed in the Garden, *"Abba, Father, everything is possible for You. Take this cup from Me. Yet not what I will, but what You will"* (Mark 14:36). Our prayers are so often motivated by our own interests and desires: we like to hear we can have anything. But God! Jesus prayed with God's interests in mind—*"Thy will be done."* Anything worth having costs something. What price are we willing to pay to gain eternal life? It cost Jesus His very life. Pray effective prayers for God's will and the good of His kingdom.

Lord, thank You for the privilege of prayer in our lives, for inviting us to bring all things before You. May our prayers be spoken out of believing hearts, for Your will, good, and glory. Thank You, Jesus! Amen.

JUNE 25TH

But as for me, it is good to be near God.
I have made the Sovereign Lord my refuge; I will tell of all Your deeds.

PSALM 73:28

Good morning! A. W. Tozer said, "To know a thing in your head is one thing, but to feel it in your heart is something altogether different. Most Christians are trying to be happy apart from having a sense of God's presence."[17]

My son, give Me your heart and let your eyes delight in My ways (Proverbs 23:26). God wants ALL of us! *Jesus replied, "'You must love the LORD your God with all your heart, all your soul, and all your mind"* (Matthew 22:37).

God invites us to draw near to Him. *Come near to God and He will come near to You* (James 4:8). Surrender your heart, your soul, your mind to God and experience His *peace which transcends all understanding* (Philippians 4:7). God's desire is that we will hunger and thirst after righteousness, and He promises we will be filled (Matthew 5:6). God tells us to seek first His kingdom (Matthew 6:33), to let the peace of Christ rule in our hearts, and to sing to God with gratitude in your hearts (Colossians 3:15-16).

So where are we in seeking God's presence, in living out His Word in our lives? God's Word holds the key to living effective, productive lives in an intimate, personal relationship with Him. There is no better way to live. Jesus is the only Way to eternal life.

Lord, we surrender our lives wholly to You. Cleanse our hearts from sin and anything that's not of You. May we seek after You with all our hearts, souls, and minds. We want to know You more. Thank You, Jesus! Amen.

---

17. A. W. Tozer, *My Daily Pursuit: Devotions for Every Day* (Bloomington, MN: Bethany House, 2013), 187.

JUNE 26TH

How lovely is Your dwelling place, Lord Almighty. My soul yearns, even faints, for the courts of the Lord; my heart and my flesh cry out for the living God. Blessed are those who dwell in Your house; they are ever praising You.

PSALM 84:1-2, 4

Good morning! Verse after verse assures us of God's presence. It is one thing to have head-knowledge of God's presence, and quite another to experience His presence in and through our lives. We inherently know the sun is in the sky but on a gloomy, rainy day we are far from experiencing its brightness and warmth.

We can meet God anywhere, at any time. God's presence is not isolated to the confines of a dedicated building or a special chosen place. He invites us to seek Him, to rest in Him, to walk with Him, and to experience relationship and fellowship with Him. To "yearn, even faint" for God's presence is the deep recognition that we cannot live without Him. He is not optional, not just a nice accessory to life. He IS life, and in Him we receive life. *In Him was life, and that life was the Light of mankind* (John 1:4).

Christians, believers in Jesus Christ, are to live in God's presence and experience the fullness of life with Him. *You make known to me the path of life; you will fill me with joy in Your presence, with eternal pleasures at Your right hand* (Psalm 16:11). To live in God's presence is to trust that His ways are better than ours (Isaiah 55:9). It's about surrendering control and letting Him guide our steps (Proverbs 3:5-6). It's about believing that no matter how dark or difficult the path may seem, His Light will always guide us home (Psalm 119:105).

Lord, thank You for the privilege of a living relationship with You, for experiencing the joy of Your presence. May others come to know You through Your Light shining brightly in and through Your presence in us. Thank You, Jesus! Amen.

JUNE 27TH

"My grace is sufficient for you, for my power is made perfect in weakness."
Therefore I will boast all the more gladly about my weaknesses,
so that Christ's power may rest on me. That is why, for Christ's sake, I delight
in weaknesses, in insults, in hardships, in persecutions, in difficulties.
For when I am weak, then I am strong.

2 CORINTHIANS 12:9–10

Good morning! The Lord is the strength that we need. When we are at our weakest, He is strong. God does not need to remove our physical, mental, or material afflictions. He demonstrates His power in and through our weaknesses. We do and will continue to have limitations. We must rely on God for our effectiveness rather than simply on our own flawed resources of limited energy, effort, or talent. God uses our weaknesses to develop Christian character and to deepen our worship. As we recognize and admit our weaknesses, we affirm and rely on God's strength. *I can do all things through him who strengthens me* (Philippians 4:13).

When we are weakest is when we need Him the most and He is waiting for us to call out to Him. *My flesh and my heart may fail, but God is the strength of my heart and my portion forever* (Psalm 73:26). God's power and strength are found in our weakness. What courage and encouragement that should bring to us! When we recognize our limitations, we can turn to God, to His strength and His way.

Lord, thank You for the strength that comes from knowing and loving You. The secret of our contentment is found in drawing on Your power and resting in Your strength. We need not fear our weakness or our enemies, as You watch over and protect us. You make a way for us in and through this world, and You use our weaknesses to draw us nearer to You. Thank You, Jesus! Amen.

JUNE 28TH

*"The God who made the world and everything in it is the Lord of heaven
and earth and does not live in temples built by human hands.
And He is not served by human hands, as if He needed anything.
Rather, He Himself gives everyone life and breath and everything else ...
God did this so that they would seek Him and perhaps reach out for Him
and find Him, though He is not far from any one of us.
For in Him we live and move and have our being."*

ACTS 17:24-25, 27-28

Good morning! God is in and close to every one of us, if we are born again. He is our Creator, sovereign and in control. Yet, God is close and personal, desiring not just to rule over our lives but to be a part of all we think, say, and do. God is close enough to want a relationship with us, but also magnificent enough that His likeness cannot be contained in a handmade idol. *We live, move, and have our being* because of God, not because of lifeless statues or false gods or made up religions and practices.

We gain nothing by our earthly position or wealth in God's eyes. He has no need we can meet for Him. *"As some of your own poets have said, 'We are His offspring'"* (Acts 17:28). We are created by the God of the Bible, and it is through the God of the Bible that we *live and move and have our being.* He created us out of His great love for us. We have life because God breathed His life into us. And we continue to live in Him because of our dependence on and need for Him. Do we know Him? Are we reaching out for Him? *Seek God and you will find Him* (Deuteronomy 4:29).

Lord, we thank You for Your deep love and affection for us. Without You, we are nothing. We came from dust and return to dust. In You, we have abundant and eternal life! Rule in us, O Lord! Thank You, Jesus! Amen.

JUNE 29TH

But they were kept from recognizing him.

LUKE 24:16

Good morning! So many seek and never find because their eyes and hearts are closed to the Truth. The disciples' problem wasn't their sight; it was their faith. They didn't expect to see Jesus, so they didn't recognize Him. The same can be true of us. We don't expect to see Jesus in the midst of our mess, our trials, and our sufferings. Faith alone can open our eyes to see Jesus!

"I do believe; help me to overcome my unbelief!" (Mark 9:24). We must edit our prayers to confront ourselves: "My kingdom go, Lord; let thy kingdom come!" We won't fully recognize Jesus in our lives until we rid ourselves of our own selfish kingdoms. *"For whoever wants to save their life will lose it, but whoever loses their life for Me will find it"* (Matthew 16:25). It is when we resign our kingship and fully surrender ourselves that Jesus Christ will become king of our lives. It is when we fully believe that Jesus is the answer to every question, the solution to all our problems, the only "Way," that we will fully see and recognize Him. *It is no longer I but Christ that lives in me* (Galatians 2:20).

Our sins died with Christ; we are no longer condemned. Relationally, we are one with Him. Our life begins when we give up ours to become one with Him. Faith, and faith alone, is what saves us.

Lord, open our eyes that we might see You, our Savior, right here with us. We want to not simply see You, but to gaze upon You and to know You more. We want to not just see You but find You. Oh, how sweet it is to know You, Lord! It is dear beyond expression! Thank You, Jesus! Amen.

JUNE 30TH

Nevertheless, we have not made use of this right, but we endure anything rather than put an obstacle in the way of the gospel of Christ.

1 CORINTHIANS 9:12

G ood morning! We are called to give up our rights so the Holy Spirit may have His way in and through our lives. Our insistence in proving that we are right is nearly always an indication of disobedience to God's teaching. *"Agree with thine adversary quickly"* (Matthew 5:25 KJV).

Paul encourages us, as he did, to be willing to lay down our rights for the gospel and the glory of God. In the current climate of this world, where everyone is fighting for and claiming their rights to this, that, and the other, and people are fearful of their rights being stripped away, what is our answer? Seek to be more like Jesus! His silence spoke volumes! We are seeking by the grace of God to follow Christ and to be conformed daily to His image. To us, His followers, Christ says, *"If anyone would come after me, let him deny himself and take up his cross daily and follow Me"* (Luke 9:23).

From His birth to His death, Christ chose the path of sacrifice and grace. He called sinners to come as they are to meet with the God of mercy to be forgiven and freed from the path of sin that leads to death.

Lord, may we focus less on our rights and more on showing the radical gospel of grace to an unbelieving world. If we make a stand, let it be for the sake of righteousness. Let our tone always be that of Your love and message of mercy, grace, and forgiveness. Thank You, Jesus! Amen.

July

JULY 1ST

But just as He who called you is holy, so be holy in all you do;
for it is written: "Be holy, because I am holy."

1 PETER 1:15–16

Good morning! God sets the standard for morality. We know that He is holy, set apart. He is not warlike, adulterous, or spiteful. He is a God of mercy and justice who cares personally for each of His followers. We, too, are set apart and as His children. We are to be different from others in this world. Our holy God expects us to imitate Him by following His high moral standards. We will never achieve perfection or sinlessness on this side of heaven. But like Him, we should be both merciful and just; like Him, we should sacrifice ourselves for others.

Therefore, I urge you, brothers and sisters, in view of God's mercy, to offer your bodies as a living sacrifice, holy and pleasing to God—this is your true and proper worship. Do not conform to the patterns of this world, but rather be transformed by the renewing of your mind (Romans 12:1-2).

God has perfect plans for us. He desires for us to be a holy people, transformed to be more like Him and living to honor and obey Him, repenting of and asking for His cleansing of our sin. We are God's people, and we should act like God's people. We know that we will fail along the way: *For all have sinned and fall short of the glory of God* (Romans 3:23). God has set the standard for us, and we should make it our standard.

Lord, we are not worthy, but You say the word and we are healed, holy, and redeemed through Your sacrifice. Cleanse our hearts in such a way that Your holiness is the desire of our hearts. May we live in a manner that is pleasing and honoring to You. Thank You, Jesus! Amen.

JULY 2ND

*As a prisoner for the Lord, then, I urge you to live a life worthy of the calling
you have received. Be completely humble and gentle;
be patient, bearing with one another in love.*

EPHESIANS 4:1-2

Good morning! Do not hide what the Lord has done and is doing
in your life! Live a life worthy of His calling that you have
received—the awesome privilege of being a child of God, a follower
of the Lord Jesus Christ! If those who know us and other people God
puts directly in our paths to minister to have no idea of and do not
experience the love of Christ in and through us, we are doing a
disservice to the very God who saved us from the mess we were in.

*Do you not know that your bodies are temples of the Holy Spirit, who is in
you, whom you have received from God? You are not your own; you were
bought with a price. Therefore honor God with your bodies* (1 Corinthians
6:19-20). Christ's death freed us from sin, and we are His. We are no
longer our own boss. We must live out God's standards, and in so doing,
honor Him. People are watching our lives. Do they see Christ in us? How
well are we representing Him? Be the church to every person you meet.
Be loving, kind, and compassionate. Represent Jesus well.

*Lord, forgive us when we fall short in loving each other and those You've set
before us. Unite Your body of believers, Your church, that we would be effective
in the ministry You've given each one of us. We were bought with Your
precious blood, and we belong to You. May we serve You well and bring many
to know who You are. Thank You, Jesus! Amen.*

JULY 3RD

O taste and see that the Lord is good:
blessed is the man that trusteth in Him.

PSALM 34:8 KJV

Good morning! Where or in whom do you put your trust? *In You, Lord my God, I put my trust. I trust in you* (Psalm 25:1-2). There is only One in whom we can trust who will never fail us or lead us astray. That One is God. Let's choose Him! *Good and upright is the Lord; therefore He instructs sinners in His ways. He guides the humble in what is right and teaches them His way* (Psalm 25:8-9). Our lives are markedly better when we live trusting in God, humble and surrendered, aware of our need for Him.

We all need the guidance and the direction of the Lord. His Word, the Bible, is our source of God's wisdom and the direction He gives for our lives. *All the ways of the Lord are living and faithful toward those who keep the demands of His covenant. For the sake of Your name, Lord, forgive my iniquity; though it is great* (Psalm 25:10-11).

David is known as a "man after God's heart," yet he committed grave sins (adultery and murder). But God! David sought after the Lord in his brokenness, repenting of his sin, trusting in God's covenant, in the mercy, grace and forgiveness He promises.

For the Lord is good; His steadfast love endures forever, and His faithfulness to all generations (Psalm 100:5). We can trust that God is good. He always acts in our best interest and out of His faithfulness to mankind. We, too, can experience the same direction, guidance, and pardon as David, if we submit to the Lord.

Lord, we put our trust in You, for You alone are worthy and faithful to those who love You. Forgive us when we fail You in our thoughts, words, and deeds. We need You to lead us and guide us in Your ways. Thank You for Your unconditional love, mercy, grace, and forgiveness. Thank You, Jesus! Amen.

JULY 4TH

For God so loved the world, that He gave His only begotten Son,
that whoever believes in Him shall not perish, but have eternal life.
For God did not send the Son into the world to judge the world,
but that the world might be saved through Him.

JOHN 3:16-17

Good morning! On July 4, 1776, the Second Continental Congress unanimously adopted the Declaration of Independence to announce the colonies' separation from the Kingdom of Great Britain. By putting their names on this paper, these men risked losing everything if the British won the American Revolution. Our country's freedom was won by their sacrifice.

But Jesus! In Him we have a Savior who sacrificed His very life that we might be set free from sin, redeemed, and sanctified. Do you know Him and recognize who He is and what He's done for you? Jesus came to save sinners, the lost, and give people eternal life. Luke 19:10 says, *"For the Son of Man has come to seek and to save that which was lost."* *"For even the Son of Man did not come to be served, but to serve, and to give His life a ransom for many"* (Mark 10:45).

Are we living in the freedom that Jesus gives, the freedom that cost Him everything? Or are we choosing to hold on tightly to our control and the self-centeredness that imprison us? We cannot have both. *"No one can serve two masters"* (Matthew 6:24). Jesus Christ came to bring salvation to each one of us, eternal life with Him forever and ever. *"So if the Son sets you free, you will be free indeed"* (John 8:36). Our true freedom is found in and through Christ Jesus.

Lord, thank You for the freedoms we enjoy from living in the United States. Protect us from the enemy that "comes only to steal, kill, and destroy." Thank You for our true freedom that is found only in and through believing, following, and knowing You. May we stand firm in our faith, boldly proclaiming Your truth. Thank You, Jesus! Amen.

JULY 5TH

Be kind and compassionate to one another, forgiving each other,
just as in Christ God forgave you.

EPHESIANS 4:32

G ood morning! I think sometimes that we are harsh people, quick
to be offended, critical, and unforgiving. We want what we want,
when we want it, and how we want it, unwilling to compromise and
unwavering in our demands of others. God calls us to have the
opposite thinking, attitude, and behavior, just as Jesus demonstrated
throughout His earthly ministry. He was compassionate, full of
mercy, grace, and forgiveness, and overflowed with loving kindness.
"But love your enemies, do good to them, and lend to them without
expecting to get anything back. Then your reward will be great, and you
will be children of the Most High, because He is kind to the ungrateful
and the wicked. Be merciful, just as your Father is merciful" (Luke 6:35–
36).

Anyone is able to love the lovable (*even sinners*, Luke 6:32). It takes
Jesus in and through us to love unlovable people, people who hurt and
wrong us. *"Do not judge, and you will not be judged. Do not condemn, and*
you will not be condemned. Forgive, and you will be forgiven. Give, and it will
be given to you" (Luke 6:37-38).

A forgiving spirit demonstrates that a person has received God's
forgiveness. We are told to *"love our enemies,"* bless and pray for them,
and share what we have with them. When we are critical or judgmental
rather than compassionate, we too will receive criticism and judgment.
However, if we are kind and treat others generously with compassion
and love, these same qualities return to us in full measure.

Lord, teach us Your ways and lead us in the way we should go. Make us more
like You in our hearts, minds, and spirits. Lord, may we be pleasing to You and
in turn to others. Thank You, Jesus! Amen.

JULY 6TH

Wait on the LORD; be of good courage,
and He shall strengthen your heart; wait, I say, on the LORD!

PSALM 27:14

Good morning! Waiting for God is not easy, but it is definitely best. Oftentimes, it may seem as if God isn't listening, as if He's not hearing our cries for help or the prayers we are uttering. Or maybe we feel as though God doesn't understand the urgency of our situation. And therein we find Satan's lies and his foothold into our lives. This kind of thinking dethrones God and implies He is not in control or that He is not fair. But God! He alone is worth waiting for!

Because of the Lord's great love we are not consumed, for His compassions never fail. They are new every morning; great is Your faithfulness. I say to myself, "The Lord is my portion; therefore I will wait for Him" (Lamentations 3:22-24). The Lord is good to those who wait for Him, to the soul who seeks Him. Waiting on and trusting in God's goodness and faithfulness makes us confident in His great promises for the future.

Now faith is confidence in what we hope for and assurance about what we do not see (Hebrews 11:1). Waiting on God increases our faith. We hope in and wait on Him, and He uses our waiting to refresh, renew, and teach us—IF we will surrender and submit to Him.

Lord, may we make good use of our times of waiting and not forge ahead on our own where the enemy waits to devour us. You have promised restoration and blessings to those who wait on and follow You. We trust in and know that Your promises are true, even when we don't understand and feel impatient to wait—but wait we will. Thank You, Jesus! Amen.

JULY 7TH

*"God did this so that they would seek him and perhaps reach out for him
and find him, though he is not far from any one of us.
'For in him we live and move and have our being.'
As some of your own poets have said, 'We are his offspring.'"*

ACTS 17:27-28

Good morning! Everything in all creation is upheld by God's mighty hand, including our very existence. God is the Creator of ALL things including each one of us. We should marvel at this thought. God made us—you and me and every single person ever in existence! *For You created my inmost being; You knit me together in my mother's womb. I praise You because I am fearfully and wonderfully made; Your works are wonderful, I know that full well* (Psalm 139:13-16).

God is Sovereign and in control, and at the very same time He is up close and personal. In Christ, we are stirred up, on the go, and everything of God is set in motion. Nothing is impossible for us because we believe that we are in Him, and in Him we move. Christ lives in us when we believe in Him, follow Him, and dedicate our lives to Him. What a glorious life we have when the Creator of the universe rules in us. *To them God has chosen to make known among the Gentiles the glorious riches of this mystery, which is Christ in you, the hope of glory* (Colossians 1:27).

Christ lives in and through us, and in the hearts of all who believe in Him. We carry on regardless of our situation or circumstances because God *Himself gives everyone life and breath and everything else* (Acts 17:25). Seek Him and you will find Him.

Lord, thank You for loving us so much! You are Lord of all—of heaven and earth—and You created us to live in fellowship with You. Who are we? And yet You love us and know us down to the number of hairs on our heads. We praise you and magnify Your Name! Thank You, Jesus! Amen.

JULY 8TH

"But if serving the Lord seems undesirable to you,
then choose for yourselves this day whom you will serve ...
But as for me and my household, we will serve the Lord."

JOSHUA 24:15

Good morning! We live in a world where there are an overwhelming number of choices! Where to eat, work, or play; what to watch, wear or consume; whether to stay or go; with whom and where. The list is endless. But there is one choice we must make that has eternal consequences. Joshua challenged the Israelites to *"choose whom you will serve,"* and nothing has changed. We must choose for ourselves whether we will serve and obey God, who is faithful and trustworthy, or the myriad of earthly idols we are chasing after.

It's easy to slip into the rebellion of doing it our own way, but there are serious consequences. God will judge those who refuse to listen to Him, and the results can be disastrous. *"Whoever believes in the Son of God has eternal life, but whoever rejects the Son will not see life, for God's wrath remains on them"* (John 3:36). At some point we must decide "our way" or "Yahweh"—God's way.

"Now then," said Joshua, *"throw away the foreign gods that are among you and yield your hearts to the Lord, the God of Israel"* (Joshua 24:23). Serving God is more than just saying the words. It is action and complete dedication to Him. We must yield our hearts to God, surrendering ourselves to Him, and prioritizing Him in our lives above all else. Make the decision today to follow Jesus and reaffirm that choice each and every day.

Lord, our hearts are set on You, surrendered in obedience to You. Teach us, guide us and show us what You would have us to do. We choose to serve You, yielding to Your control in and of our lives. Thank You, Jesus! Amen.

JULY 9TH

Peter followed at a distance ... The Lord turned and looked straight at Peter ...
And he went outside and wept bitterly.

EXCERPTS FROM LUKE 22:54-62

Good morning! Are we following Jesus from a distance? If so, what is keeping us from Him? Just as Jesus had spoken, Peter three times denied even knowing Jesus. *Then Peter remembered the words Jesus had spoken: "Before the rooster crows, you will disown Me three times." And he went outside and wept bitterly* (Matthew 26:75). Peter's fear of the consequences of knowing Jesus, of being recognized as one of His chosen, caused him to deny Jesus, his teacher, friend, and Savior. Are we living any differently?

We need to be aware of our own breaking points of standing firm in our faith, places where we might become overconfident or self-sufficient. Maybe we have let self-indulgence rule or are exercising a vengeful spirit, or a lukewarm attitude. Or maybe worldliness has distanced us from God. It broke Peter's heart to come face-to-face with the knowledge that he had not only denied his Lord but turned away from his very dear friend, the person who had loved and taught him for three years—Peter *wept bitterly.* When we fail—and we all will—our sins separate us from God, but they can be forgiven. *For all have sinned and fall short of the glory of God, and all are justified freely by His grace through the redemption that came by Christ Jesus* (Romans 3:23-24).

From this humiliating experience, Peter learned much that would help him later as a leader in the ministry and building of the church. God will use even our failures to glorify Him when we repent and return to Him.

Lord, thank You for the privilege of sitting and walking with and knowing You. We desire fellowship with You, Lord, without the hindrances of our sin and rebellion. We can only do that through You, our Lord Jesus Christ. Thank You, Jesus! Amen.

JULY 10TH

*In the same way, faith by itself, if it is not accompanied by action, is dead.
But someone will say, "You have faith; I have deeds." Show me your faith
without deeds, and I will show you my faith by my deeds [by what I do].*

JAMES 2:17-18

Good morning! Have you ever thought or said these words out
loud: "I can't wait for retirement!"? Or possibly we are hoping
for, and maybe even living for, the time we can "just relax" and "do
what we want, when we want." Let this not be so when it comes to
our faith! Jesus never taught us to live a remote, retired, and
secluded life, particularly when it comes to being His disciples.
*"Therefore go and make disciples of all nations, baptizing them in the
name of the Father and of the Son and of the Holy Spirit, and teaching
them to obey everything I have commanded you"* (Matthew 28:19-20).

Jesus was all about "going" and putting faith to work. Faith and
action go hand-in-hand. We don't earn our salvation by our works, but
we are called to have a servant's heart and be obedient to the things and
work that God calls us to do. *As the body without the spirit is dead, so faith
without deeds is dead* (James 2:26). Our deeds are our faith in action,
demonstrating that our commitment to God is authentic and real. They
are a verification of our faith in Christ Jesus. We must not simply rest on
our laurels, using God for the sake of blessings, peace, and joy, and
getting our enjoyment of Him. Jesus Christ never encouraged the idea of
retirement from serving others and Him.

*Lord, may we not be lazy about the work You have given us to do. May our
faith be filled with a firm confidence that results in action. Show us, Lord, what
You would have us do for You this day, and may we respond in faith with
action. "And I said, 'Here I am. Send me!'" (Isaiah 6:8). Thank You, Jesus!
Amen.*

JULY 11TH

Praise be to the God and Father of our Lord Jesus Christ,
the Father of compassion and the God of all comfort,
who comforts us in all our troubles, so that we can comfort those in any
trouble with the comfort we ourselves receive from God.

2 CORINTHIANS 1:4

Good morning! We are in the midst of perilous times, and for
some, life seems to be too much, nearly unbearable. What do we
do? The more we suffer, the more comfort God gives! When we are
feeling overwhelmed, we must go to the great Comforter. God is the
source of mercy and comfort to the hurting. *And the God of all grace,*
who called you to His eternal glory in Christ, after you have suffered a
little while, will Himself restore you and make you strong, firm and
steadfast (1 Peter 5:10).

We do not experience life in a vacuum for only ourselves! In good or
bad experiences, we share life as a family of God, and our stories are for
mutual benefit. With every trial we endure, we are being prepared to
comfort and be a help to other people who are suffering similar troubles.

God may use our challenges and trials as a means of teaching or
correcting us. We are strengthened so that we may endure in and
through Christ Jesus for sharing with others to help heal, build
relationships, and walk in faith together. Comforting each other, as
God has comforted us, is a way to encourage fellowship and serve
one another in Christ Jesus.

Thank You, Lord, for the privilege of coming alongside others to comfort as
You have comforted us. You use everything for building up Your kingdom in
this world. Help us to be willing to share our experiences with others in a way
that brings glory to You. Thank You, Jesus! Amen.

JULY 12TH

"Greater love has no one than this: to lay down one's life for one's friends."

JOHN 15:13

G ood morning! A song sung by artist Johnny Lee talks about "Lookin' for love in all the wrong places."[18] That can be said about so many people, sometimes even us. But God! There is no greater love than His! God loved us enough to sacrifice His one and only Son, Jesus Christ! *He made Himself nothing by taking the very nature of a servant, being made in human likeness. And being found in appearance as a man, He humbled Himself by becoming obedient to death—even death on a cross* (Philippians 2:7-8).

This is not the definition of love Johnny Lee sang about! God's love is sacrificial, steadfast, and unfailing. *This is love: not that we loved God, but that He loved us and sent His Son as an atoning sacrifice for our sins* (1 John 4:10). God's redeeming love pursues us where we are. Through His love, He forgives us, no matter our sins. Only His love can transform us and make us whole again. He restores all who repent and return to Him.

There's another song by Stuart Townend: *How deep the Father's love for us, / How vast beyond all measure, / That He should give His only Son / To make a wretch His treasure. / How great the pain of searing loss – / The Father turns His face away, / As wounds which mar the Chosen One / Bring many sons to glory.*[19]

Do we know this Chosen One? The only One who sets us free? The One God sent for all humanity, that we would experience life with Him—full, abundant, eternal life?

Thank You, Lord, for a love like no other—unconditional, unwavering, constant and pure. We could never earn Your blessing of love that cost so much. We could never understand Your loss. May we learn to love more like You. Thank You, Jesus! Amen.

---

18. Wanda Mallette, Bob Morrison, and Patti Ryan, "Lookin' for Love" (Los Angeles: Sunset Sound Recorders, Full Moon Label, 1980).
19. Stuart Townend, "How Deep the Father's Love" (Thankyou Music, 1995).

JULY 13TH

Surrender to the Lord YAHWEH, all you nations and peoples.
Surrender to him all your pride and strength.
Confess that YAHWEH alone deserves all the glory and honor.

PSALM 96:7-9

G ood morning! What if our daily prayer was something like this: "Lord, let our lives overflow with Your presence every day"? We would need to surrender ourselves wholly to God, humbling ourselves and recognizing His Sovereignty. *The Lord does whatever pleases Him, in the heavens and on the earth, in the seas and all their depths* (Psalm 135:6).

Surrendering involves trusting God with our concerns, resting in His peace, and letting go of our pride and our need to control. God expects us to surrender every part of our life to Him, trusting in His thoughts and His ways. *"For My thoughts are not your thoughts, neither are your ways My ways,"* declares the Lord. *"As the heavens are higher than the earth, so are My ways higher than your ways and My thoughts than your thoughts"* (Isaiah 55:8-9).

We could never measure up to the Lord in all His grandeur, His wisdom, power, and love. And yet, He is interested in every part of our lives. We need to submit every aspect of our lives to God, to walk in the Spirit in everything we do. *Those who belong to Christ Jesus have crucified the flesh with its passions and desires. Since we live by the Spirit, let us keep in step with the Spirit* (Galatians 5:24-25).

God's presence will overflow in our lives as we surrender to Him and keep doing what He calls us to do, following Jesus and trusting in God for the results.

Lord, thank You for Your constant presence in our lives. Take from us all things that hinder and block us from knowing and following You. May we live fully surrendered to You, with our hearts fixed on You. Thank You, Jesus! Amen.

JULY 14TH

For in Christ all the fullness of the Deity lives in human form,
and in Christ you have been brought to fullness.
He is the head over every power and authority.

COLOSSIANS 2:9-10

Good morning! Do you want to experience the fullness of God in your life? Submit everything to Him—surrender all—and fully trust that what He says is the final word and truth. The more we know God's Word, the better off we will be! In Paul's letter to the Ephesians, we read, *and to know this love [Christ's love] that surpasses knowledge—that you may be filled to the measure of all the fullness of God* (Ephesians 3:19).

God's love is total. It reaches every corner of every experience of our lives and surpasses any knowledge we could ever have. The *fullness of God* is expressed only in Christ. God was in Christ's human body, and when we have Christ, we have everything we need. Stop searching for fulfillment in the things of this world or in ourselves. Fulfillment is only found in Jesus.

Paul closes his prayer with these powerful encouraging words of truth and praise: *Now to Him who is able to do immeasurably [exceedingly, abundantly] more than all we ask [think] or imagine, according to His power that is at work within us, to Him be glory in the church and in Christ Jesus throughout all generations, for ever and ever! Amen!* (Ephesians 3:20-21).

Yes, we have all the fullness of God available to us and we must appropriate that fullness through faith and through prayer as we live daily for Him.

Thank You, Lord, for Your Holy Spirit, who fills every aspect of our life to the fullest as we pursue our faith and remain "rooted and established" in Your love. Everything we are, everything we do, and everything we have come from You. We praise You and magnify Your Holy Name! Thank You, Jesus! Amen.

JULY 15TH

I waited patiently for the LORD; He turned to me and heard my cry.
He lifted me out of the pit of despair, out of the mud and the mire.
He set my feet on solid ground and steadied me as I walked along.
He put a new song in my mouth, a hymn of praise to our God.

PSALM 40:1-4

Good morning! All we have to do is this: obey God. But instead, we choose to live on our own resources, making decisions from our flesh. We rebel and dishonor until we've made such a mess of our lives, and then we cry out, "Why, God?" or "Help me, God!"

When I came to the end of myself, desperate and broken, God was there. Wherever we find ourselves today, swimming along joyfully or struggling miserably through difficulties or somewhere in the middle, God is there. *Jesus replied, "What is impossible with man is possible with God"* (Luke 18:27).

Jesus is the answer to every question, and He is all we need. Are we surrendered to God? We are to live in obedience to His Word and do what it says. Our hearts and our wills are to be aligned with God's will, and we must base our decisions and actions on what God's Word says. *But if anyone obeys His word, God's love is truly made complete in Him. This is how we know we are in Him: Whoever claims to live in Him must walk as Jesus did* (1 John 2:5-6). Do what Christ says and live as Christ wants!

Thank You, Lord, for showing us the way to live. You set our feet on solid ground, and You show us the Way we are to go. We surrender our lives to You, for we are made complete in You. Your will, not ours, be done. Thank You, Jesus! Amen.

JULY 16TH

"In the same way [as a lamp "gives light to everyone in the house"],
let your light shine before others, that they may see your good deeds
and glorify your Father in heaven."

MATTHEW 5:16

Good morning! When we come across something with great
benefit, something valuable, how quickly we move to tell others
all about it. But how quickly or how far are we willing to go to share
who God is and what He has done and is doing in our lives? We must
be willing to live for Christ and glow like lights, showing others who
Jesus is and what He is like. There is no light in this world apart from
Jesus.

Jesus sought out the lost, and He rejoiced when they were found. *"Or*
suppose a woman has ten silver coins and loses one. Doesn't she light a lamp,
sweep the house and search carefully until she find it? And when she finds it,
she calls her friends and neighbors together and says, 'Rejoice with me; I have
found my lost coin'" (Luke 15:8-9). Jesus uses this parable to teach that
God cares about restoring those who have fallen and that people should
celebrate when that happens. *"In the same way, there is rejoicing in the*
presence of the angels of God over one sinner who repents" (Luke 15:10).

Be bold in sharing what God has given you, what He's done and is
doing in your life. *For it is by grace you have been saved, through faith—and*
this is not from yourselves; it is the gift of God—not by works, so that no one
can boast. For we are God's handiwork, created in Christ Jesus to do good
works, which God prepared in advance for us to do (Ephesians 2:9-10). Be
willing to bring the hope of Jesus to someone in need.

Lord, may we have a renewed confidence and boldness to share who You are
and the message of Your saving grace so others will come to receive the
message of who You are and all that You do, that they would come to know
and follow You. Thank You, Jesus! Amen.

JULY 17TH

Each one of you should use whatever gift you have received to serve others,
as faithful stewards of God's grace in its various forms.
If anyone speaks, let them speak as the oracles [the very words] of God. If
anyone serves, they should do so with the strength God provides,
so that in all things God may be praised through Jesus Christ.
To Him be the glory and the power for ever and ever. Amen.

1 PETER 4:10–11

Good morning! Every good thing we have is a gift from God and is ours only by His grace and is intended to be used for His purposes. That is not how most people view their talents, resources, and belongings. But, as believers and followers of Christ Jesus, we are to be set apart in fulfilling God's purposes. Are we using the gifts God has given us to faithfully serve others?

Our gifts are not intended exclusively for our enjoyment. God has equipped each one of us as He sees fit in order that His body would be built up. *To equip His people for works of service, so that the body of Christ may be built up until we all reach unity in the faith and in the knowledge of the Son of God and become mature, attaining to the whole measure of the fullness of Christ* (Ephesians 4:12–13).

Combining our gifts together, we can obey God more fully than we could alone. We need each other to serve all the needs put before us and express the fullness of God. We are to love one another and use God's gifts to serve each other with God's power in and through us, for His glory and so others might be drawn to Him.

Lord, thank You for the gifts You have entrusted to us. May we use them for Your glory and the fulfillment of Your kingdom, that many would be drawn to You and come to know and believe. Thank You, Jesus! Amen.

JULY 18TH

Jesus answered, "I am the Way, the Truth and the Life.
No one comes to the Father except through Me."

JOHN 14:6

Good morning! Do not seek religion. Seek Jesus! Oswald Chambers wrote, "Many a soul begins to come to God when he flings off being religious, because there is only one Master of the human heart, and that is not religion but Jesus Christ."[20]

Jesus is both God and man. Following Him leads us to God. By uniting our lives with Jesus, we are united with God. Knowing Jesus is not about rules, rituals, and regulations but a living, loving relationship with our Savior. *"Now this is eternal life: that they know You, the only true God, and Jesus Christ, whom You have sent"* (John 17:3). Knowing God the Father Himself through His Son Jesus Christ is how we get eternal life, by entering into a personal relationship with God in Jesus.

When we repent and turn away from our sin, Christ's love lives in us by His Holy Spirit. Nowhere in God's Word are we told to seek religious practices. *"Seek first His kingdom and His righteousness, and all these things will be given to you as well"* (Matthew 6:33). Turn to God first to pursue His kingdom, trusting in His righteousness, and leave it to God to fulfill our basic needs.

We are to fill our thoughts with His desires, and to take on His character as our own, serving and obeying Him in everything. Is God first in our lives?

Thank You, Lord, for the privilege of living in relationship with You. May we always prioritize You as first in our lives and pursue Your righteousness. Help us to not get caught up in religious practices but to seek after You! You alone are sovereign and good. We can attain nothing of lasting value apart from You. Thank You, Jesus! Amen.

---

20. Oswald Chambers, *My Utmost for His Highest*, July 18 entry.

JULY 19TH

Be diligent in these matters; give yourself wholly to them, so that everyone may see your progress. Watch your life and doctrine closely. Persevere in them, because if you do, you will save both yourself and your hearers.

1 TIMOTHY 4:15-16

G ood morning! We are not able to *"go and make disciples"* (Matthew 28:19) if we are not disciples ourselves. We cannot give away what we ourselves don't have! God gave Jesus authority over heaven and earth. On the basis of that authority, Jesus told His disciples to make more disciples as they preached, baptized, and taught. Jesus had prepared them through His time with them in prayer and teaching.

We too are called *to go and make disciples,* and we too must be prepared. To be disciples of Christ we must be disciplined and genuinely committed to Him. Our lives must be reflective of Christ—His Word and His character. We need to be disciplined, attuned to the Spirit until we are in harmony with God's planning and purpose for us. *But in your hearts revere Christ as Lord. Always be prepared to give an answer to everyone who asks you to give the reason for the hope that you have* (1 Peter 3:15).

Each day we have many opportunities to support and encourage those around us—not of ourselves but of the Christ in us.

Lord, may we always be prepared to share our faith with those You put before us. Forgive us for the times we live without self-discipline and devotion to You. We pray to be attuned to Your Spirit in harmony with You, for Your glory and the purpose of ministering with and discipling others. Thank You, Jesus! Amen.

JULY 20TH

But those who hope in the Lord will renew their strength.
They will soar on wings like eagles; they will run and not grow weary,
they will walk and not faint.

ISAIAH 40:31

Good morning! We all want peace in our lives, but the question is, how or where do we find it? Depend on God's presence in your life and put your hope in the Lord! When we live in the expectation of His promise of strength in our lives to rise above life's distractions and difficulties, we will find God's peace. *And the peace of God, which surpasses all understanding, will guard your hearts and minds in Christ Jesus* (Philippians 4:7).

God's peace is a deep-seated harmony with Him. He protects our hearts and minds. We are able to live in confidence and relax in His promises that are right and good. The Lord has the power to control all of life—yes, even your life! Those who *will walk and not faint* choose to look upon Jesus, to walk as He walked, in and with character, and to walk alongside Him.

Jesus assured His disciples (and us), *"And surely I am with you always, to the very end of the age"* (Matthew 28:20). God is omnipresent, which means He is close to, next to, anywhere, everywhere. No matter where we are, He is there! *Whoever dwells in the shelter of the Most High, will rest in the shadow of the Almighty. I will say of the Lord, "He is my refuge and my fortress [hiding place], my God, in whom I trust"* (Psalm 91:1-2). There is no one and nothing that compares to God and the peace that His presence brings to our lives.

Lord, our hope and trust are in You. Thank You for the strength and peace we find in Your presence! Nothing compares to walking with and loving You! Thank You, Jesus! Amen.

JULY 21ST

Let the peace of Christ rule in your hearts,
since as members of one body you were called to peace.

COLOSSIANS 3:15

Good morning! Our hearts can be a center of conflict because it is there that our feelings and desires clash. How do we deal with our hearts' conflicts? Whatever we let *rule in our hearts* is what is in charge of how we live. To live in peace requires us to work together through and in love despite our differences. To live in love leads to peace. By using the "rule of peace" we are choosing that which promotes peace to the benefit of all concerned. We choose hope over fear, trust over distrust, love over jealousy.

And the peace of God, which transcends all understanding, will guard your hearts and your minds in Christ Jesus. Finally, brothers and sisters, whatever is true, whatever is noble, whatever is right, whatever is pure, whatever is lovely, whatever is admirable—if anything is excellent or praiseworthy—think about such things. Whatever you have learned or received or heard from me, or seen in me—put it into practice. And the God of peace will be with you (Philippians 4:7-9).

True peace is not found in positive thinking, in absence of conflict, or in good feelings. It comes from knowing God is in control— of all things, even of our hearts and minds. Let God be God of your life.

Lord, we pray that Your peace would guard our hearts and minds against all conflicts born of this world and the darkness it holds. We know our citizenship in Your kingdom is sure, our destiny is set, and we can have victory over sin. Thank You, Jesus! Amen.

JULY 22ND

"But when you are invited, take the lowest place, so that when your host
comes, he will say to you, 'Friend, move up to a better place.'
Then you will be honored in the presence of all the other guests.
For all those who exalt themselves will be humbled,
and those who humble themselves will be exalted."

LUKE 14:10-11

Good morning! We live in a me-first society, one that is filled with hurry for the most, the best, to impress, to have the highest status and position of prestige. But God! God promotes humility! Rather than a position of worldly reward and prestige, our place is meant to be one in which to serve God and others. He will open the doors to serve on a wider scale as He sees fit and as we allow Him to work in and through our lives.

But He gives us more grace. That is why Scripture says: "God opposes the proud but shows favor to the humble" (James 4:6). Pride makes us self-centered and leads us to the wrong conclusion, one of greed and grasping for more than we need. Instead, we are to do all in the character of Christ. In that, we will realize our sinfulness and understand our limitations. *Humble yourselves, therefore, under God's mighty hand, that He may lift you up in due time* (1 Peter 5:6).

We mustn't be concerned about our position and status or getting recognition for what we do. It is God's recognition that counts more than human praise. And God will bless in due time as He sees fit.

Lord, humble us to see ourselves as You see us. Use us as You will, that the desires of our hearts would be found in living to serve others and to glorify You! Thank You, Jesus! Amen.

JULY 23RD

"Lord, what do You want me to do?"

ACTS 9:6

G ood morning! Saul's response to the Lord on the road to Damascus is the example of a man yielding his will to God's will and is one that we should each aspire to daily. Are we willing for God to have His way with us today? There is nothing we could ever plan or have on our agendas, our to-do lists, or whatever daily checklist we follow, that will ever compare to what God is calling us to do. *Many are the plans in a person's heart, but it is the Lord's purpose that prevails* (Proverbs 19:21).

God wants to change our faith today to see that it is not obtained through our struggling and working and longing but in and through His Holy Spirit in our lives. *For it is God who works in you to will and to act in order to fulfill His good purpose* (Philippians 2:13).

God comes alongside us and within us to give us the desire and the power to do what pleases Him. The secret to a changed life is to submit to God's control and let Him work. *"Apart from Me you can do nothing"* (John 15:5). It is the living faith within us, and the power of God through our faith that leads us to do what God wants us to do. Wonderful things will take place when we get nearer and nearer to Him!

Lord, we thank You for loving us so much that You gave up Your throne in heaven to save us. Your ministry in and through us begins as soon as we yield ourselves to Your will. Surrendered obedience leads to our freedom and to glorifying You. Show us what You would have us do, Lord. Thank You, Jesus! Amen.

JULY 24TH

*"For I tell you that unless your righteousness surpasses
that of the Pharisees and the teachers of the law,
you will certainly not enter the kingdom of heaven."*

MATTHEW 5:20

Good morning! We all want the benefits of following Jesus, but we are not all willing to do what's necessary to receive them. What is Jesus telling us here? The Pharisees were exacting and scrupulous in their attempts to follow their laws, rules, and regulations. Their weakness was their contentment with external obedience without allowing God to change their hearts and attitudes. Our righteousness comes from what God does in us, not what we can do ourselves. *This righteousness is given through faith in Jesus Christ to all who believe* (Romans 3:22).

We must be God-centered, not self-centered, in our thoughts and actions. Our righteousness is based on reverence for God, not approval from people, and it goes beyond keeping laws to living in unity with Christ Jesus and allowing His Holy Spirit to lead, guide, and work in and through us. We must be willing to allow God to change our hearts to impact our attitudes and behaviors.

Know that a person is not justified by the works of the law, but by faith in Jesus Christ (Galatians 2:16). Laws can never make us acceptable to God and cannot possibly save us, although they can guide us to live as God requires. It is by our faith in Jesus that our righteousness of God comes.

Lord, we pray for righteousness that comes through our faith in You. Teach us and show us, Lord, that we would live as You require, and that Your Spirit would dwell in and work through us. Thank You, Jesus! Amen.

JULY 25TH

The Lord replied, "My Presence will go with you, and I will give you rest."
Then Moses said to Him, "If Your Presence does not go with us,
do not send us up from here."

EXODUS 33:14-15

G ood morning! Why do we run far from the Lord? In contrast, Moses told the Lord, "Without Your Presence, don't send us. We don't want to go without You." God knows us. God is with us, and one of His greatest gifts is allowing us to know Him and experience His Presence in and through our lives.

God's Presence is clear and convincing. There is no mistaking it! There is nowhere we can go away from His Presence. *If I go up to the heavens, You are there; if I make my bed in the depths, You are there* (Psalm 139:8). We experience God's Presence in our lives as we humbly and earnestly seek Him, as He reveals Himself to us. He is with us in times of prayer and sweet times of fellowship with Him. *You know when I sit and when I rise; You perceive my thoughts from afar. You discern my going out and my lying down; You are familiar with all my ways* (Psalm 139:2-3).

God is omnipotent, meaning all-powerful; omniscient, meaning all-knowing; and omnipresent, meaning present everywhere at all times. God's attributes are inseparable. He is Lord, God Almighty, Magnificent and Holy. His manifest presence should fill our hearts with praise and thanksgiving, for He is so, so good to us.

Thank You, Lord, for Your Presence in our lives. We praise You for the marvelous wonder of who You are and all that You do. May we draw near to You, seeking You with devoted hearts, desiring an intimate relationship with You. Thank You, Jesus! Amen.

JULY 26TH

*"I am sending you to them to open their eyes, in order to turn them
from darkness to light, and from the power of Satan to God,
so that they may receive forgiveness of sins and an inheritance [a place]
among those who are sanctified by faith in Me."*

ACTS 26:17-18

Good morning! I read this quote this morning: "The church has many tasks but only one mission." Oh, if only we could remain focused on just that one mission set before us! *Jesus said, "For the Son of Man came to seek and to save the lost"* (Luke 19:10). And He told His disciples to *"go and make disciples"* (Matthew 28:19).

Discipleship is all about the right relationship with God, self, and others. We are to find people to encourage toward Christ, humbly share what Jesus has and is doing in our own lives, and help them to do the same toward others. Discipleship is all about loving. *"Love the Lord your God with all your heart and with all your soul and with all your mind. This is the first and greatest commandment. And the second is like it, 'Love your neighbor as yourself'"* (Matthew 22:37-39).

God's love changes people to be more like Him, opening their hearts to receive the message of forgiveness, redemption, and salvation. We have a message to share. *Do the work of an evangelist* (2 Timothy 4:5). Jesus sent His disciples—the Church, including us—to share and be an example of His way of life in this world. *"By this everyone will know that you are My disciples, if you love one another"* (John 13:35).

Thank You, Lord, for the mission to seek and save the lost. Give us a renewed passion and focus for Your mission and show each one of us how best to be of service in bringing the lost to know You. Help us to boldly proclaim the gospel and to set an example of Your love, that many will come to know You. Thank You, Jesus! Amen.

JULY 27TH

"You unbelieving generation," Jesus replied, "how long shall I stay with you? How long shall I put up with you? Bring the boy to me."

MARK 9:19

Good morning! There is no bargaining with God. We either believe or we don't. The disciples failed to heal a demon-possessed boy, and his father said to Jesus, *"But if You can do anything, take pity on us and help us."* How many times do we question whether or not God is able to help us? *"If You can."* The God who spoke all of creation into existence, who breathes life into the dead! *"If You can?" said Jesus. "Everything is possible for one who believes."* Immediately the boy's father exclaimed, *"I do believe; help my unbelief!"* (Mark 9:23-24).

Nothing is too difficult for God! And nothing is impossible for God! So, the issue doesn't lie with God's ability. We cannot have or expect to receive everything we pray for like a spoiled child or as if by magic. But with faith, by believing, we can have everything we need to serve God and others. The attitude of trust and confidence that the Bible calls belief or faith is not something we can obtain or conjure up. The disciples asked Jesus, *"Why couldn't we drive it out?"* He replied, *"This kind can come out only by prayer and fasting"* (Mark 9:28-29). Prayer and fasting are the keys that unlock faith in our lives.

Believe in God and in what His Word tells us. Spend time in earnest prayer, having an attitude of complete dependence on and the action of a surrendered asking. Prayer demonstrates our reliance on God as we humbly invite Him to fill us with faith and power. Fasting unlocks sacrificial obedience and a deeper relationship with God.

Lord, we believe; help our unbelief! There is no substitute for prayer and fasting, especially in circumstances that seem impossible. We humbly come before You, never in self-sufficiency but in seeking Your renewing of our spirits, always trusting in You. Thank You, Jesus! Amen.

JULY 28TH

"I have finished the work which You have given Me to do."

JOHN 17:4

Good morning! Probably most of us have asked for more hours in the day so we could accomplish everything we needed to do. At one point, Julius Caesar mandated a new solar calendar that caused one year to have 445 days and became known as the "Year of Confusion." The secret to getting all our work done is not adding hours to our day or days to the year. It's doing only what our Heavenly Father has put before us to do. *The disciples asked Jesus, "What must we do to do the works God requires?" Jesus answered, "The work of God is this: to believe in the One He has sent"* (John 6:28-29). Our purpose is not found in the work we do, but in whom we believe.

Our lives are a testimony to the Son of the living God, satisfying our Creator and His plans and purposes. *"For I know the plans I have for you," declares the Lord, "plans to prosper you and not to harm you, plans to give you hope and a future. Then you will call on Me and come and pray to Me, and I will listen to you"* (Jeremiah 29:11-12).

Ask God for His agenda each day. Don't let the urgent usurp the important. Do everything while under His power and resting in Him. The only "must do" on our "to do" is the work that God gives us to do.

Lord, we give to You this day and all the minutes and hours within it. We are Yours to do what You would have us to do for the good of others and Your kingdom. Prepare us; make us and keep us ready to do exactly what You appoint us to do. Thank You, Jesus! Amen.

JULY 29TH

"Behold, He cometh with clouds."

REVELATION 1:7 KJV

Good morning! What if God isn't so much trying to teach us something in our trials as He is wanting us to unlearn something? Oswald Chambers said, "God's purpose in the cloud is to simplify our belief until our relationship with Him is exactly that of a child."[21]

Jesus answered and said to Him, "Most assuredly, I say to you, unless one is born again, he cannot see the kingdom of God" (John 3:3). We are born with sin, and we are living in the devil's world. This is his kingdom. Everything is different from God's kingdom. We learn to get by grasping instead of giving. We learn to be first instead of last. Everything needs to be unlearned. That's one of the reasons Jesus said we must be born again. *And whatever you do, whether in word or deed, do it all in the name of the Lord Jesus, giving thanks to God the Father through Him* (Colossians 3:17).

When we become followers of Jesus and find ourselves doing things, thinking and acting differently from the ways of this world, rejoice! God told the Israelites in the desert, *"See, I am doing a new thing! Now it springs up; do you not perceive it?"* (Isaiah 43:19). When we are born again in Christ Jesus, we are learning a new and better way to live.

Lord, may our answer be "yes" to the question, "Have I been born again?" May we be willing to surrender and unlearn the devil's lies, his ways of living, thinking, and doing. May our hearts be set on You as we seek after You, learning the ways of living for You and in Your Kingdom. Thank You, Jesus! Amen.

---

21. Oswald Chambers, *My Utmost for His Highest*, July 29 entry.

JULY 30TH

*"Choose for yourselves this day whom you will serve. ...
But as for me and my household, we will serve the Lord."*

JOSHUA 24:15

Good morning! We used to tell our children that the choices they make today impact their tomorrows. This truth continues throughout our lifetime. Joshua challenged the Israelites: the choice to follow the Lord is life-giving and life-changing. He rescues us out of darkness and brings us into His everlasting light. *God is Light; in Him there is no darkness at all. If we claim to have fellowship with Him and yet walk in the darkness, we lie and do not live out the truth. But if we walk in the Light, as He is in the Light, we have fellowship with one another, and the blood of Jesus, His Son, purifies [cleanses] us from all sin"* (1 John 1:5-7).

When we choose to commit our lives to Jesus and identify ourselves with Him, His death becomes ours, and we are covered by the blood of Jesus. *In Him we have redemption through His blood, the forgiveness of sins, in accordance with the riches of God's grace that He lavished on us* (Ephesians 1:7). And just as Jesus rose from the grave, we rise up to a new place of fellowship with Him. Our decision to choose Light and life today impacts every day we live, all the way into eternity.

Lord, we love You! We choose Light and life! We choose You! We live in gratitude for and awe of You. The choice to follow You has a greater impact on today and our tomorrows than any other choice or decision we will ever make. Thank You for making a way for us! Thank You, Jesus! Amen.

JULY 31ST

May the God who gives endurance and encouragement give you the same attitude of mind toward each other that Christ Jesus had, so with one mind and one voice you may glorify the God and Father of our Lord Jesus Christ.

ROMANS 15:5-6

G ood morning! Paul is essentially praying for the Roman church (and for us) for God to provide strength to persevere and the ability to live in acceptance of one another, getting along despite differences. The Roman church was a diverse community, divided, so it was difficult for people to accept one another. Years have passed but the divisive nature of man and sin lives on in the world and within God's church. Paul goes on in verse 7 to say, *Accept one another, just as Christ accepted you, in order to bring praise to God.*

We will never bring others to Christ through harsh judgment, rudeness, and avoidance. Our thoughts, words, and actions are to demonstrate the love of Jesus to those we interact with. Jesus told His disciples, *"A new commandment I give to you, that you love one another: just as I have loved you, you also are to love one another"* (John 13:34). Where there is division, we are choosing wrong thinking, acting, and belief. When we are in the Spirit, we have life, and we will love everybody, even those with whom we disagree.

Lord, we aspire to live in, by, and through Your Spirit. Help us to live by Your grace, dying to ourselves and living for You. Teach us to surrender and submit to Your ways, to be humble, compassionate, kind, and loving. Teach us to become more like You. Thank You, Jesus! Amen.

August

AUGUST 1ST

Blessed is the man who trusts in the LORD, whose trust is the LORD.
He is like a tree planted by water, that sends out its roots by the stream,
and does not fear when heat comes, for its leaves remain green, and is not
anxious in the year of drought, for it does not cease to bear fruit.

JEREMIAH 17:7–8 ESV

Good morning! Trusting in God allows no room for worry or anxiety. Trusting in the Lord gives us abundant strength, not only to meet our own needs but even the strength to meet the needs of others. Like a well-watered tree, we flourish and bear good fruit to share. Trusting in the Lord supplies strength to face adversity, difficulties, and times of crisis. We find joy in the Lord and praise Him. *The LORD is my strength and my shield; my heart trusts in Him, and He helps me. My heart leaps for joy, and with my song I praise Him* (Psalm 28:7).

Throughout Scripture, we are told, "do not fear," "do not be discouraged," and "be anxious for nothing." Why? Because God is our refuge and strength, our fortress, our help in times of trouble. *You keep him in perfect peace whose mind is stayed on You, because he trusts in You* (Isaiah 26:3).

When we put our trust in God, we find confidence, faith, courage, humility, peace, contentment, hope, and reassurance. Those who trust in God are blessed!

Lord, You are our only source of true safety. You protect us and provide for us. We have no need for fear and anxiety when we are trusting in You. Our perfect peace is found in You. Lord, may we live surrendered lives, obedient to and trusting in You. Thank You, Jesus! Amen.

AUGUST 2ND

"You say, 'I am rich, I have acquired wealth, and do not need a thing.'
But you do not realize that you are wretched, pitiful, poor, blind, and naked."

REVELATION 3:17

Good morning! There was a contrast of views between Jesus and the church of Laodicea. The wealth of the city and church of Laodicea led the people to assume their material possessions were a sign of God's spiritual blessings. But they did not take a stand for anything. They were indifferent, idle, and neglectful of doing anything of value for Christ or others. They prioritized material wealth and didn't realize its fleeting value in comparison to the unseen and eternal wealth that comes from God.

No matter how many material possessions or how much financial wealth a person may have, it pales in comparison to a vital relationship with Jesus. *"Do not store up for yourselves treasures on earth, where moths and vermin destroy and where thieves break in and steal. But store up for yourselves treasures in heaven ... For where your treasure is, there your heart will be also"* (Matthew 6:19-21). The things of this world distract us and cause us to live in greed or to be envious of those who appear to have an easier way of life, coveting what they have. But God! We must refocus our gaze away from temporary worldly prosperity to the lasting rewards of God.

Temporary wealth gives way to death, but the righteousness found in Christ has eternal value. What we treasure the most controls us. Choose well. Choose Jesus and eternity.

Thank You, Lord, for the rich blessings that come from Your hand. Thank You for the treasure of knowing You, for You are our Provider, rich in mercy, grace, love, and forgiveness. May we prioritize our relationship with You and the hope of heaven over all else. Thank You, Jesus. Amen.

AUGUST 3RD

"And I will be their God, and they shall be my people."

JEREMIAH 31:33

Good morning! We are the children of God, invited to come to Him, to bring everything before Him in prayer and to live in a personal, intimate relationship with Him. God is all things: Creator, Provider, Protector, Lover of our souls. He is the One true God—glorious and magnificent. He is our shield to protect us, our guide to direct us. He is the God who stills the raging storms simply by speaking, *"Peace. Be still!"* (Mark 4:39). He is the Lord, my Shepherd who takes care of our needs, the Alpha-Omega, Beginning and End.

As God has said: "I will live with them and walk among them, and I will be their God, and they will be My people." ... And, "I will be a Father to you, and you will be My sons and daughters," says the Lord Almighty (2 Corinthians 6:16, 18). God is always with us, for He dwells within us. We are His temple, and we are His people. He is the Creator and overseer of our lives, and His Word is alive and active (Hebrews 4:12).

Live in His Presence and experience His power and peace. There is no other like our God!

Thank You, Lord, for Your covenant promises with us, Your people. Forgive us when we wander from You and try to navigate our lives alone, neglecting fellowship with You and rebelling against Your Word. We repent and turn to You, Lord, surrendering ourselves wholly to You. Thank You, Jesus! Amen.

AUGUST 4TH

John answered and said, "A man can receive nothing unless it has been given to him from heaven."

JOHN 3:27 NKJV

Good morning! Have we gotten to the place of understanding that all we have and all we need comes from God? Will not the Father, the Creator, take care of His children, His creation? Jesus shared the heart of God: unselfish, not begrudging or stingy. We don't have to beg or plead, bargain or grovel. He is compassionate, loving, and kind. He knows our needs before we ask, and His desire is that we live in a manner worthy of His calling. *"For everyone who asks receives, and he who seeks finds, and to him who knocks it will be opened"* (Matthew 7:7-8).

Jesus taught His disciples (and us) how much the heavenly Father delights in their coming to Him. He told them to seek the Father and ask Him to provide for their needs. God knows how to give good gifts. *"If you then, though you are evil, know how to give good gifts to your children, how much more will your Father in heaven give the Holy Spirit to those who ask Him?"* (Matthew 7:11, Luke 11:13).

We can trust that God will always meet our needs. *And my God will meet all your needs according to the riches of His glory in Christ Jesus* (Philippians 4:19). Whatever we need on earth, He will supply. Whatever we need in heaven, He will supply. We may not get all we want, but assuredly He meets our needs. By trusting in Christ, our attitudes and appetites can change from wanting everything to accepting His provision and the power He supplies to live for Him.

Lord, move us from wanting and needing to that place of recognizing our sufficiency is found in knowing and trusting in You. Lord, build in us the faith, focus, and follow-through to know You. Our efforts are never in vain. All we need is found in You. Thank You, Jesus! Amen.

AUGUST 5TH

"My grace is sufficient for you, for My power is made perfect in weakness."

2 CORINTHIANS 12:9

Good morning! Why do we ask God for something He's already given and not trust that what He's given is exactly what we need? God may not answer our prayers in the way we think is best, but God answers in the way HE knows is best. How many times in our lives do we encounter circumstances or situations that make us question God? I've had a few big ones!

"My grace is sufficient for you, for My power is made perfect in weakness." Just as God did not take away Paul's affliction, He may not remove ours, but we can be assured God will demonstrate His power in our lives, just as He did in Paul's. The fact that God's power is displayed in weakness should give us courage and be an encouragement to us during times that weaken our faith. God is able to use people, circumstances, and difficulties in ways we cannot even begin to fathom.

Don't question what God has stated as fact: *"My grace is sufficient for you, for My power is made perfect in weakness."* Our effectiveness comes from our reliance on God, not our own simple energy, effort, or talent. He uses our weakness to develop and increase our Christian character, deepen our worship, and affirm God's strength and presence in our lives.

Take God at His Word: *"My grace is sufficient for you, for My power is made perfect in weakness."*

Lord, increase our faith in Your Word, that we would respond by placing our trust fully in You. Thank You for Your sufficient grace. May our reliance on You increase, as our self-sufficiency decreases. Thank You Jesus! Amen.

AUGUST 6TH

Praise be to the God and Father of our Lord Jesus Christ,
the Father of compassion and the God of all comfort,
who comforts us in all our troubles, so that we can comfort those
in any trouble with the comfort we ourselves receive from God.

2 CORINTHIANS 1:3-4

Good morning! Out of the depths of a broken heart comes the capacity to love in the most compassionate and understanding ways. God's comfort isn't necessarily to take troubles away but to teach us how to comfort others. We must understand that being comforted can also mean receiving strength, encouragement, and hope to deal with our troubles. The more we suffer, the more comfort God gives us. Are we willing to go to any lengths to be a comfort to others as God has done for us?

Therefore, I urge you, brothers and sisters, in view of God's mercy, to offer your bodies as a living sacrifice, holy and pleasing to God—this is your true and proper worship (Romans 12:1). When we dedicate our bodies as living sacrifices to God, we don't just sit around and enjoy the experience of knowing God and of His comfort. We willingly go out and serve, comforting others as God has comforted us. We must be willing to enter into discomfort for the sake of others and to go where God sends us for the sake of others and His glory.

Let's make the effort to leave our comfort zone to go out to the places and people God invites us in order to share the comfort He has shared with us.

Lord, thank You for who You are and what You've done and are doing in our lives. May we set aside ourselves to go where You send us, to trust You to lead and guide us into areas of need, that we would be a comfort to others as You have been a comfort to us. Thank You, Jesus! Amen.

AUGUST 7TH

The plans of the LORD stand firm forever,
the purposes of His heart through all generations.

PSALM 33:11

Good morning! Let God have His way with you! Nothing in life will go as it's intended until we allow Him to be Lord of and in our lives. We will miss out on the life God intends when we're clutching on to all the details of our lives that we have no control over—constantly trying to maneuver and manipulate to make things happen or change what was, is, or might be to what we think or want it to be.

Let God be God! *I will instruct you and teach you in the way you should go; I will counsel you with my eye upon you. Do not be like the horse or mule, which have no understanding but must be controlled by bit and bridle or they will not come to you* (Psalm 32:8-9).

God longs to guide us in His love and wisdom, and He offers us the best way to go. Are we following God's way and His written Word, or are we stubbornly insisting on our own way, continually rebelling in disobedience that requires His discipline or punishment?

Many are the woes of the wicked, but the Lord's unfailing love surrounds the one who trusts in Him. Rejoice in the Lord and be glad, you righteous; sing all you who are upright in heart! (Psalm 32:10-11).

Lord, You are the Way, the Truth, and the Life. May we be counted among the righteous, surrendering ourselves to You in obedience to Your Word and Your way. We praise You for who You are and all that You do. Thank You, Jesus! Amen.

AUGUST 8TH

Why, you do not even know what will happen tomorrow. Instead, you ought to say, "If it is the Lord's will, we will live and do this or that.

JAMES 4:14, 15

Good morning! Oh, the time and effort we waste projecting and predicting! Experts are forecasting the economy, the weather, sports season outcomes, fashion trends, color palettes—the list is endless. Ultimately, no one has the ability to see even five minutes into the future! God knows! While it is good to have goals, goals can disappoint us if we leave God out of the equation.

There is no point in making plans as though God doesn't exist, because the future, and all things, are in His Hands. We must include God as part of our planning process through prayer and submitting to what His Word says.

To man belong the plans of the heart, but from the Lord comes the reply of the tongue. All a man's ways seem innocent to him, but motives are weighed by the Lord. Commit to the Lord whatever you do, and He will establish your plans (Proverbs 16:1-3). We can plan ahead, but we must hold on to our plans loosely. When we put God's desires at the center of our planning, He will never disappoint us. We make our plans, but God has the last word.

Lord, we prayerfully make our plans, holding them loosely, and surrendering them all to You. Help us, Lord, to remember to always seek You first for the plans and decisions we need to make. We trust in Your ways, Your timing, and Your will to be done in our lives. Thank You, Jesus!

AUGUST 9TH

Pray without ceasing [continuously, never stop].

1 THESSALONIANS 5:17

Good morning! One of the most powerful tools we have is prayer, and we are told throughout Scripture to use it! We are to always have an attitude of prayer, built upon the acknowledgment of our need for and dependence on God. We must constantly recognize His presence within us and determine to obey Him fully. *And pray in the Spirit on all occasions with all kinds of prayers and requests. With this in mind, be alert and always keep on praying for all the Lord's people* (Ephesians 6:18).

How can we be praying *on all occasions?* Prayer must always be foundational in our lives as a consistent response. *"Then you will call on Me and come and pray to Me, and I will listen to you"* (Jeremiah 29:12). We can make quick, brief prayers our habitual response to every situation and need we have throughout the day. *I call on you, my God, for You will answer me; turn Your ear to me and hear my prayer* (Psalm 17:6). We can offer frequent and spontaneous prayers of praise and thanksgiving. And we can order our life around God's desires and teachings, so our very life becomes a prayer.

Do not be anxious about anything, but in every situation, by prayer and petition, with thanksgiving, present your requests to God (Philippians 4:6). A life of prayer means that prayer is a part of every aspect of our life, and not just something that happens at certain times. Pray continually—without ceasing!

Thank You, Lord, for the privilege of prayer. Help us to prioritize our prayer life so our prayers will be heartfelt, personal, and authentic and never a ritual or task. We live in a world desperate for You, Lord. May we pray for each other, for increased faith and to encourage each other in faithful surrender and obedience to You. Thank You, Jesus! Amen.

AUGUST 10TH

This is the verdict: Light has come into the world, but people loved darkness instead of light because their deeds were evil. Everyone who does evil hates the Light, and will not come into the Light for fear that their deeds will be exposed. But whoever lives by truth comes into the Light, so that it may be seen plainly that what they have done has been done in the sight of God.

JOHN 3:19-21

Good morning! We all know someone, maybe even within our own families or circle of friends, who avoids the Light we share. This should not be surprising to us. Many people don't want their lives exposed to God's Light because they fear what will be revealed. They don't want to be asked to change. It can appear threatening to others when our lives are changing and we desire to obey what God commands and follow Jesus.

Fear can lead people to wrong actions and places. *Fear of man will prove to be a snare, but whoever trusts in the Lord is kept safe* (Proverbs 29:25). Fear drives people to put their faith in the wrong things and to live misguided lives in darkness, ignoring the love of God and the freedom He offers us. *For God so loved the world that He gave His one and only Son, that whoever believes in Him shall not perish but have eternal life. For God did not send His Son into the world to condemn the world, but to save the world through Him* (John 3:16-17).

Don't give in to discouragement. Keep shining God's Light into the darkness.

Lord, there are so many who need Your Light. We live in a dark world filled with those You came to save. We continue to pray for the lost, the sick, the suffering, and for all those who are choosing to live separated from You in darkness. Lord, may we shine Your Light into their lives that they might come to know You. Thank You, Jesus! Amen.

AUGUST 11TH

Love must be sincere. Hate what is evil; cling to what is good.
Be devoted to one another in love. Honor one another above yourselves.
Never be lacking in zeal, but keep your spiritual fervor, serving the Lord.
Be joyful in hope, patient in affliction, faithful in prayer.
Share with the Lord's people who are in need. Practice hospitality.

ROMANS 12:9–13

Good morning! Is our love genuine and sincere? Many of us have guarded hearts and mastered the art of politeness in love. We use kind words, avoid hurting others, appear to take interest in conversations, and maybe even are moved by compassion when we hear of needs or injustice done to others. We monitor our responses and filter sharing our beliefs so as not to offend.

But God is calling us to a deeper love, a sincere love that goes beyond pretense, pretending, and politeness. Sincere love requires honesty, concentration, and effort. Sincere love demands our time, money, resources, and personal involvement. *Above all, love each other deeply, because love covers a multitude of sins* (1 Peter 4:8). Sincere love always looks for ways to impact others' lives with and for Christ Jesus.

There are entire communities of people who need and don't know Jesus. That should break our hearts and move us out of our chairs and into action!

Thank You, Lord, for Your unconditional love, that while we were yet sinners, You came to save us. Help us to see people through Your eyes, to hear their cries through Your ears. Move in our hearts to love as You love, with sincerity, fullness, compassion and kindness. Thank You, Jesus! Amen.

AUGUST 12TH

*His divine power has given us everything we need for a godly life
through our knowledge of him who called us by his own glory
and goodness. Through these he has given us his very great and precious
promises, so that through them you may participate in the divine nature,
having escaped the corruption in the world caused by evil desires.*

2 PETER 1:3-5

Good morning! God has given us everything we need to lead the life He is calling us to lead. We are fully equipped in His Word, and Jesus is our guide. But we have a choice whether or not to be obedient in our spiritual life, to lead the good and godly lives God has called us to. This requires surrender, submission, and obedience on our part. But God! He desires for us to make use of Him, for His covenant blessings are not simply meant to be looked at. They are to be put into action, having been given to us for present use.

When we are born again, God, by His Spirit, empowers us with His own moral goodness. We don't have what it takes on our own to be good, to be holy. The power to grow does not come from us but from God and His Holy Spirit within us. God's divine nature keeps us from sin and helps us live for Him. God's Word of promise is meant to be an everyday source of strength and comfort.

Lord, we pray our faith deepens and results in action, growth in Your character in us, and the practice of moral discipline. Our deep desire is to know You more, to grow in knowledge, to do Your will, and to love others. Thank You, Jesus! Amen.

AUGUST 13TH

Therefore, as God's chosen people ... Bear with each other and forgive one another if any one has a grievance against someone. Forgive as the Lord forgave you.

COLOSSIANS 3:12-13

Good morning! Have you ever thought or said, " I can never forgive (fill in the blank)" or "I'll forgive, but I'll never forget." Friends, that is not in the Word of God. What if God held forgiveness in the same vein as we often do—limited and with conditions? His Word commands us to *forgive as the Lord forgave you.* The key to forgiveness is remembering how much God has forgiven us. How can we withhold our forgiveness of another when we acknowledge that God has forgiven us so much?

Stop and realize God's infinite love and forgiveness. We must pray for Him to help us love and forgive others, especially those we are struggling to release from our unforgiveness and judgment. God is the only one who can judge. *"It is mine to avenge; I will repay," says the Lord* (Romans 12:19).

Unforgiveness is poison to our souls and leads to death. *"And when you stand praying, if you hold anything against anyone, forgive them, so that your Father in heaven may forgive you your sins"* (Mark 11:25). It is not by our forgiving others that God forgives us but because of his great mercy toward us. As we come to understand His mercy, however, we grow in the desire to become more like Him. Having received so great a mercy and His forgiveness, we will pass forgiveness on to others. Those unwilling to forgive have not become one with Christ, who was willing to forgive even those who crucified Him. Can we say, as He did, *"Father, forgive them, for they do not know what they are doing"* (Luke 23:34)?

Lord, help us to forgive as You have forgiven us, for it is in such mercy that we are set free to fully love and be loved. Lord, we pray for our hearts to be pure and holy, for our lives to become more like Yours each day, bringing honor and glory to You. Thank You, Jesus!

AUGUST 14TH

*"In this world you will have trouble but take heart;
I have overcome the world."*

JOHN 16:33

Good morning! Trials and tribulations are promised. Our response reflects our spiritual condition and greatly impacts our life at the moment and into the future. Jesus' words to His disciples (and to us) should give us courage. In spite of the inevitable struggles we face, we are not alone. Jesus never abandons us in our struggles. Our response must be grounded in the truth that our ultimate victory has already been won and we can claim the peace of Christ in the most troublesome times.

My brethren, count it all joy when you fall into various trials, knowing that the testing of your faith produces perseverance (James 1:2-3). God's Word doesn't say "if" but "when" we experience trials and trouble—we WILL encounter them. But God! Our proper response is in Christ Jesus! It isn't a pretense of happiness but a confidence in the victory already won, a positive outlook based on what God's already done and will continue to do in our lives.

Troubles taken upon ourselves without Jesus can crush us. Troubles surrendered to the Lord share in His victory: *"I have overcome the world."*

Lord, help us to not respond to troubles of this world with sin but trusting in the victory You've already won. Lord, grow us in Your character, mature us in our faith, that we would be more like You and draw others to come to know Your grace, mercy, love, and forgiveness. Thank You Jesus! Amen.

AUGUST 15TH

Then Jesus said to His disciples, "Whoever wants to be my disciple must deny
themselves and take up their cross and follow me. For whoever wants to save
their life will lose it, but whoever loses their life for me will find it."

MATTHEW 16:24-25

ood morning! In Chapter 5, "How It Works," of the *Big Book of*
Alcoholics Anonymous, we read these words: *At some of these [the*
12 Steps] we balked. We thought we could find an easier, softer way. But we
could not. With all the earnestness at our command, we beg of you to be
fearless and thorough from the very start. Some of us have tried to hold on
to our old ideas and the result was nil until we let go absolutely. There is
"no easier softer way." We either follow the way that sets us free from
bondage or we remain living in the same imprisoned condition we are in.[22]

There are those of us who may be looking for "an easier, softer way"
to follow Jesus Christ. We don't want to have to "deny ourselves" or
"pick up our cross." There is no other way to follow Jesus than the way
He commands. If we want what God is offering us, there is no way other
than Jesus! Real discipleship implies real commitment—pledging our
whole existence to His service. And when we surrender our lives wholly
in service to Jesus Christ, we discover the real purpose of living. *Jesus*
answered, "I am the way and the truth and the life. No one comes to the
Father except through Me. If you really knew Me, you would know my Father
as well" (John 14:6-7). The only way is the Jesus way! Surrender yourself,
follow Jesus, and be set free.

Lord, may we willingly surrender all in exchange for following You. We are
unashamed to worship You, the One who died on a cross to save us, that we
might have life, full and eternal. We lay down our rights and our lives, that we
would find You—the One, the best, the most fulfilling Life ever. Thank You,
Jesus! Amen.

---

22. Bill W., *Alcoholics Anonymous, Third Edition* (Alcoholics Anonymous World Services,
Inc., 1976), 58.

AUGUST 16TH

Yet the Lord longs [waits] to be gracious to you;
therefore He will rise up to show you compassion.
For the Lord is a God of justice; blessed are all those who wait for Him.

ISAIAH 30:18

Good morning! Waiting can feel like a huge waste of time, especially in our world of "hurry up and get it done." But God! His Word has much to say about the value that surrounds and comes out of waiting. Waiting is never easy. Waiting for God is harder still. In our times of waiting, we may feel unheard, unworthy, lost, anxious, or defeated. But God is worth waiting for! *The Lord is good to those whose hope is in Him, to the one who seeks Him; it is good to wait quietly for the salvation of the Lord* (Lamentations 3:25-26). Hope in and wait for the Lord!

God oftentimes uses our waiting to refresh, renew, grow, and teach us. If we're fussing and fighting in our times of waiting, we'll miss its benefits. *Wait for the Lord; be strong and take heart and wait for the Lord* (Psalm 27:14). Instead, we can make good use of our waiting times by discovering what God may be trying to teach and accomplish in us. God's timetable is different from ours. Waiting draws us closer to God and teaches us to be patient. Our trust in God is increased in times of waiting, and clarity of purpose is often revealed. God's timing is always perfect.

Lord, increase our faith during times of waiting. Help us to diligently seek after You, deepening our knowledge of who You are and trusting in Your perfect timing and the work You are doing in us. You alone are God, and we will wait patiently on You. Thank You, Jesus! Amen.

AUGUST 17TH

Be still, and know that I am God.

PSALM 46:10

Good morning! In the chaos of life, even in our attempts to minister and serve others, and within our prayer life, are we seeking after the Source of all? Or is our noise and the demand to be in control dominating our lives? The phrase *be still* uses a Hebrew term that implies an act of surrender, a release of striving and hostility. Relax, let go, or stop. *Be still* and faithfully trust God as our source of strength. To know that He is God requires us to trust and submit, like a child to a protective parent. *Be still, and know that I am God* invites us to surrender ourselves to Him in trust and submit to His authority, honoring Him, His power and majesty.

At the end of our days, we will stand quietly before the Lord God Almighty. *For we will all stand before God's judgment seat. It is written: "As surely as I live," says the Lord, "every knee will bow before Me; every tongue will acknowledge God." So then, each of us will give an account of ourselves to God* (Romans 14:10-12).

Should we not be sitting reverently before Him now, honoring Him and acknowledging His power and majesty? *Yes, my soul, find rest in God; my hope comes from Him. Truly He is my rock and salvation; He is my fortress, I will not be shaken. My salvation and my honor depend on God; He is my mighty rock, my refuge. Trust in Him at all times, you people; pour out your hearts to Him, for God is our refuge* (Psalm 62:5-8).

When we are resting in God's strength, nothing can shake us. When we trust Him, our entire outlook on life changes.

Lord, may we learn to sit still before You, trusting in You! Quiet the chaos of our lives and shift our hearts and minds to You, our refuge and strength. We are set free from our earthly captivity when we are resting in Your presence. Thank You, Jesus! Amen.

AUGUST 18TH

Yet when I surveyed all that my hands had done and what I toiled to achieve,
everything was meaningless, a chasing after the wind;
nothing was gained under the sun.

ECCLESIASTES 2:11

Good morning! We are not a people who settle for less when it
comes to our earthly lifestyle and activities. Are we as insistent
in our pursuit of the things of Christ and as concerned about our
spiritual condition? *But our citizenship is in heaven. And we eagerly*
await a Savior from there, the Lord Jesus Christ (Philippians 3:20). This
should give us a much different perspective on our lives and what we
are willing to settle for, and where. Our homeland is in heaven, not
here on earth. Our ultimate destiny is with the Lord in heaven. We
belong to the kingdom of God. Our earthly pursuit must be after the
things of God, seeking after Him. *"Therefore I tell you, do not worry*
about your life, what you will eat; or about your body, what you will
wear. For life is more than food, and the body more than clothes. ...
But seek His kingdom, and these things will be given to you as well"
(Luke 12:22-23, 31).

Pursuing God is about taking the time to ask ourselves who or what
is our priority and deciding to direct our time, energy, and heart in that
direction. *"But seek first His kingdom and His righteousness, and all these*
things will be given to you as well" (Matthew 6:33).

God should always be first. We should be pursuing Him first in
thought, word, and deed. Our thoughts should be His desires for our
lives; our character should be taking on His character as our pattern. And
we must serve and obey Him in everything.

Forgive us, Lord, when we fall short in our pursuit of You. Lead us and guide us
this day as we look to follow You. Thank You, Lord, for Your faithfulness in
meeting all our needs, and for Your unconditional love. May we grow in Your
character as we live in surrendered obedience to You. Thank You, Jesus! Amen.

AUGUST 19TH

Great is the Lord and most worthy of praise; His greatness no one can fathom. One generation commends Your works to another; they tell of Your mighty acts. They speak of the glorious splendor of Your majesty—and I will meditate on Your wonderful works.

PSALM 145:3-5

Good morning! There is no better way to lift our spirits than to praise God for who He is and all He's done. And while some contemporary Christian music does a wonderful job, there's little that compares to the lyrics found in hymns of old and words of praise within the pages of Scripture. David invites us to join together to praise God in recognition of His mighty acts, His greatness, and His goodness. Praise reminds and teaches us that acknowledgement and worship of God's nature should be part of every heart throughout all generations.

The hymn "How Great Thou Art" by English missionary Stuart K. Hine (based on the original poem "O Store Gud" written in 1885 by Swedish preacher Carl Boberg) is one of my old time favorites from my childhood. As the title suggests, it is all about the greatness of God.

Oh Lord, my God, When I in awesome wonder, Consider all the worlds Thy hands have made. I see the stars, I hear the rolling thunder, Thy power throughout the universe displayed. Then sings my soul, my Savior God to Thee. How great Thou art, how great Thou art.[23]

Our God is worthy to be praised! There is no one like Our God. Whatever is happening in your life today—the good, the bad and the ugly—praising God is certain to lift your spirits!

Lord, You alone are worthy of our praise! Forgive us when we get so caught up in earthly matters that we neglect You, the One from whom all good things come. Your mercy, grace, and forgiveness are undeserved, yet freely given. Lord, may our lives be an anthem to Your greatness! Thank You, Jesus!

---

23. Stuart K. Hines, "How Great Thou Art" (The Stuart Hine Trust, 1949, 1953).

AUGUST 20TH

"If you love those who love you, what reward will you get? Are not even the tax collectors doing that? And if you greet only your own people, what are you doing more than others? Do not even pagans do that? Be perfect, therefore, as your Heavenly Father is perfect."

MATTHEW 5:46-48

Good morning! There are some people who are easy to love—just naturally pleasant and lovable. But if we're honest, we all have encountered a person or two we might have thought "only a mother could love." Seriously though, there are people who are obstinate, or "always right," or the cranky person we just can't please. But God calls us to love all people.

There are no exclusions to whom we are to love. There are no footnotes or passes that give us an excuse for the difficult ones. *"My command is this: Love each other as I have loved you. Greater love has no one than this: to lay down one's life for one's friends"* (John 15:12-13). We are to love others as Jesus loves us, and He loved us enough to give His life for us. *But God demonstrates His own love for us in this: While we were still sinners, Christ died for us* (Romans 5:8).

God sent Jesus to die for us, not because we were good enough and not because we were lovable, but because He loved us. So who is it in our lives God has put in front of us to love? We must give all the love we can, and then try and give a little more. Listen, help, encourage, give—love like Jesus!

Lord, forgive us when we withhold our love from others, when we judge someone unlovable. Pierce our hearts, cleanse us from our sin. Make us whole and holy in You, through Your Holy Spirit living is us. As we experience Your love, may we share that love with others. Thank You, Jesus! Amen.

AUGUST 21ST

For by grace you have been saved through faith and this is not your own doing; it is the gift of God—not the result of works, so that no one may boast.

EPHESIANS 2:8-9

Good morning! We all need and have received God's grace. But there are many who have experienced the depth of God's grace in more profound ways, who were desperate, or recognized how deep a mess they were in. The ones who, if the Lord had not come along to save them, might not be here now. *If the Lord had not been on our side ... they would have swallowed us up alive...the flood would have engulfed us, the raging waters would have swept us away* (Psalm 124:1-5).

Do we know God's grace? Have we experienced it? It is only by His grace that we have been saved. Salvation's source is God's grace. The means of salvation is faith. We believe by faith to be saved, but we would never choose to believe apart from the grace of God operating in our lives. Grace is God's unmerited favor, a gift we could never earn, yet one He freely gives. God's grace is a power that brings blessing and joy. God's grace is a reflection of His loving character and His gracious nature. His grace is a divine influence that works to regenerate and sanctify us.

Amazing grace! How sweet the sound / That saved a wretch like me! / I once was lost, but now am found / Was blind, but now I see. / 'Twas grace that taught my heart to fear / And grace my fears relieved / How precious did that grace appear / The hour I first believed![24]

Thank You, Lord, for the gift of Your grace, undeserved, unearned, freely given. We thank You for who You are in our lives and pray we grow in faith and character to be more like You, Lord, that we would draw people to know You. Thank You, Jesus! Amen.

---

24. John Newton, "Amazing Grace" (public domain, 1779).

AUGUST 22ND

*"I baptize you with water for repentance. But after me comes one
who is more powerful than I, whose sandals I am not worthy to carry.
He will baptize you with the Holy Spirit and fire."*

MATTHEW 3:11

G ood morning! Have we come to the end of ourselves, where God
is our "All in all" and Jesus is our everything? We cannot do a
thing on our own. It is only through Christ in and through us—His
Holy Spirit beginning to do the things no one or nothing else can
do—that we begin to understand repentance. The biblical definition
of repentance is the act of changing one's mind and turning from sin
to begin a new relationship with God. If there is anything remaining
in us that says we can do it on our own, we are not fully in
repentance. We must have an inward conviction, a realization of our
utter helplessness and unworthiness.

It is the work of the Holy Spirit that leads to a changed life. The Holy
Spirit is God's guarantee of what is to come. *Now the One who has
fashioned us for this very purpose is God, who has given us the Spirit as a
deposit, guaranteeing what is to come* (2 Corinthians 5:5). His work in our
lives today assures us that the healing process will be thoroughly
completed in Christ's presence. Transformation takes time and requires
patience. We must get to a place where we let God and His Spirit rule in
our lives.

*Lord, we pray that nothing be in the way of Your work in and through our
lives. Take us to the place of complete surrender. Drag into light our sin, that
we would put everything at Your feet. We are unworthy, but say the word and
our souls will be healed. Thank You, Jesus! Amen.*

AUGUST 23RD

The Son is the radiance of God's glory and the exact representation of his being, sustaining all things by his powerful word. After he had provided purification for sins, he sat down at the right hand of the Majesty in heaven.

HEBREWS 1:3

G ood morning! Who is on the throne of your life? Unless our answer is "Jesus is Lord over my life," nothing we attempt will be successful and of eternal value—no enterprise, relationship, or endeavor. God exalted Jesus Christ to His rightful place as King. "*God exalted Him to His own right hand as Prince and Savior that He might bring Israel to repentance and forgive their sins*" (Acts 5:31).

Jesus is not only the exact representation of God, but He is God Himself—the very God who spoke all creation into existence. *The Word became flesh and made His dwelling among us. We have seen His glory, the glory of the One and only Son, who came from the Father, full of grace and truth* (John 1:14).

When Jesus was born, God became a man. Jesus was completely human and completely divine. *Beyond all question, the mystery from which true godliness springs is great: He appeared in the flesh, was vindicated by the Spirit, was seen by angels, was preached among the nations, was believed on in the world, and was taken up in glory* (1 Timothy 3:15-16). Paul is affirming the humanity and divinity of Christ, revealing the heart of the gospel.

We will never please God on our own. We need and must depend on Jesus. Do not deny the One who is the only God! Make Him Lord in, of, and over your life.

Lord, You became man, lived a perfect life, and are the perfect example for how we are to live. Thank You for Your power to do what is right, according to Your wisdom and plan. We are only able to live a godly life through following You. Thank You, Jesus! Amen.

AUGUST 24TH

"A new command I give you: Love one another. As I have loved you,
so you must love one another. By this everyone will know that
you are My disciples, if you love one another."

JOHN 13:34-35

Good morning! Are we willing to give up ourselves for another?
There is, as my husband says, a "nugget" to be found in these
verses: *"as I have loved you"*—that's how we are to love. Paul goes on
to say, *Love does no wrong to a neighbor. Therefore, love is the*
fulfillment of the law (Romans 13:10).

We are to imitate the love of God, of Christ Jesus. What does that look
like? *"By this, everyone will know you are My disciples!"* The word *this*
refers to our love toward other people—as Jesus loved us. *This* is how
everyone will know we are His disciples. Not by our church attendance,
spouting Bible verses, wearing a cross or Christian t-shirts, or
displaying a fish decal on the back bumper of our cars. By our love! We
are to be compassionate and kind. Don't slander or gossip. Take time to
listen and be generous with the resources God has provided. People
matter to God, so they should matter to us, and we must live accordingly.

The world is watching—what Jesus do they experience in and
through us? God commands us to *"love one another,"* and the bar is set
high! *"As I have loved you"*!

Lord, forgive us when we fall short in how we love others. You are the perfect
example for us. Help us, Lord, to surrender ourselves to You—to love as You
love us—with reckless abandon, wholeheartedly, and in obedience to Your
calling. Thank You, Jesus! Amen.

AUGUST 25TH

*"Therefore do not worry about tomorrow, for tomorrow
will worry about itself. Each day has enough trouble of its own."*

MATTHEW 6:34

Good morning! What is distracting us from living in today? We are given only one day at a time in which to live, and that day is today. Yesterday is gone, and tomorrow is not promised. All the worrying in the world has no power to change anything. *"Can any one of you by worrying add a single hour to your life?"* (Matthew 6:27). There is only one answer to the worry and anxiety that this world can bring, and that is to surrender it all to the One who is in control: God. *Do not be anxious about anything, but in every situation, by prayer and petition, with thanksgiving, present your request to God* (Philippians 4:6).

An effective solution to worry is prayer. We've heard it said, "Want to worry less? Pray more!" or "Stop, drop, and pray."

And the peace of God, which transcends all understanding, will guard your hearts and your minds in Christ Jesus (Philippians 4:7). Praying produces peace from knowing that God is in control. That leads to trusting in Him more. *You will keep in perfect peace those whose minds are steadfast, because they trust in You* (Isaiah 26:3).

When we are trusting in God, worrying about tomorrow is a waste of time and offers no benefit. Worry or not, tomorrow will come just the same. So, why worry? Live in today, trusting God to supply your needs and sustain you. Jesus is always our answer, the only solution we need today, tomorrow, and always.

Thank You, Lord, for Your everlasting presence and peace. May we trust You moment by moment and rest in Your daily provision. You are faithful to supply for all our needs through You. Thank You, Jesus! Amen.

AUGUST 26TH

For we are God's handiwork, created in Christ Jesus to do good works, which God prepared in advance for us to do.

EPHESIANS 2:10

Good morning! We are God's creation, His workmanship, crafted with skill and purpose. We are intentionally made by the hands of God! *For You created my inmost being; You knit me together in my mother's womb. Your eyes saw my unformed body; all the days ordained for me were written in Your book before one of them came to be* (Psalm 139:13, 16). Before we were even born, God had a plan for our lives. *"For I know the plans I have for you," declares the LORD, "plans to prosper you and not to harm you, plans to give you hope and a future"* (Jeremiah 29:11).

He knew us, He appointed us, and He set us apart (Jeremiah 1:5). Nothing in our lives is a surprise to Him. God, our loving Heavenly Father, wants us to find joy and His purpose. He created a plan for us to grow, live by faith, and return to live with Him forever.

Have we opened our hearts to God? To His plan and purpose for our lives? *Search me, God, and know my heart; test me and know my anxious thoughts. See if there is any offensive way in me, and lead me in the way everlasting* (Psalm 139:23-24).

Invite God to search your heart, to set you on His path and the plan He has already purposed for your life.

Thank You, Lord, for loving us so much that You created us in Your image, with a plan and a purpose, to do good works! Cleanse our hearts of any sin that blocks us from Your righteousness and lead us in Your way. May our lives be living sacrifices to Your glory. Thank You, Jesus! Amen.

AUGUST 27TH

Although the Lord gives you the bread of adversity and the water of affliction, your teachers will be hidden no more; with your own eyes you will see them. Whether you turn to the right or to the left, your ears will hear a voice behind you, saying, "This is the way; walk in it."

ISAIAH 30:20-21

Good morning! Adversity has a purpose in our lives as we grow and learn valuable lessons from hardships. God is in control, and He provides the wisdom and direction we need to overcome our difficulties and continue on the right path. *"I will instruct you and teach you in the way you should go; I will counsel you with My loving eye on you"* (Psalm 32:8).

Many times, following God can be painful, but God always acts out of His love for us. God uses adversity for His good, and His goal is for us to become more like Christ. *And we know that in all things God works for the good of those who love Him, who have been called according to His purpose. For those God foreknew He also predestined to be conformed to the image of His Son, that He might be the firstborn among many brothers and sisters* (Romans 8:28-29).

Even God's own Son, Jesus Christ, learned through adversity. *Son though He was, He learned obedience from what He suffered* (Hebrews 5:8). True faith looks to God, trusts in His plans, relies on His strength and believes in His purposes.

Thank You, Lord, for Your plan and purpose for our lives, for Your promise to be with us, and for Your voice that directs us in the way we should go. May we be obedient to and listen for Your voice. Thank You, Jesus! Amen.

AUGUST 28TH

Now it is God who makes both us and you stand firm in Christ.
He anointed us, set His seal of ownership on us, and put His Spirit
in our hearts as a deposit, guaranteeing what is to come.

2 CORINTHIANS 1:21-22

G ood morning! Feelings are not facts. Human feelings and
thoughts are fluid, constantly changing, and they can steal from
us God's anointing. Grab hold of God's Word and His Truth! As
believers in Christ Jesus, we have the privilege of belonging to God
and receiving the gift of the Holy Spirit. *"But the Advocate [the*
Comforter], the Holy Spirit, whom the Father will send in My name, will
teach you all things and will remind you of everything I have said to you"
(John 14:26).

We must fill ourselves with Truth, and Jesus promises that the
Holy Spirit will help us remember what He has taught and continues
to teach us. As we study God's Word, we can trust Him to plant Truth
in our minds and reveal God's will.

Therefore, my dear brothers and sisters, stand firm [be steadfast]. Let
nothing move you [be immovable]. Always give yourselves fully to the
work of the Lord, because you know that your labor in the Lord is not in
vain (1 Corinthians 15:58). Nothing we do is in vain when we know
and believe Christ has won the ultimate victory. We must do the good
we have the opportunity to do, knowing our work is for eternal
results. Don't let feelings stand in the way of God's Truth moving in
your life.

Thank You, Lord, for Your Word and the Truth You reveal in and through it.
Thank You that Your Holy Spirit will help us remember Your Word so we can
speak it clearly and concisely into the lives of those You send us. Thank You,
Jesus! Amen.

AUGUST 29TH

Be alert and of sober mind. Your enemy the devil prowls around like a roaring lion looking for someone to devour. Resist him, standing firm in the faith, because you know that the family of believers throughout the world is undergoing the same kind of sufferings.

1 PETER 5:8–9

Good morning! Don't believe the lies! There is nothing in this world that will fulfill, fix, restore, or make us right. When we are so focused on what we lack or the troubles and suffering in our lives, we lose sight of and forget to watch for the danger we are in. This is right where the devil wants us—feeling defeated—and we are open to his attack and fall prey to believing his lies. But God! *Keep your eyes on Jesus!* (Hebrews 12:2). Shift your focus from the lies to the Truth. *Submit yourselves, then, to God. Resist the devil, and he will flee from you* (James 4:7). Satan is a defeated foe. Treat him as such.

We can resist the devil's attempts through the Holy Spirit's power in us. *No temptation has overtaken you except what is common to mankind. And God is faithful; he will not let you be tempted beyond what you can bear* (1 Corinthians 10:13).

We serve a Mighty God who helps us and gives us a way out of temptation. Believe in the One who came to set us free, to give us life, to make us a new creation. Stand firm in faith and surround yourself with a family of believers to fight against the enemy in prayer together.

Thank You, Lord, for the Truth that set us free. Protect us from the enemy's lies and the deception in this world. You are faithful and just, and You are near to us. We stand firm in our faith and join together with other believers to fight against the one who is already defeated. In You, we have the victory that's already been won. Thank You, Jesus! Amen.

AUGUST 30TH

Therefore, my dear friends, as you have always obeyed—not only in my presence, but now much more in my absence—continue to work out your salvation with fear and trembling, for it is God who works in you to will and to act to fulfill His good purpose.

PHILIPPIANS 2:12-13

Good morning! We must be careful about what we believe and how we live. The secret to a changed life is to submit to God's control and let Him work. It is the work that God does through us that counts, not what we think we are doing for Him.

Being confident of this, that He who began a good work in you will carry it on to completion until the day of Christ Jesus (Philippians 1:6). The good work of transformation and change in our lives is initiated and completed by God, not our own efforts. Our true faith should be placed in God's ongoing work within us. Our focus must be on what God is doing in us, not on our own activities, abilities, or achievements.

God will fulfill His purpose in and through us. *"But seek first His kingdom and His righteousness, and all these things will be given to you as well"* (Matthew 6:33). When we pursue God's kingdom and trust His righteousness, we can leave it up to Him to take care of the rest. We want to live in right relationship to Jesus, to be connected to God. God doesn't need us to accomplish anything. We need Him! It isn't about what we do; it's about Who we know!

Lord, may our first priority always be a right relationship with You. Our fulfillment of Your plans and purposes for our lives is a byproduct of being rightly related to You and done through Your Spirit living in and through us. May our hearts be set on You and living in surrendered obedience. Have Your way, Lord; have Your way. Thank You, Jesus! Amen.

AUGUST 31ST

And yet I will show you the most excellent way.

1 CORINTHIANS 13:1

Good morning! The "love chapter" of the Bible is 1 Corinthians 13. Anyone who has attended a marriage ceremony—believers, unbelievers, church-goers, and unchurched alike—has most likely heard excerpts from its popular verses that share what love is. But I don't recall ever hearing or reading this first verse: *And yet I will show you the most excellent way.* Oh, yes, please show us and teach us the "most excellent way" of love!

How many of us feel we've tried and somehow totally missed something along the way? We're so busy doing, trying to put to use our spiritual gifts and talents, that love is often not even in the mix of it at all, totally lacking in the equation. Great faith, acts of dedication or sacrifice, and miracle-working power without the presence of love are useless. *If I do not have love, I am nothing, ... I gain nothing* (1 Corinthians 13:2, 3).

God's kind of love is directed outward toward others, not inward toward ourselves. God's kind of love goes against our natural inclinations, and it is only possible to practice with His help. We must set aside our own desires and instincts so we can love with no ulterior motives, expecting nothing in return.

The more we grow to become like Jesus, the more we exhibit the kind of love Christ demonstrated to us. Take time to read and meditate on 1 Corinthians 13. Love is indispensable. *And now these three remain: faith, hope and love. But the greatest of these is love* (1 Corinthians 13:13).

Lord, thank You for loving us—the greatest gift ever given—the only One we will ever need. Teach us, Lord, to love more like You each moment of our lives—a love that endures, is everlasting. Love is the greatest attribute of all human qualities and can only be found and exhibited in and through You. Thank You, Jesus! Amen.

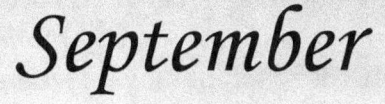

September

SEPTEMBER 1ST

So God blessed the seventh day and made it holy, because on it
God rested from all his work that he had done in creation.

GENESIS 2:3

Good morning! Long before Labor Day was ever even a thought, God commanded man to rest. Labor Day originated in the eight-hour movement: eight hours for work, eight for recreation, eight for rest. We live in a world of constant movement and perpetual activity, always seeming to have something to do or somewhere to be and always at the expense of rest and relaxation. Yet God demonstrated that rest is appropriate, right, and needed. Consider if God Himself rested from His work, how much more should we?

Jesus also demonstrated this principle to His disciples. After having fed the five thousand, He said to them, *"Come with Me by yourselves to a quiet place and get some rest"* (Mark 6:31). God's rest in Genesis was not because He was tired, but because He was finished with His work of creation. But we do need rest! Jesus took the disciples away. He recognized that for effectiveness in ministry or any other work, times of rest and renewal are needed.

There are several Scriptures that encourage us to rest. *Better one handful of rest [with tranquility] than two handfuls of labor [with toil] and striving [chasing] after wind* (Ecclesiastes 4:6). *"Come to Me, all who are weary and burdened, and I will give you rest"* (Matthew 11:28). *There remains, then, Sabbath-rest for the people of God; for anyone who enters God's rest also rests from their works, just as God did from His. Let us, therefore, make every effort [be diligent] to enter that rest* (Hebrews 4:9-11). We must make every effort to grab hold of what God has already provided—His rest.

Lord, we come to You for rest. You promise to always go with us and give us rest, and You invite us to come to You weary and burdened, and You will give us rest. Thank You for this day, Your constant presence, and provision of rest. Thank You, Jesus! Amen.

SEPTEMBER 2ND

I have been crucified with Christ and I no longer live,
but Christ lives in me.

GALATIANS 2:20

Good morning! God lives in us, but in order for Him to shine through us, there is much work that needs to be done. We must die to ourselves. But what does that mean? God looks at us as if we had died with Christ. *For we know that our old self was crucified with Him so that the body ruled by sin might be done away with, that we should no longer be slaves to sin* (Romans 6:6). We must daily allow God to crucify our sinful desires, the things that block us from and keep us away from following Jesus, a kind of dying.

Then He said to them all: "Whoever wants to be My disciple must deny themselves and pick up their cross daily and follow me" (Luke 9:23). Being Jesus' disciples means putting aside our selfish desires, shouldering our cross, and following Him. It means understanding that we belong to Jesus and that we live to serve His purposes. *You were taught, with regard to your former way of life, to put off your old self, which is being corrupted by its deceitful desires; to be made new in the attitude of your minds; and to put on the new self, created to be like God in true righteousness and holiness* (Ephesians 4:20-22).

Living for Jesus is a process. Although we have a new nature, we don't automatically think new thoughts and express all the right attitudes. But God! If we keep listening to Him, we will continue to change over time. *For those God foreknew He also predestined to be conformed to the image of His Son* (Romans 8:29). God's ultimate goal is to make us more like Jesus. Start by saying "yes" to Jesus!

Lord, we cannot fathom the depths of Your mercy, grace, forgiveness, and love, that You would care so much for us that You made a way for us to live as one with You. May we choose to follow You, to give up our selfish ways to live in Your kingdom and share Your love with others—to be Your light in the darkness of this world. Thank You, Jesus! Amen.

"And I will ask the Father, and He will give you another Helper, to be with you forever, even the Spirit of truth, whom the world cannot receive, because it neither sees Him nor knows Him. You know Him, for He dwells with you and will be in you."

JOHN 14:16-17

Good morning! There is no straining and striving in the accomplishment of the work God gives us to do. God Himself is doing the work He assigns to His children in and through us. When Jesus was about to leave His disciples, He told them the Father would *"give them another advocate to help them"* (John 14:16).

Those who have been baptized, who confess that Jesus is Lord and follow Him, have received the Advocate, the Spirit of God Himself, to care for and guide them. The Holy Spirit is the very presence of God within us and all believers, helping us live as God wants, building up His church on earth, and doing the works we're called to do. By faith we can appropriate the Spirit's power in and through God's assignments. *For it is by grace you have been saved, through faith—and this is not from yourselves, it is the gift of God—not by works, so that no one can boast. For we are God's handiwork, created in Christ Jesus to do good works, which God prepared in advance for us to do* (Ephesians 2:8-9).

We are saved by God's grace, and given work to do, acts of service that He's given us in and through His Spirit (the Advocate, the Helper) to accomplish.

Lord, out of gratitude for Your gift of mercy, grace, and forgiveness, for our salvation, we seek to help and serve others with kindness, love, and compassion. Thank You that we are never alone, that You are our Provider and Protector. We can "cease all striving and know that You are God. Exalted among the nations; exalted in the earth" (Psalm 46:10). Thank You, Jesus! Amen.

SEPTEMBER 4TH

"Not everyone who says to me, 'Lord, Lord,' will enter the kingdom of heaven, but only the one who does the will of my Father who is in heaven."

MATTHEW 7:21

Good morning! This got me thinking, "It is when you get out of the will of God that you have a hard time." So then, what IS the "will of God"? Jesus is more concerned with our walk than our talk. Many people say the right words and know all the right verses in Scripture, but their hearts are far from the Lord and others. *Do not be conformed to this world, but be transformed by the renewal of your mind, that by testing you may discern what is the will of God, what is good and acceptable and perfect* (Romans 12:2). God's will is that we would be a transformed people with renewed minds, living to honor and obey Him, because God's will is what is best for us, and He gave His Son Jesus to make our new lives possible.

He has told you, O man, what is good; and what does the Lord require of you but to do justice, and to love kindness, and to walk humbly with your God? (Micah 6:8). This world is passing away. *The world and its desires pass away, but whoever does the will of God lives forever* (1 John 2:17). We should be very concerned that we know and are doing the will of God.

God's will for us is revealed throughout the Scriptures. Study and know His Word and put it into action. It is God's will that we love Him and others (Mark 12:29-31). It is God's will that we go and make disciples (Matthew 28:19). It is God's will that we follow His commandments. All that God has called us to in Scripture is His will for us. May His will be done.

Lord, we humbly submit ourselves to You. Teach us and show us Your ways. Lord, our desire is to do what pleases You, what is acceptable in Your sight, and to be included as Your good and faithful servants. May Your will be done, Lord. Thank You, Jesus! Amen.

SEPTEMBER 5TH

But they that wait upon the Lord shall renew their strength;
they shall mount up with wings as eagles, they shall run, and not be weary,
and they shall walk, and not faint.

ISAIAH 40:31

Good morning! WAIT. How many read that one word and felt the weight of impatience come over them? We're told repeatedly to "wait on the Lord"—but why? Isaiah 40:31 contains a promise of renewed strength that comes from waiting. His strength is our source of strength that rises above life's distractions and difficulties. Oh, the confidence that comes in knowing God's purposes are right! God has the power to control all of life—why would we not wait on Him?

The Lord is good to those who wait for Him, to the soul who seeks Him. It is good that one should wait quietly for the salvation of the Lord (Lamentations 3:25-26 ESV). God is worth waiting for! But in our impatience, we want God to act now! To change our circumstances, move here or there, answer our prayers. And He wants us to change! To increase our faith, to trust Him, to let Him do the work that needs to be done to become more like Him. Waiting gives us God's perspective on our lives and reminds us we are at His mercy on the timing.

Wait for the Lord; be strong, and let your heart take courage; wait for the Lord! (Psalm 27:14). Waiting patiently says we are faithfully trusting the Lord and His timing. He uses our times of waiting to test, teach, and train us for what lies ahead. We need these periods to sanctify us. And when we live faithfully in the midst of them, God will use them to transform us.

Lord, thank You for times of waiting and the work that's accomplished in the midst of them. Help us to lean into You, humbling ourselves to accept waiting as a gift from You that matures us for Your work and glory. Thank You, Jesus! Amen.

SEPTEMBER 6TH

"Do not judge, or you too will be judged.
For in the same way you judge others, you will be judged,
and with the measure you use, it will be measured to you."

MATTHEW 7:1-2

Good morning! Are we exhibiting judgment or mercy and grace to others? Our answer is indicative of the condition of our hearts and a measure of our faith. God's Word is clear: *"Do not judge."* We make excuses for feeling justified in our judgment of others with statements like, "You don't know them like I do" or "You don't know what he or she did" or "They do this all the time" or "They deserve what they got." We claim people are unforgivable. But God's Word is clear: *"Why do you look at the speck of sawdust in your brother's eye and pay no attention to the plank in your own eye?"* (Matthew 7:3).

I have heard it said, "Keep your own side of the street clean." Meaning that we are to be responsible for our own actions and to focus on what we can change—ourselves. And that, in itself, can sometimes be a full time job!

Jesus went on to say, "You hypocrite, first take the plank out of your own eye, and then you will see clearly to remove the specks from your brother's eye" (Matthew 7:5). Oftentimes, the traits in others that bother us most are the very ones we struggle with or have disliked in ourselves. Our untamed bad habits and behavior problems are the very ones we point out or try to change in others. But it's not our job to fix or change other people. We are to deal with others the same way the Lord Jesus Christ has dealt with us—full of mercy, grace, love, and forgiveness.

Lord, forgive us when we look at others with a critical, judgmental eye. Help us instead to build others up, to carry Your Light into dark places, and to be kingdom builders who exhibit the kind of grace, mercy, and love You so freely gave to us. Thank You, Jesus! Amen.

SEPTEMBER 7TH

"As you go, proclaim this message: 'The kingdom of heaven has come near.'
Heal the sick, raise the dead, cleanse those who have leprosy,
drive out demons. Freely you have received; freely give."

MATTHEW 10:7-8

Good morning! They were waiting for the Messiah to usher in His kingdom but not in the way that He came, nor for the purpose He came to fulfill. Jesus, the Messiah, brought freedom with Him, but not from the Romans and not in a political or military kingdom. Jesus was talking about a spiritual kingdom.

Our favor with God was won on the cross of Calvary. It cost God His only Son, Jesus Christ, given as a sacrifice for our sins, the sin of all mankind, and none committed by Him. The mercy of God led Christ to Calvary, freely given that we might freely receive.

The gospel today is that the kingdom is still near. Jesus has begun His kingdom on earth in our hearts, His followers. Jesus gave us, His disciples, a principle to guide our actions as we minister to others: *"Freely you have received: freely give."* The gifts we have received are not earned, bought, or bargained for. God showered us with His blessings so we would bless others. Are we giving generously to others of our time, love, talents, gifts, and possessions? Whatever God has given to us will be used for His glory when we freely give it back to Him for another's benefit.

Thank You, Lord, for Your gifts freely given. May we bless others as You have blessed us and boldly share the gift of Your gospel with others. Thank You, Jesus! Amen.

SEPTEMBER 8TH

For the word of God is alive and active [powerful]. Sharper than any double-edged sword, it penetrates even to dividing soul and spirit, joints and marrow; it judges the thoughts and attitudes of the heart.

HEBREWS 4:12

Good morning! What draws so many people to read the myriad of self-help books available today and attend self-improvement seminars at sold-out capacity while their Bibles sit collecting dust on a shelf, unopened, or perhaps even nonexistent in their homes? If we are truly interested in improving ourselves, in becoming the best people we can be, or living successful lives, we might be going to the wrong teachers. Should we not be going to the One who created us and is the Source of all wisdom and knowledge?

The *word of God* is written in and is the Bible. The Bible is not simply a collection of words and stories or a vehicle for communicating ideas. It is *alive and active [powerful].* The Bible is life-changing and dynamic as it works within us, teaching us about who God is, what He has done, and how we are to respond.

All Scripture is God-breathed and is useful for teaching, rebuking, correcting and training in righteousness, so that the servant of God may be thoroughly equipped for every good work (2 Timothy 3:16-17). The Bible is filled with God's truth. It leads, guides, and directs us in how to become more like Jesus, and to know and love God more—our ultimate earthly goal.

God's Word reveals who we are and who we are not, distinguishing between good and evil within us. God's Word demands decisions. We must not only read and listen to it, but we must also allow it to guide, direct, and shape our lives.

Thank You, Lord, for Your written Word, the Bible. You have given us everything we need to know and follow You, to live surrendered and obedient to You, to serve You and others, and to one day be with You for all eternity. Thank You, Jesus! Amen.

SEPTEMBER 9TH

*I want to know Christ—yes, to know the power of His resurrection and
participation in His sufferings, becoming like Him in death,
and so somehow, attaining to the resurrection from the dead.*

PHILIPPIANS 3:10-11

Good morning! Paul lived with passion! He had experienced a complete transformation through his experience with Jesus on the road to Damascus. Paul had set out on another mission to persecute and even kill believers and was stopped in his tracks, made blind, and awakened to the power of God. Oh yes, the Lord got Paul's attention, and his passion was set anew to save lives through the power of Jesus Christ!

Have we experienced the passion that comes through knowing Jesus Christ? Paul said that his goal was to know Christ, to be like Christ, and to be all Christ had in mind for him to be. What about us? *Not that I have already obtained all this, or have already arrived at my goal, but I press on to take hold of that for which Christ Jesus took hold of me. I press on toward the goal to win the prize for which God has called me heavenward in Christ Jesus* (Philippians 3:12, 14).

We should not let anything distract us from the goal of knowing and following Jesus and becoming more like Him. *But our citizenship is in heaven. And we eagerly await a Savior from there, the Lord Jesus Christ* (Philippians 3:20). Let us live in a manner worthy of the prize of our heavenly citizenship.

Thank You, Lord, that You came to save us, to bring Your resurrection power to our lives. As You did for Paul, awaken our passion for You, Lord. We want to know You more, to press into what You have in store for us to be and to do to build Your kingdom. Thank You, Jesus! Amen.

SEPTEMBER 10TH

There is a time for everything, and a season
for every activity under the heavens.

ECCLESIASTES 3:1

Good morning! Just as the seasons transition from summer to fall, so it is with different periods of our lives, causing us to adapt and change. God orchestrates change in our lives, and we can trust Him to guide us through the different seasons. God is in control and is constantly at work in our lives to teach us and grow us. We are being made new, transformed to be more like Him. *You were taught, with regard to your former way of life, to put off your old self, which is being corrupted by its deceitful desires; to be made new in the attitude of your minds; and put on the new self, created to be like God in true righteousness and holiness* (Ephesians 4:22–24).

Grab hold of that promise: *created to be like God in true righteousness and holiness*! As Christ followers, we should experience a profound change in our lives, a new nature. Just as the leaves change with the seasons and new growth happens in the spring, our thoughts turn to good and our attitudes change to a new direction, impacting positive actions. When we make a conscious decision to daily surrender our lives to God, He will lead, guide, and direct our way. We are told to put on a "new self" and have a new way of thinking that the Holy Spirit gives. We have a new mindset in which we put behind old habits of sin in order to be more fully present to Him.

Lord, You provide for us a new way where the world claims there is no way. You offer us a new path ahead, a path of promises and blessings. Lord, break down the strongholds, bring Light to the darkness, and transform our hearts to be more like Yours. We are made new creations in and through You! Thank You, Jesus! Amen.

SEPTEMBER 11TH

For our struggle is not against flesh and blood, but against the rulers,
against the authorities, against the powers of this dark world
and against the spiritual forces of evil in the heavenly realms.

EPHESIANS 6:12

Good morning! There is much evil in our world. Today, we remember the 911 attacks, an atrocity that stopped our nation. We banded together in prayer. Strangers reached out to those in need. We were unified in compassion, love, and support.

We face a powerful army whose goal is to defeat Christ's church. Our true enemy is sin. The devil may use other people or things as part of his attack against us, but sin is what separates us from God. And although we are assured of victory, we must engage in the struggle until Christ returns, because Satan is constantly battling against all who are on the Lord's side.

Have our hearts hardened? Have we put our blinders on to the sin of this world facing us? Spiritual battles surround us at all levels and throughout this world. *Therefore put on the full armor of God, so that when the day of evil comes, you may be able to stand your ground, and after you have done everything, to stand* (Ephesians 6:13). As believers in Christ Jesus, we must be prepared for all types of attacks by putting on God's armor. We must band together in the unity and strength of God.

Finally, all of you, be like-minded, be sympathetic, love one another, be compassionate and humble (1 Peter 3:8). These qualities will go a long way toward helping us serve God effectively amidst the darkness of our world.

Lord, thank You for sending Your Son, Jesus Christ, as living evidence of Your great love for us, for showing us the difference true faith, love, and compassion can make. Let our lives be evidence of Your truth as we share Your gospel with people in desperate need of Your saving grace, mercy, and forgiveness. Thank You, Jesus! Amen.

SEPTEMBER 12TH

The Lord does not look at the things people look at.
People look at the outward appearance, but the Lord looks at the heart.

1 SAMUEL 16:7

Good morning! God is after our hearts, that they would be wholly devoted to Him. How often we look at someone's outer appearance and wrongly determine the condition of their life, the depth of their character, or the degree their life is rightly put together. Appearance does not necessarily reveal what people are really like or what their values and characters are.

King David wrote, *Search me, God, and know my heart; test me and know my anxious thoughts. See if there is any offensive way in me, and lead me in the way everlasting* (Psalm 139:23-24). David sought God and asked Him to search his heart and mind to point out any wrong motives in him.

Our concern needs to shift from the condition of other people's standing, which is not for us to judge, to the condition of our own heart, mind, and soul. The questions we should be answering have nothing to do with other people but rather with ourselves: What is my spiritual condition? Am I conforming to God's will?

One of the most difficult things for us to do is to admit our hearts are not always right in God's sight. *Examine yourselves to see whether you are in the faith; test yourselves. Do you not realize that Christ Jesus is in you—unless you fail the test?* (2 Corinthians 13:5). Paul urges us to give ourselves a spiritual checkup and look for a growing awareness of Christ's presence and power in our life. If we aren't moving closer to God, we're moving away from Him.

Thank You, Lord, for Your grace. May we exhibit that same grace toward others. Lord, cleanse our hearts from the sin, which separates us from You. May our focus shift from the sins and shortcomings of others to the sin in our own lives, that we would repent and turn back to You. Thank You, Jesus! Amen.

SEPTEMBER 13TH

"Come, all you who are thirsty, come to the waters;
and you who have no money, come, buy and eat!"

ISAIAH 55:1

Good morning! Is there any sweeter invitation than the Lord's bidding to *"Come to Me"*? Stop for a moment and consider His invitation. God Himself invites us, mere mortals, to commune with Him! What stops us from responding to the greatest, most important invitation we'll ever receive, the only invitation that brings us everything we need?

God's invitation is nourishment that feeds and gives rest to our souls. *"Come to Me, all who are weary and burdened, and I will give you rest. Take my yoke upon you and learn from Me, for I am gentle and humble in heart, and you will find rest for your souls. For My yoke is easy and My burden is light"* (Matthew 11:28–30). God's invitation promises love, healing, and peace with Him. His invitation is into a relationship with Him that changes our meaningless, wearisome toil into a life of spiritual progress, productivity, and purpose. Suddenly we are joined together with a Partner—our Creator, the Giver of Life. His invitation is to join Him in His kingdom, yielding our whole hearts to Him.

Jesus simply says, *"Come. Follow Me."* When we accept His invitation, our lives are changed, made new. God alone provides nourishment for our souls, spiritual satisfaction, and everlasting life.

Thank You, Lord, for the greatest invitation we will ever receive: to come and follow You. There is no one like You, Lord. We surrender all to You! We accept Your invitation, yielding our hearts to You. Our deepest desire is to know You more and to share who You are with others in our lives and those You put before us. Thank You, Jesus! Amen.

SEPTEMBER 14TH

But one thing I do: Forgetting what is behind and straining toward
what is ahead, I press on toward the goal to win the prize
for which God has called me heavenward in Christ Jesus.

PHILIPPIANS 3:13–14

Good morning! Is there something in our past that keeps us from realizing the present and future God intends for us? We must make knowing Christ our goal and move forward in the right direction! We must not let anything distract us away from being an effective Christian and knowing Christ Jesus. Paul had to forget his past sins. We've all done things we're ashamed of, and we may be faced with the tension of knowing what we used to be.

Like the prodigal son, we may have come to a point in our lives where we are destitute. *"The son said to him, 'Father, I have sinned against heaven and against you. I am no longer worthy to be called your son'"* (Luke 15:21).

But there is hope for this moment when our hope is in Christ Jesus. We can let go of past guilt and look forward to great love that extends to find lost sinners and welcome them home. *"So he got up and went to his father. But while he was still a long way off, his father saw him and was filled with compassion for him; he ran to his son, threw his arms around him and kissed him. 'For this son of mine was dead and is alive again; he was lost and is now found.' So they began to celebrate"* (Luke 15:20, 24). God's great love for us reaches out and finds lost sinners no matter how or why they got lost.

Thank You, Lord, that You came to save the lost, the sick, and the brokenhearted, people just like us. Your love reaches out with grace, mercy, and forgiveness. Say the word and we are healed, made into new creations, and set free from the bondage of sin and shame. Thank You, Jesus! Amen.

SEPTEMBER 15TH

Then Jesus came to them [the disciples] and said, "All authority on heaven and earth has been given to Me. Therefore go and make disciples of all nations, baptizing them in the name of the Father and of the Son and of the Holy Spirit, and teaching them to obey everything I have commanded you. And surely I am with you always, to the very end of the age."

MATTHEW 28:19-20

Good morning! Are we so concerned about offending someone by talking about Jesus that we shy away from or even change our conversation altogether? If we are believers in and followers of Jesus, having accepted the gospel, we are commissioned as His ambassadors. Jesus spoke what His Father told Him—with *all authority*. He then told us (His disciples) what we are to do—"*go and make disciples ... baptizing and teaching.*" And we aren't doing this on our own—"*I [Jesus] am with you always.*"

What if the people in our lives and those we encounter have been placed before us intentionally by God Himself for us to share the salvation message?

Preach the word; be prepared in season and out of season; correct, rebuke and encourage—with great patience and careful instruction (2 Timothy 4:2). We must be ready to serve God in and through the opportunities He puts in front of us, whether or not it is convenient or comfortable. Be willing to be inconvenienced and uncomfortable. Be sensitive to the opportunities God gives you. Be ready to share the gospel at all times. That opportunity may be the only time someone hears about or comes in contact with Jesus and is ready to listen.

Lord, give us a renewed spirit of boldness to speak truth and to share the gospel. Give us Your eyes to see, words to speak, and hearts to love. And may all we think, say, and do be pleasing to You and further Your kingdom work here in this world. Thank You, Jesus! Amen.

SEPTEMBER 16TH

*It is for freedom that Christ has set us free. Stand firm, then,
and do not let yourselves be burdened again by a yoke of slavery.*

GALATIANS 5:1

Good morning! There is so much conversation about freedoms and rights, and yet the greatest freedom offered to us is greatly ignored. It is the offer of freedom that was paid with a price none of us could ever afford, yet it was freely given. It is the gift of grace, mercy, and forgiveness that awaits each man, woman, and child who comes to say "yes" to Jesus, to know Him, and follow Him! *"So if the Son sets you free, you will be free indeed"* (John 8:36).

In saying that one word—*yes*—we receive freedom from sin, darkness, and death. Now that's something to talk about! Christ came to set us free from sin. He did not come so we could do whatever we please or live in the slavery of our selfish desires, sin, and despair. *You, my brothers and sisters, were called to be free. But do not use your freedom to indulge the flesh; rather, serve one another humbly in love* (Galatians 5:13).

Christ died to set us free from sin and to know the truth. *"And you will know the truth, and the truth will set you free"* (John 8:32). We are now free and able to do what was impossible before—to live unselfishly, to accept His gracious gift through faith, to know truth, to resist temptation, and to serve others.

Thank You, Lord, for the freedom of abundant life found in You. There is nothing that compares with knowing, loving, and following You! Lord, set our hearts on fire, that we would be like the faithful before us, with a confident faith in action, sharing who You are and what You have done with others so they, too, would be set free. Thank You, Jesus! Amen.

SEPTEMBER 17TH

Therefore, holy brothers and sisters, who share in the heavenly calling, fix your thoughts on Jesus.

HEBREWS 3:1

Good morning! We are not to be blown about like grass in a field by the storms of life and the ups and downs of this world. Our strength and our hope are not found in earthly things or circumstances. We find them in Christ Jesus. Our lives need to be grounded in Christ, *fixing our eyes on Jesus, the pioneer and perfecter of faith* (Hebrews 12:2).

We must give up whatever distracts us from, interferes with, or endangers our relationship with God. We are not moved by the things of this world, for we know everything here is all temporary. *So we fix our eyes not on what is seen, but on what is unseen, since what is seen is temporary, but what is unseen is eternal* (2 Corinthians 4:18). Our ultimate hope is not and will never be found or satisfied in or by this world. Our home is being prepared in heaven.

"Do not let your hearts be troubled. You believe in God; believe also in Me. My Father's house has many rooms; if that were not so, would I have told you that I am going there to prepare a place for you? And if I go and prepare a place for you, I will come back and take you to be with Me that you also may be where I am" (John 14:1-3). Jesus' words share that the way to eternal life, though unseen, is as secure as our faith and trust in Jesus. *"I am the way, and the truth, and the life. No one comes to the Father except through Me. If you really know Me, you will know My Father as well"* (John 14:6-7). The only unsettled issue might be our willingness to believe—our faith in the One and only Way.

Thank You, Lord, for making the Way for us to the Father. We believe in and are confident in our heavenly home because You promised it to all who believe in You. May we live our earthly lives as testimony to our belief in and our love for You. Teach us and grow us to be instruments of Your will. Thank You, Jesus! Amen.

SEPTEMBER 18TH

The Lord confides in those who fear him;
he makes his covenant known to them. My eyes are ever on the Lord,
for only he will release my feet from the snare.

PSALM 25:14-15

G ood morning! Do you have a special time and place where you sit with God? For us, during fair weather months, it is mornings spent on the front porch. Maybe for you it is evening walks or midday breaks. The when and where are much less important than the necessity of making certain to do so. Why? Because it is the very thing that Jesus did!

Have you just received difficult news? *Jesus, after hearing about John the Baptist's fate at the request of Herodias, withdrew by boat to a solitary place* (Matthew 14:6-13). Do you have a long day ahead of you? *Before preaching throughout Galilee, very early in the morning, while it was still dark, Jesus got up, left the house and went off to a very solitary place, where He prayed* (Mark 1:35). Are you facing a big decision? Before choosing the twelve disciples *Jesus went out to a mountainside to pray and spent the night praying to God* (Luke 6:12).

If Jesus recognized the need and took the time to spend time with His Father, how much more should we? *God is good to those who hope in and seek Him* (Lamentations 3:25). *He gives strength and power to His people* (Psalm 68:35).

Look to the Lord and His strength; seek His face always (Psalm 105:4). God's Word encourages us to look to Him, to seek Him, spend time with Him, and talk to Him—to pray.

Thank You, Lord, for Your example of standing on Your Word and going to a solitary place to pray. The busyness will wait, and You will strengthen us through our time with You. Lord, instruct us, teach us, and strengthen us for Your work in and through our lives. Thank You, Jesus! Amen.

SEPTEMBER 19TH

"For I have come down from heaven not to do my will but to do the will of him who sent me. And this is the will of him who sent me, that I shall lose none of all those he has given me, but raise them up at the last day. For my Father's will is that everyone who looks to the Son and believes in him shall have eternal life, and I will raise them up at the last day."

JOHN 6:38-40

Good morning! I think that so much of our trouble comes from our unwillingness to yield to God's authority in our lives. Like strong-willed children, we fuss and fight over the direction He is leading us. Jesus succumbed to the will of His Father, even to the point of death. *"My Father, if it is possible, may this cup be taken from Me. Yet not as I will, but as You will"* (Matthew 26:39). He knew what the Father's will was, and He dedicated His life to obedience in it. Jesus' purpose was to do the will of His Father, not to satisfy His human desires.

When we make the decision to follow Jesus, we must have the same surrender and obedience. *Submit yourselves, then, to God. Resist the devil, and he will flee from you. Come near to God and He will come near to you. Humble yourselves before the Lord, and He will lift you up* (James 4:7-8, 10).

We are to yield to God's authority and will, commit our lives to Him and His control, and have a willingness to follow Him. *Commit to the Lord whatever you do, and He will establish your plans* (Proverbs 16:3). Do not waiver but always trust God's will in everything and commit yourself and your life fully to Him.

Lord, we surrender our will to You this day, trusting in Your sovereignty, plans, and goodness. You are faithful, and Your desire is for our lives to be joined to You, that one day we might see You face to face. Oh, what a glorious day that will be! Thank You, Jesus! Amen.

SEPTEMBER 20TH

Watch your life and doctrine closely. Persevere in them, because if you do, you will save both yourself and your hearers.

1 TIMOTHY 4:16

Good morning! We must be constantly vigilant and guard against falling into sin that can so easily contaminate and destroy us. And we must watch what we believe just as closely. Wrong beliefs, misguided thinking, and corrupt emotions can lead us into sin. *"These people honor Me with their lips, but their hearts are far from Me. They worship Me in vain; their teachings are merely human rules"* (Matthew 15:8-9). When we claim to honor God when our hearts are far from Him, our worship is in vain.

"For out of the heart come evil thoughts—murder, adultery, sexual immorality, theft, false testimony, slander. These are what defile a person" (Matthew 15:19-20). God examines the condition of our hearts. The way we are deeply matters most to God. He changes us from the inside. *"But seek first His kingdom and His righteousness"* (Matthew 6:33).

Before anything else, we must spend time with our Lord and Savior. He gives us all we need. Our clarity comes from seeking Him, His will, His direction, His Word. Even Jesus sought His Father in solitude and prayer. *After He had dismissed them, He went up on a mountainside by Himself to pray* (Matthew 14:23).

Our first responsibility is to God. We cannot be of service to Him if we aren't rightly connected to and with Him. God is our Source!

Lord, may our outward proclamation of faith and good works be generated from a deep inward understanding and relationship with You. Protect us from deception and the devil's work. May we seek You and follow You. Teach us, Lord, Your ways. Guide us, direct us, and lead us. Thank You, Jesus! Amen.

SEPTEMBER 21ST

"But seek first His kingdom and His righteousness,
and all these things will be given to you as well."

MATTHEW 6:33

Good morning! Pause for a moment and consider: what is the routine of your day? Some jump in with a list already made, mental or written. Others check their calendar of appointments and meetings, all before setting feet on the floor. If you ask most people what their biggest challenge is, many will answer "too much to do," "too busy," or "not enough time." But God! What does He say and where does He fit in?

Give this and every day to God—first thing! Thank Him for the blessing of another day and ask Him what He has for you to do. Turn to God for help, to fill your thoughts with His desires, to take His character for your pattern, and to serve and obey Him in everything. Actively choose to give God first place in every area of your life.

Pray continually, give thanks in all circumstances; for this is God's will for you in Christ Jesus (1 Thessalonians 5:17-18). Choose to have an attitude of prayer and praise at all times. This attitude is built upon acknowledging our dependence on God, realizing His presence within us, determining to obey Him fully, and thanking Him in everything!

Changing our daily routine to be led by the Lord with joy, prayer, and gratitude changes everything! We will begin to see our lives, other people, and circumstances from a new perspective—through the Light of the Lord!

Lord, renew in us a fervor for Your will in and through our lives. We long for a deeper walk with You leading, guiding, and directing our lives. Not our plans, Lord, but those You have already set in place for us. Today we are trading our to-dos for Your higher purpose. Thank You, Jesus! Amen.

SEPTEMBER 22ND

Praise the Lord. Praise the Lord, my soul. I will praise the Lord all my life;
I will sing praise to my God as long as I live.

PSALM 146:1-2

Good morning! What are we most grateful for? We have
experienced a lifetime of the grace of God. Should that not result
in a lifetime of gratitude? *I will extol the Lord at all times; His praise
will always be on my lips* (Psalm 34:1). If you are a follower of Christ,
you have experienced the grace of God. We did nothing to deserve
God's grace. It is by His great love for us that we've received this gift.
*But because of His great love for us, God, who is rich in mercy, made us
alive with Christ even when we were dead in transgressions—it is by
grace you have been saved* (Ephesians 2:4-5).

We should turn ourselves to God's name in praise, offering to Jesus a
continual sacrifice of praising Him! *Through Jesus, therefore, let us
continually offer to God a sacrifice of praise—the fruit of lips that openly
profess His name* (Hebrews 13:15).

Living a life of praise is a powerful way to change our lives and is one
of the most enjoyable ways to live. *Ascribe to the Lord the glory due His
name; worship the Lord in the splendor of His holiness* (Psalm 29:2).
Sacrificial praise is honoring and pleasing to the One who is most due
our gratitude.

*Lord, You alone are worthy of all honor and praise. We lift our hands and
voices to You in an anthem of praise, glorifying Your holy name in gratitude
for who You are and all You do! Thank You, Jesus! Amen.*

SEPTEMBER 23RD

For the Spirit God gave does not make us timid,
but gives us power, love and self-discipline.

2 TIMOTHY 1:7

Good morning! What are the fears that are stealing away the victory Christ has already won for us? If we believe in Christ Jesus as Lord and Savior, having surrendered our lives to Him in obedience to God, we will be saved and *will never be put to shame* (Romans 10:11). Do not let circumstances or other people steal the promises of God already won and given! *No, in all these things we are more than conquerors through Him who loved us* (Romans 8:37).

Believers have had to face hardships throughout the ages that could cause them to fear. But God! It is impossible to be separated from God and His unconquerable love. Nothing can stop Christ's constant presence with us. The power of the Holy Spirit is available to help us overcome fear and anxiety so we can live effective lives for Christ Jesus.

God is our refuge and strength, an ever-present help in trouble. Therefore we will not fear, though the earth give way and the mountains fall into the heart of the sea, though its waters roar and foam and the mountains quake with their surging (Psalm 46:1-3). There is nothing we can't face with God! He is our eternal refuge, and He can (and will) provide strength in any circumstance.

Lord, You did not give us the spirit of fear or anxiety. From You "every good and perfect gift comes down" (James 1:17). Lord, we lay our fears and anxieties down, and instead we place our lives in Your hands to lead, guide, and direct us. We claim victory in You! Teach us and show us. Make us, Lord, the people You desire us to be, workers to build Your kingdom. Thank You, Jesus! Amen.

SEPTEMBER 24TH

But you, man of God, flee from all this, and pursue righteousness, godliness, faith, love, endurance and gentleness. Fight the good fight of the faith. Take hold of the eternal life to which you were called ...

1 TIMOTHY 6:11-12

Good morning! Rise up and take hold of what God intends for us— yes, for you—to have and to be! The Christian life is a life of action! Flee, pursue, fight, take hold. We are not to be passively waiting around but must have an active faith, training, working hard, sacrificing, and doing whatever we know is right in the eyes of God. Our discipline and obedience to Christ Jesus defines who we are, what we believe, and is our living testimony to others.

Jesus said, *"I have set you an example that you should do as I have done for you"* (John 13:15). We are to live and lead by Christ's example, following in His footsteps. We are not left alone in this—God will equip us and give us everything we need. *Now may the God of peace ... equip you with everything good for doing His will* (Hebrews 13:21).

Do not be complacent. Put your faith to work. *His divine power has given us everything we need for a godly life through our knowledge of Him who called us by His own glory and goodness. Through these He has given us His very great and precious promises, so that through them you may participate in the divine nature* (2 Peter 1:3-4). When we truly belong to the Lord, we must not ignore how we are to live and what we are to do.

Thank You, Lord, for who You are in our lives. May we continue to pursue and seek after You, that we would increase in our knowledge of You and our faith and works would grow in order to glorify You. Your kingdom come; Your will be done. Thank You, Jesus! Amen.

SEPTEMBER 25TH

*Do everything without grumbling or arguing, so that you may
become blameless and pure, children of God without fault
in a warped and crooked generation. Then you will shine among them
like the stars in the sky as you hold firmly to the word of life.*

PHILIPPIANS 2:14–16

Good morning! If we are still muddling about in gossip,
complaining, and the petty things of the natural life, we will
not be living in the spiritual realm of God in a capacity that will
effectively demonstrate the gospel of Christ. Have a life and live a life
that is worthy of Christ! Out of our mouths comes the condition of
our hearts and minds. Are we transformed or still living on the
fringes of darkness? We must be aware at all times of what we are
thinking before our thoughts become spoken words and actions. We
serve the risen Christ, and it must be done without complaint,
grumbling, and disputing.

*If anyone speaks, they should do so as one who speaks the very words
[the oracles] of God. If anyone serves, they should do so with the strength God
provides, so that in all things God may be praised through Jesus Christ. To
Him be the glory and the power for ever and ever. Amen* (1 Peter 4:11).

Everything Jesus said and did was out of love. He is our example.
Pause to pray before speaking and doing. We must seek the Lord in all
things so we can lead effective, productive lives in and for Christ Jesus.
Remember whose we are and whom we serve.

*Lord, forgive us for our grumbling and complaining words and attitudes.
Guard our minds and our mouths, that our thoughts and words would be
pleasing to You, Lord. Our desire is that we would effectively share Your love
and always represent You well—that we would be productive workers in
building Your kingdom. Thank You, Jesus. Amen.*

SEPTEMBER 26TH

Therefore, since we have these promises, dear friends,
let us purify ourselves from everything that contaminates body and spirit,
perfecting holiness out of reverence for God.

2 CORINTHIANS 7:1

Good morning! The definition of the word *contaminated* is "having been made impure by exposure to or addition of a poisonous or polluting substance." We are to protect ourselves from the things of this world that contaminate the mind, body, and spirit. We are to turn away from sin, repent, and turn toward God. Our goal should always be to work at maturing our faith. We are perfected through our relationship with God, not this world, constantly growing deeper in living God's way of life.

In Matthew 15:18, we are told the things that come out of our mouths from the heart are what make us "unclean." The way we are deep down inside is of much more concern to God than our outward appearance which is easily cleaned up and made to look attractive. What is the condition of our hearts, and what are the thoughts we are entertaining?

Whatever happens, conduct yourselves in a manner worthy of the gospel of Christ (Philippians 1:27). God chose us to be Christ's representatives on this earth. Paul is challenging us to live pure lives worthy of the calling we received. *I urge you to live a life worthy of the calling you have received* (Ephesians 4:1). We must not compromise our standards to fit into a world we do not belong to, allowing ourselves to be contaminated and poisoned by sin and destruction.

Lord, we count it a privilege to be called Your children, to represent You in this world. We pray for strength to fight against the evil here, to protect ourselves from all that would take us away from You and the ministry You have given us to do. May our lives bring glory and honor to Your name. Thank You, Jesus! Amen.

SEPTEMBER 27TH

"A new command I give you: Love one another.
As I have loved you, so you must love one another. By this everyone will
know that you are My disciples, if you love one another."

JOHN 13:34-35

Good morning! There is one characteristic above all that will point
others to Jesus. The command to love others is not new. *"Do not*
seek revenge or bear a grudge against anyone among your people, but
love your neighbor as yourself. I am the Lord" (Leviticus 19:18). What is
a new command is to *"love as I have loved you."* Christ died for us!
Jesus is talking about a sacrificial love! A love so deep, so profound,
that it touches unbelievers and believers alike. A love that is centered
in Christ, that knows no limitations, that is pure and reveals itself in
action.

Jesus was a living example of God's love, and He commanded us to
be living examples of His love. I read this description of how we can love
others as Jesus loves us: "By helping when it's not convenient, by giving
when it hurts, by devoting energy to others' welfare rather than our
own, by absorbing hurts from others without complaining or fighting
back."[25] It is a kind of love that is hard to do, which is why people notice
and are drawn by it. Jesus said, *"By this everyone will know that you are My*
disciples, if you love one another" (John 13:35).

We are not able to love "as Christ loved us" without first being
surrendered and obedient to God. It is a Christlike love that is
empowered by the Holy Spirit in and through us.

Lord, we submit our lives to You, surrendering all to You in obedience to Your
Word. Teach us to love others as You have loved us, that we would be effective
workers in drawing others to You and building up Your church. More of You
and less of us. Thank You, Jesus! Amen.

---

25. "Gospel of John App," *Filament Bible Collection* (Carol Stream: Tyndale House Publishers, Inc.), "Reflections" section.

SEPTEMBER 28TH

"I am coming to You now, but I say these things while I am still in the world, so that they may have the full measure of My joy within them."

JOHN 17:13

Good morning! Are we looking in the right place for our blessings, joy, and peace? True satisfaction will never come from other people, an occupation, financial independence, material possessions, status, popularity, or anything else this world boasts. All these are temporary and subject to change. God desires for us—disciples, believers, followers—to be joyful because of the blessings that are ours in Christ Jesus. *"I have told you this so that My joy may be complete in you and that your joy may be complete"* (John 15:11).

Joy comes from a consistent relationship with Jesus Christ. When our lives are intertwined with His, when our hearts are set on His Word, His teachings, and commandments, we will find the blessing of peace, joy, and true fulfillment. The world takes away; Jesus gives. *"The thief comes only to steal and kill and destroy; I have come that they may have life, and have it to the full"* (John 10:10).

If we are feeling disappointed and frustrated, questioning if this is all there is in life, we are most likely looking in the wrong places for our satisfaction and fulfillment. *Do not be anxious about anything, but in every situation, by prayer and petition, with thanksgiving, present your requests to God. And the peace of God, which transcends all understanding, will guard your hearts and your minds in Christ Jesus* (Philippians 4:6-7). True satisfaction and fulfillment come from only one place: look to Jesus!

Lord, we look to You, seeking after Your will for our lives. You alone are able to lead us, to guide and direct the way in which we should go. When You are first in our hearts and minds, all else follows in proper order. Thank You, Jesus! Amen.

SEPTEMBER 29TH

Be on your guard; stand firm in the faith;
be courageous; be strong. Do everything in love.

1 CORINTHIANS 16:13-14

Good morning! Don't settle for a watered down faith! We must be prepared for the challenges, obstacles, and spiritual enemies we will face. We are promised trouble in this world, and our victory comes from knowing Jesus and believing in the victory He has already won. *"I have told you these things, so that in Me you may have peace. In this world you will have trouble. But take heart! I have overcome the world"* (John 16:33).

Jesus made it clear that we will experience hard times, the difficulty that comes from living in a sin-stained world. This should not be a surprise to us. We were given the answer: *stand firm in faith*. We are told to hold fast in faith, trusting in God, as did the heroes of faith before us. *Consequently, faith comes from hearing the message, and the message is heard through the word about Christ* (Romans 10:17).

We can increase our faith by spending time and growing more in love with God. Study and know His Word, and put it into action. *Do not merely listen to the word, and deceive yourselves. Do what it says* (James 1:22). Don't neglect time with other believers. Be an encouragement to each other. All these things can increase our faith as we share in the love God so freely gives.

Lord, thank You for sharing Your Word with us, for strengthening and showing us how we are to live in You. We are overcomers through the victory You have already won. May our faith increase as we rely on You and share with others the gift of Your grace, truth, and love. Thank You, Jesus. Amen.

SEPTEMBER 30TH

"Peace I leave with you; My [perfect] peace I give you;
I do not give to you as the world gives. Do not let your hearts be troubled."

JOHN 14:27

Good morning! In this turbulent, chaotic world, we are offered peace. Our lives are easily filled with the turbulence from all that's going on in this world. We experience stress, fear, anxiety, and depression. Our peace is stolen away as we witness all the divisions at war in this world. But God! He's offered us a way of peace, a confident assurance, through His Son, Jesus Christ, and His Holy Spirit. Have we accepted His peace? *May the God of hope fill you with all joy and peace as you trust in Him, so that you may overflow with hope by the power of the Holy Spirit* (Romans 15:13).

God's peace is not subject to worldly circumstances. It is the result of the Holy Spirit working in and through our lives. *And the peace of God, which transcends all understanding, will guard your hearts and your minds in Christ Jesus* (Philippians 4:7). True, lasting peace comes from knowing that God is in control. His peace fills our hearts and protects our minds. It restores our hope and gives us strength that is built on the firm foundation of Christ Jesus. There is nothing in this world that can separate us from His love and nothing that can take away His promised peace. Live in His truth and experience His peace.

Thank You, Lord, for the assurances we have in You—of unending peace, everlasting hope, and unconditional love. All You ask is for us to believe in You, to live lives worthy of Your calling. We believe! And we surrender ourselves to Your will and Your ways. Thank You, Jesus! Amen.

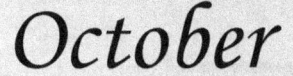

October

OCTOBER 1ST

Therefore, if anyone is in Christ, the new creation has come:
The old has gone, the new is here!

2 CORINTHIANS 5:17

Good morning! We've flipped the calendar to another new month, and now it's October. In the Midwest, where we live, the month is marked by the leaves changing from green to vibrant autumn colors of orange, yellow, and red before falling to reveal the bare branches of the winter months. The changing seasons repeat each year, timed with Earth's tilt and orbit around the sun, predictable and sure.

Change. God has a plan for change in our lives that includes hope and a future. When we seek after Jesus, come to know Him, and live in vital union with Him, we are changed—new creations under a new Master. *And we, who with unveiled faces all reflect the Lord's glory, are being transformed into His likeness with ever increasing glory, which comes from the Lord, who is the Spirit* (2 Corinthians 3:18). This change is an entirely new being and way of living under Jesus' authority. We see people, life, and all of creation in a new way. We are changed from within, and we experience the power of Christ and the Holy Spirit in and through us.

God made Him who had no sin to be sin for us, so that in Him we might become the righteousness of God (2 Corinthians 5:21). When we put our trust in Christ, we exchange our sin for His righteousness. He paid the price for our sin so that we might be changed to *become the righteousness of God.*

Lord, we praise You. You made a way to change us from wandering, lost, and dying to purposeful, found, and alive. We are new creations in You! Thank You, Jesus! Amen.

OCTOBER 2ND

So whether you eat or drink or whatever you do,
do it all for the glory of God!

1 CORINTHIANS 10:31

Good morning! How different our lives and the impact we have on other people's lives would be if we were more mindful of our thoughts, words, and actions! A good measure of our lives is whether or not we are glorifying or honoring God by our thoughts, words, and everything we do. There are no categories of living that are off-limits to God.

We aren't supposed to be living "Jekyll and Hyde" lives or have an attitude of drudgery or disinterest! *Whatever you do, work at it with all your heart, as working for the Lord, not for human masters, since you know that you will receive an inheritance from the Lord as a reward. It is the Lord Christ you are serving* (Colossians 3:23-24).

Everything we do, everything we are, should be considered an act of worship or service to God. *For none of us lives for ourselves alone, and none of us dies for ourselves alone. If we live, we live for the Lord; and if we die, we die for the Lord. So, whether we live or we die, we belong to the Lord* (Romans 14:7-8). Our lives belong to Him and thus, should be lived dedicated to and reflective of Christ and His character in us.

Lord, forgive us when we live as though You are outside of the equation of our lives. Renew in us an attitude of gratitude and thanksgiving, a posture of praise, and a focus on life that reflects our love for You and allows Your Spirit to be evident in and through us. Thank You, Jesus! Amen.

OCTOBER 3RD

"He must become greater; I must become less."

JOHN 3:30

Good morning! Have we allowed God to touch our hearts and change our lives? Our natural desire is to be self-centered, as we are born sinners. But God intends that we surrender our lives in obedience to Him so we will lead others to Him—disciples making disciples. Our focus must move from ourselves to God. He must increase in us in a way that fully realizes any success in our lives comes from God. What we do should always point to God through a changed life.

What shall we say, then? Shall we go on sinning so that grace may increase? By no means! We are those who have died to sin; how can we live in it any longer? (Romans 6:1-2). Jesus paid for our forgiveness with His life to set us free and to open the way to a living relationship with God through Him. We must consciously choose to live in our new life with Jesus, giving Him the credit for our change and any success.

Since, then, you have been raised with Christ, set your hearts on things above, where Christ is, seated at the right hand of God. Set your minds on things above, not on earthly things. For you died, and your life is now hidden with Christ in God (Colossians 3:1-3). Knowing our real home is where Christ lives is a truth that should reach our hearts and impact how we live our lives, giving all praise to Him.

Lord, please change our hearts, that they might be set on things above, with heavenly priorities. We pray that our earthly lives would have a heavenly perspective based on what You desire for us and that we might impact others to come to know You. May we see what You see, hear with discerning ears, and love with hearts filled with Your love. Thank You, Jesus! Amen.

OCTOBER 4TH

*When I consider Your heavens, the work of Your fingers,
the moon and the stars, which You have set in place, what is mankind
that You are mindful of them, human beings that You care for them?*

PSALM 8:3-4

Good morning! We human beings think too highly of ourselves, for if it weren't for God, where would we be? *If it had not been the Lord who was on our side—they would have swallowed us alive* (Psalm 124:1, 3). Of all of God's creation, He chose mankind to be made in His image, to have dominion over all creation, and He blessed them (Genesis 1:26-30). The reality is, in comparison to the greatness and vastness of all of God's creation, mankind is not much larger than a speck or a tiny insect. After all, we were made from dust! *Then the Lord God formed a man from the dust of the ground and breathed into his nostrils the breath of life, and the man became a living being* (Genesis 2:7).

We often lack the humility this reality should bring to our perspective and the proper respect of exactly how great our God is. *Lord, our Lord, how majestic is Your name in all the earth!* (Psalm 8:9). We will shrink in size when compared to the magnitude of who God is and the entirety of His creation. And yet, God still cares for us and loves us. How benevolent He is!

Lord, we are in awe of You! Nothing is too much for You! Change our perspective to see and to marvel at how great You are. Thank You for loving us so much that You call us Your own: children of the King! That You made a way for us to come before You in prayer. We humble ourselves before You, in honor, praising and worshiping You. Thank You, Jesus! Amen.

OCTOBER 5TH

"Blessed are those who hunger and thirst for righteousness,
for they will be filled."

MATTHEW 5:6

Good morning! Are we urgently pursuing after doing right in the sight of and for God? To Jesus, "blessed" means experiencing hope and joy, separate from our outward circumstances. As Christ followers, we seek after God, and our attitudes are different from those of this world.

"But seek first His kingdom and His righteousness, and all these things will be given to you as well" (Matthew 6:33). We turn to God first for help, to fill our minds with His thoughts and His desires. We live to take on and develop in His character, and to serve and obey Him. And we receive in return God's promises. *"I, the Lord, have called you in righteousness; I will take hold of your hand. I will keep you and make you to be a covenant for the people and a light for the Gentiles, to open the eyes that are blind, to free captives from prison and to release from the dungeons those who sit in darkness"* (Isaiah 42:6-7).

When we seek after God, He works in and through us to open people's eyes to see who He is, to free them from the prison of the hold of this world and release them into His light. What a privilege to be part of the mission of Christ Jesus! It starts with seeking His righteousness before we can demonstrate it and share it with others.

Lord, we thank You for including us in Your earthly mission—for allowing us to help open eyes, minds, and hearts and bring Your light into the dark places of the souls of Your people. It is only by Your Holy Spirit working in and through us that we are so blessed. Thank You, Jesus! Amen.

OCTOBER 6TH

For the Spirit God gave us does not make us timid, but gives us power, love and self-discipline. So do not be ashamed of the testimony about our Lord.

2 TIMOTHY 1:7-8

Good morning! Are we prepared to share our faith and the hope we have been given with others? So many are more concerned about offending man than pleasing God. If we believe in Jesus Christ, who He is and what He has done, we should be a changed people, living new lives in Him. *Therefore, if anyone is in Christ, the new creation has come: the old has gone, the new is here!* (2 Corinthians 5:17). We began a new life under Christ Jesus, made whole and new in union with Him. Do our lives reflect what Jesus has and continues to do in and through us? If so, others should notice the difference, and we must be prepared to share our faith, to give an answer about why we are different.

But in your hearts revere Christ as Lord. Always be prepared to give an answer to everyone who asks you to give the reason for the hope that you have. But do this with gentleness and respect (1 Peter 3:15). Can others see our hope in Christ? He has displaced our old way of thinking and living with His way. The Holy Spirit has breathed new life in us. We should not be the same anymore.

Stop and consider what knowing, believing in, and following Jesus has done in your life. Be ready to share the testimony of what Christ has done and continues to do in your life. Be Jesus to someone today, as if they were touched by His love through you.

Lord, when we were yet sinners, You loved us enough to come and die for us. You have changed our lives, given us new birth and a hope everlasting. Help us to be bold for you, to share the life-saving, life-changing message of the gospel to the ones You put before us. Thank you, Jesus! Amen.

OCTOBER 7TH

But just as He who called you is holy, so be holy in all you do;
for it is written: "Be holy; because I am holy."

1 PETER 1:15-16

Good morning! We are not called to a "holier-than-thou" attitude that is offensive and steeped in an attitude of moral superiority. Holiness means we are totally devoted to God, set aside for His special use and set apart from sin and sin's influence. God set the example for our morality. He is merciful, full of grace, loving kindness and justice.

Paul wrote to the Corinthians, *Follow my example, as I follow the example of Christ* (1 Corinthians 11:1). We are to imitate Jesus, to be set apart and to be different. Are we like our Heavenly Father and His Son Jesus? Or are we compromising ourselves to the world we live in?

In your relationships with one another, have the same mindset as Christ Jesus (Philippians 2:5). The qualities of God living in and through us are what makes us different. We are not holy on our own but through Christ Jesus. *And by that will, we have been made holy through the sacrifice of the body of Jesus Christ once and for all. For by one sacrifice He has made perfect forever those who are being made holy* (Hebrews 10:10, 14).

God is not finished with us. We must pursue after Him in all areas of our lives, be open to the discipline and guidance of Christ, and be willing to relinquish the control of our lives to Him.

Lord, we are wholly Yours. Continue to make us, Lord, into vessels of Your will, that we would be made holy as You are holy. Teach us, Lord, Your ways. Mold us into the people You created us to be, humble yet holy for You. Thank You, Jesus. Amen.

OCTOBER 8TH

*"In the same way, let your Light shine before others,
that they may see your good deeds and glorify your Father in heaven."*

MATTHEW 5:16

Good morning! We should not be surprised or disheartened by the darkness and trouble in this world. My husband and I live in a more rural area with very few street lights (limited light pollution, so to say). The stars appear brighter and more numerous, but in reality, they just shine brighter because of the darkness surrounding them. And so it should be with those who live for Jesus. We should be shining brightly, showing others what Jesus is like and who He is.

For God, who said, "Let light shine out of darkness," made his light shine in our hearts to give us the light of the knowledge of God's glory displayed in the face of Christ (2 Corinthians 4:6). Lights do not need to be turned on amidst the light but in the darkness. Are we being the Light of Christ to those in need, to those struggling in the darkness of the world's chaos and the devil's lies?

"You are the Light of the world" (Matthew 5:14). We are called to share the Light of Christ—to speak His Truth, to stand out from the crowds, to deny sin in our lives, to be ready to share the gospel message, and to respond to the needs of the people God puts before us. It is time to be bright and bold for Jesus! Shine the Light wherever you go.

Lord, it seems the darkness permeates this world more and more. May we obey Your Word that tells us to be Light, to introduce others to who You are, to show them what You are like, and to share Your love with them. Help us, Lord, to shine brightly for You! There are so many lives who need to see Your Light and to know You. Thank You, Jesus! Amen.

OCTOBER 9TH

So the other disciples told him [Thomas], "We have seen the Lord!" But he said to them, "Unless I see the nail marks in His hands and put my finger where the nails were, and put my hand into His side, I will not believe."

JOHN 20:25

Good morning! Are you a "doubting Thomas," needing proof of the resurrected Christ? Thomas needed proof that Jesus was alive. He wanted not just to see Him, but to touch the wounds of His death. Jesus is not limited to a physical presence. He is alive in His Holy Spirit given those who believe. Even John the Baptist had his moment of doubt sitting in prison after preparing the way for Christ's coming. *When John, who was in prison, heard about the deeds of the Messiah, he sent his disciples to ask Him [Jesus], "Are you the one who is to come, or should we expect someone else?"* (Matthew 11:1-2).

Satan does not want us to believe; he wants us to doubt. And he will do what he needs to do in order to plant seeds of doubt and to distract us from Jesus. Jesus' reply sent to John was of the evidence seen and heard in His earthly ministry and ended with Jesus saying, *"Blessed is anyone who does not stumble on account of Me"* (Matthew 11:6).

Look at the evidence of Jesus in Scripture and the change in our lives. His identity is obvious. *"Stop doubting and believe"* (John 20:27). When you doubt, don't look away, but, just as John did, turn to Him for His answers.

Lord, there is no doubting who You are and the price You paid for our salvation, redemption, and lives. We believe and stand firm in our faith. And if doubts should arise, we will turn to You, to the Truth found in Your Word, at the cross, and in Your resurrection. Thank You, Jesus! Amen.

OCTOBER 10TH

"If you love me, obey [keep] my commandments."

JOHN 14:15

Good morning! Obedience comes from and is a sign of our love for God. We live in a world that preaches and pushes freedom and rights, rejecting authority and rankling at the mention of obedience to anyone or anything other than ourselves. This is not the way of God or spiritual maturity. Adam and Eve rejected God's authority. Their disobedience destroyed the state of man's perfect communion with God. Our obedience is born in trusting God's sovereignty and wisdom, and a sign of our respect, honor, and praise of who He is.

Therefore, with minds that are alert and fully sober, set your hope on the grace to be brought to you when Jesus Christ is revealed at His coming. As obedient children, do not conform to the evil desires you had when you lived in ignorance (1 Peter 1:13-14). Are we living in obedience to God and loving Him?

As we love God and live in obedience to His Word (commands), Jesus remains in us through the "Advocate"—the Spirit of God Himself—to care for and guide us. *"If you love me, keep my commands. And I will ask the Father, and He will give you another advocate to help you forever—the Spirit of truth"* (John 14:15-17).

God's way is not just better; it is best. Obeying God leads us into a deeper understanding of who He is and fellowship with Him.

Lord, we thank You for making a way for us out of our sin and rebellion by loving You through our obedience and trust. You have set us free at the cost of Your Son Jesus, given us Your Word to study and follow and Your Spirit to guide and direct us. May we abandon ourselves, surrendering to Your will, and live in love and obedience to You. Thank You, Jesus! Amen.

OCTOBER 11TH

Draw [come] near to God, and He will draw [come] near to you.

JAMES 4:8

Good morning! Invite God into your life, into your day and all the activities it will hold. So many have forgotten God or make Him an afterthought to their days, when He should be our priority and the first thought we have. When we invite God to come close, He always accepts our invitation. *Whoever dwells in the shelter of the Most High will rest in the shadow of the Almighty* (Psalm 91:1).

Sit with Him awhile in the safety and peace of His presence. God is our Protector and our Provider. He will lead and guide us in the way we should go, giving us clarity in this muddled and crazy world. *Whether you turn to the right or to the left, your ears will hear a voice behind you, saying, "This is the way; walk in it"* (Isaiah 30:21).

When we ignore God, we will find ourselves wandering off His intended path, but He is always there to correct us if we return to Him. God's desire is that we seek Him first, and He assures us that we will find Him. *"You will seek Me and find Me when you seek Me with all your heart"* (Jeremiah 29:13). We can call on God in confidence, knowing that He is waiting, He listens for us, He hears, and He will answer. No matter what our circumstances or where we are, we can find God when we seek Him wholeheartedly.

Thank You, Lord, that You listen for and hear Your people. You invite us to come to You, and You assure us You will always be there. Whether we are in need or bringing our praise to You, we are met with the response of Your presence. Thank You, Jesus! Amen.

OCTOBER 12TH

Joseph's master took him and put him in prison,
the place where the king's prisoners were confined.

GENESIS 39:20

Good morning! Have you ever had a door closed on you that you thought was opening to the right direction? How did you respond? Joseph spent two years in that prison, accused of a crime he didn't even commit! If anyone had reason to rebel against a closed door, it was Joseph! *But while Joseph was there in the prison, the Lord was with him; He showed him kindness and granted him favor in the eyes of the prison warden* (Genesis 39:20-21).

Joseph had every reason to rebel, but he chose to trust in God and respond with diligence and purpose. *"Call on Me in the day of trouble; I will deliver you, and you will honor Me"* (Psalm 50:15). The Lord is our answer to all situations, even the open and closed doors we face.

Our character is being developed in and through our experiences, and our responses reflect the condition of our hearts. *Not only so, but we also glory in our sufferings, because we know that suffering produces perseverance; perseverance, character; and character, hope. And hope does not put us to shame, because God's love has been poured out into our hearts through the Holy Spirit, who has been given to us* (Romans 5:3-5).

Doors will close. We will experience disappointments and suffering. But God will always make a way for us if we remain in Him. *And we know that in all things God works for the good of those who love Him, who have been called according to His purpose* (Romans 8:28). Closed doors (troubles) are part of life. Our response will influence what's next. *Trust in the One who is able* (Ephesians 3:20).

Lord, You are God, and we are not. We choose to put our trust in Your will and Your ways. No matter what today or tomorrow may bring, You have promised to be with us, leading and guiding all the way. Thank You, Jesus! Amen.

OCTOBER 13TH

Therefore, I urge you [beseech you], brothers and sisters, in view of God's mercy, to offer your bodies as a living sacrifice, holy and pleasing to God—this is your true and proper worship.

ROMANS 12:1

Good morning! Challenge: Are we behaving in a way that is pleasing to God? God wants us to offer ourselves to Him—living sacrifices—abandoning our ways to follow Him. Our energy and resources belong to Him. They are for His glory. *Do not conform to the patterns of this world, but be transformed by the renewing of your mind. Then you will be able to test and approve what God's will is—His good, pleasing and perfect will* (Romans 12:2).

The world tells us "What's mine is mine. I earned it." God's Word tells us *not to conform to the patterns of this world. Be pleasing to God.* He wants what's best for us, for us to be transformed people with renewed minds, living to honor and obey Him. We aren't to be "playing church," checking off boxes on a religious list: church, check; read the Bible, check; help someone, check. God isn't interested in rules and a checklist faith. He's all about going deeper in a living relationship with Him, setting aside ourselves to follow and trust Him.

"For my thoughts are not your thoughts, neither are your ways My ways," declares the LORD. "As the heavens are higher than the earth, so are My ways higher than your ways and My thoughts than your thoughts" (Isaiah 55:8-9).

Live in a way that puts God first, in which we strive to seek His will, His plans, His ways: *transformed.*

Lord, forgive us when we live in the folly of this world, ignoring You and acting holy by going through the motions of being "good." Our desire is to be pleasing to You, Lord. "Let the words of my mouth and the meditation of my heart be pleasing in Your sight, O Lord, my Rock and my Redeemer" (Psalm 19:14). Thank You, Jesus! Amen.

OCTOBER 14TH

For in Christ all the fullness of the Deity lives in bodily form, and in Christ you have been brought to fullness. He is the head over every power and authority.

COLOSSIANS 2:9-10

Good morning! What is our "everything"? If it doesn't start and end with Jesus, we will not be whole. All of God was in Christ's human form. When we have Jesus, we have everything we need for salvation and right living. *The Son is the image of the invisible God, the firstborn over all creation. For in Him all things were created ... all things have been created through and for Him* (Colossians 1:15-16).

Jesus not only reflects God, He is the exact representation of Him, and He reveals God to us. He is Lord of all, completely holy. Fully believe in the deity of Christ, supreme over all creation! Keep all your focus on Jesus. Everything in spiritual and physical worlds was created by and is under His authority. He has no equal or rival. He is Lord over all! And our lives are found in Him.

For you died, and your life is now hidden with Christ in God. When Christ, who is your life, appears, then you will also appear with Him in glory! (Colossians 3:3-4). We are concealed and safe in and with Christ Jesus. Our service and conduct are results of our salvation. He has given us the power to live in and through Him and given us a hope for tomorrow.

Jesus deserves the highest place of honor in our lives. He is our everything, and everything worth having and being comes from Him.

Lord, You are our All in all. Everything we need is of You and comes from You. We seek only what You desire, breaking the chains of this world's pleasures and its empty religiosity in exchange for a deeper understanding of and relationship with You. Lord, help us to view this world as You do, and to be vessels of Your love and service to those You put before us. Thank You, Jesus! Amen.

OCTOBER 15TH

My sacrifice, O God, is a broken spirit;
a broken and contrite heart you, God, will not despise.

PSALM 51:17

Good morning! God uses broken things! Throughout Scripture, we read and are shown how God uses brokenness for His greater purpose. We will never please God by outward appearances and activity of our own doing, no matter how good our intentions, if our hearts are not humble and right. The people God uses most are those who are completely broken with no motives of their own. *The Lord is close to the brokenhearted; and saves those who are crushed in spirit* (Psalm 34:18).

So often we are looking for ways out of our brokenness—out of pain, sorrow, grief, and despair—through our own methods. But God! He is our source of power, courage, healing, and strength. His desire is to rescue us from our brokenness. He uses those who may seem totally hopeless, lost, and helpless. *He gives strength to the weary and increases the power of the weak* (Isaiah 40:29).

God uses broken things for His glory. Let us never forget that it was the broken body of His Son, Jesus Christ, that paid for our sins and redeemed us into salvation and new life. We must be willing and allow God to grab ahold of our hearts, even in the midst of brokenness, and surrender to what His plan and purpose is. Watch and see what the Lord will do!

Lord, there is no other like You. You use broken things and broken people for Your glory. Thank You for choosing us as a people worthy of Your love, that You care for us in our brokenness, to save and redeem us. Grip us with Your Spirit and use us as You will. Thank You, Jesus! Amen.

OCTOBER 16TH

Then He said to His disciples, "The harvest is plentiful,
but the workers are few. Ask the Lord of the harvest, therefore,
to send out workers into His harvest field."

MATTHEW 9:37-38

Good morning! Jesus was referring to the crowds surrounding Him as a plentiful harvest, ready to give their lives to Him. It is no different today! Look around and see all those who need or are ready to hear about Jesus. We are His disciples being given the same instruction: *"Pray to the Lord of the harvest."* Pray that many would respond to the need for believers to share the gospel—*"send out workers into His harvest field."* There is so much work to be done. Look at the crowds of people who don't know and aren't living in the kingdom of God. This should break our hearts and move us into the response of prayer! And then be prepared for God to answer and use us to show others the way to Him.

We are therefore Christ's ambassadors, as though God were making His appeal through us. We implore you on Christ's behalf: Be reconciled to God (2 Corinthians 5:20). We are official representatives of Christ Jesus, called to be disciples and therefore make disciples. *"Therefore go and make disciples of all nations, baptizing them in the name of the Father and of the Son and of the Holy Spirit, and teaching them to obey everything I have commanded you. And surely I am with you always, to the very end of the age"* (Matthew 28:19-20).

We dare not take this responsibility lightly! We must pray, share the good news of salvation, and live a life that represents Jesus well through our thoughts, words, and deeds.

Lord, we pray that we would be Your ambassadors, instruments to share Your love with others. Give us the words and the courage to speak about Your truth, so people might come to know You and experience Your grace, that many will be reconciled to You! Thank You, Jesus! Amen.

OCTOBER 17TH

For from him and through him and for him are all things.
To him be the glory forever! Amen.

ROMANS 11:36

Good morning! What are we doing with the gifts God has given us? Everything comes from God and exists by His power and is intended for His glory. *"So take the bag of gold from him and give it to the one who has ten bags. For whoever has will be given more, and they will have an abundance. Whoever does not have, even what they have will be taken from them"* (Matthew 25:28-29).

The parable of the loaned money can be misinterpreted as the master being harsh, even cruel, until its meaning is understood. There are two attitudes we can have toward the gifts God (the Master) has given us. We can be diligent in preparing for Christ's return by investing the gifts and resources we've been given to serve God. Or we can be self-centered and negligent, concerned with just ourselves, bearing no fruit for God's kingdom.

Each of you should use whatever gift you have received to serve others, as faithful stewards of God's grace in its various forms (1 Peter 4:10). Our talents, abilities, and resources should be faithfully used to serve others, to grow God's kingdom, and to bring Him glory. Everyone has been given gifts and talents. We must find ours and put them to use as the Spirit leads. *"Let your light shine before others, that they may see your good deeds and glorify your Father in heaven"* (Matthew 5:16).

When we see a need, we should seek to meet it. Through a willingness to serve, we often discover the gifts we've been given.

Lord, thank You for all You've blessed us with: gifts, talents, and resources intended to be used for Your glory. May we willingly pursue after areas You reveal to us and direct us toward, that others might see You in us and be drawn to You. Thank You, Jesus! Amen.

OCTOBER 18TH

And we know that in all things God works for the good of those who love Him, who have been called according to His purpose.

ROMANS 8:28

Good morning! My husband and I memorized this verse a few years ago during a particularly difficult time in our lives. We encouraged each other by repeating it to one another, sometimes multiple times a day.

Skeptics will question: "ALL things? How can loss, pain, suffering, and death be for our good?" The story doesn't end with the experiences and circumstances we're living in or going through. God is in control of ALL things, and He is a part of our story. God knew us before we were even born, recording our days in His book of life. *Your eyes saw my unformed body; all the days ordained for me were written in Your book before one of them came to be* (Psalm 139:16-17).

God has plans for us that are meant to prosper us, give us hope, and give us a future (Jeremiah 29:11). There are times God will discipline those He loves, called to be His children, to build us up and ensure our story is complete. *And have you completely forgotten this word of encouragement that addresses you as a father addresses his son? It says, "My son, do not make light of the Lord's discipline, and do not lose heart when he rebukes you, because the Lord disciplines the one he loves, and he chastens everyone he accepts as his son." Endure hardship as discipline; God is treating you as his children. For what children are not disciplined by their father?* (Hebrews 12:5-7).

Trust God's Word and His Ways. Know His truth, that in ALL things God works for the good of those who love Him.

Lord, we thank You that You are in control of our story, that You love us so much You orchestrate our lives to mature our faith and bring us to a deeper knowledge of who You are and into a lasting relationship with You. Thank You, Jesus. Amen.

OCTOBER 19TH

And my God will supply every need of yours
according to his riches in glory in Christ Jesus.

PHILIPPIANS 4:19

Good morning! We fight and try so hard to see or find all the things God has already prepared for us, and yet, all are waiting if we would simply surrender ourselves to Him. God has a storehouse of goodness beyond anything we could ever imagine waiting for us. Whatever we need on earth, God is able to supply, even the courage to face the discomfort of breaking the chains that hold us in perpetual fear, anxiety, and earthly idols. What's more, He is inviting us to come to Him and take, participate in, and experience His richness. *Taste and see that the LORD is good; blessed is the one who takes refuge in Him. Fear the Lord, you His holy people, for those who fear Him lack nothing* (Psalm 34:8-9).

When we take that first step of surrender, of obedience in following God, we will discover who He really is—His kindness and goodness, mercy and grace. Our fear is a reverence, a humble attitude and posture of genuine worship. And as we trust Him more and begin to experience His goodness firsthand, we come to know Him personally and realize that He loves us more than we can ever imagine. We are invited to feed on His truth that changes our lives from the inside out.

Trust God and seek Him. He is our source of protection and provision. He is all we need.

Lord, thank You for Your constant invitation to come to You, to know You and experience Your goodness. Lord, may we abandon ourselves to You in complete surrender, obedient to Your will, and grow in the knowledge of who You are. All we need is Yours to give and ours to hold. You are our Lord and Savior. Thank You, Jesus! Amen.

OCTOBER 20TH

"Do not store up for yourselves treasures on earth, where moths and vermin destroy, and where thieves break in and steal. But store up for yourselves treasures in heaven, where moths and vermin do not destroy, and where thieves do not break in and steal. For where your treasure is, there your heart will be also."

MATTHEW 6:19-21

Good morning! We live in a world of plenty that promotes more. But this earthly wealth is fleeting and should not be our life's desire and focus. Our focus should be to intentionally seek the fulfillment of God's purposes in all we do, not how much money we have and make and what we plan to do with it. If money and what it brings become our treasure, our hearts will be led in the wrong place and eaten up by wasted concerns and thinking.

What we treasure most is what will consume us—our time, effort, and peace. Our hope is not found in any earthly treasure but in God, who knows what we need and how to provide for us. *Command those who are rich in this present world not to be arrogant nor to put their hope in wealth, which is so uncertain, but to put their hope in God, who richly provides us with everything for our enjoyment* (1 Timothy 6:17).

Rich or poor, our true wealth comes from God. Be rich then in good deeds, generosity, and sharing. No matter what our bank account balance says, our lives should demonstrate that it is God we serve, and He is our ultimate provider.

Lord, forgive us when our priorities shift from heavenly to earthly pursuits. We know and trust that You know how to care for us and that You know how to give good gifts that matter most. May we live this day with generous hearts set on loving You and loving others in a way that brings glory and honor to You. Thank You, Jesus! Amen.

OCTOBER 21ST

Grace and peace be yours in abundance.

1 PETER 1:2

Good morning! Peter wrote this opening to the Jewish Christians who had been scattered in foreign lands (from Jerusalem to throughout Asia Minor). One might wonder, where is the grace and peace to be found in that! Our response to each and every situation demonstrates the condition of our faith and our character. *These have come so that the proven genuineness of your faith—of greater worth than gold, which perishes even though refined by fire—may result in praise, glory and honor when Jesus Christ is revealed* (1 Peter 1:7).

We are being prepared for Christ's return! That should fill us with such excitement and a fervor to perfect our faith! *"However, when the Son of Man comes [returns], will He find faith on earth?"* (Luke 18:8). Our trials and suffering are part of the refining process that burns away the impurities in our hearts, minds, and souls, in order to prepare us for the glorious day in which we will meet our Savior, Jesus Christ. We are not to be dragging ourselves through life, bickering and complaining, living out of defeat and despair, but to live in the knowledge of His abundant grace and peace.

Jesus made a huge sacrifice so we would have such abundance in Him. *"I have told you these things, so that in Me you may have peace. In this world you will have trouble. But take heart! I have overcome the world"* (John 16:33). Are we putting our emphasis on the troubles or on Christ's overcoming? Let us be all about living in such a way that we will one day hear the Lord's precious words, *"Well done, good and faithful servant"* (Matthew 25:23).

Lord, Your grace, mercy, and love far surpass anything we could ever fully know. You desire our hearts in faithful surrender, for our obedience in pursuing after You. May we choose to rejoice, even in the midst of trials, with grateful hearts and ceaseless prayer and praise. Oh, that we will be amongst Your faithful. Thank You, Jesus! Amen.

OCTOBER 22ND

As God has said: 'I will dwell in them and walk among them.
I will be their God, and they shall be My people."

2 CORINTHIANS 6:16

Good morning! If we are looking to find God on the mountaintop, we are looking in the wrong place, for God is among us, His people. In Paul's letter to the church in Corinth, he is quoting from Isaiah, that those who follow Jesus are the temple of God. The church is not where we go, it is who we are. God isn't waiting for us up on top of a mountain. He is within us amidst our daily routines, through the difficulties and in the good times. God not only lives among us— we are the house in which He dwells. *And I heard a loud voice from the throne saying, "Look! God's dwelling place is now among the people, and He will dwell with them. They will be His people, and God Himself will be with them and be their God"* (Revelation 21:3).

God came down in His Son, Jesus Christ, to be among His people. No matter what we are going through, we can know that God has the final word in our lives. We were made to be in close fellowship with God within us. *Be still, and know that I am God; I will be exalted among the nations, I will be exalted in the earth* (Psalm 46:10).

Take time to be quiet and sit with God, to exalt Him. Our mountaintop experience is not far away. It is held in our hearts when we experience God within, no matter what is going on around us.

Lord, as we take time today to sit quietly before You, as we study Your Word, journal, or pray, You are with us. You walk among us, and You dwell within us. Thank You, Jesus, that we are able to experience You in and through our lives always. Amen.

OCTOBER 23RD

*"For My thoughts are not your thoughts,
neither are your ways My ways," declares the Lord.*

ISAIAH 55:8

Good morning! Do we trust only what we understand? What kind of trust and faith is that? God sees more than we can ever see and knows far more than we will ever know. He works in ways well beyond our comprehension. If we trust only what we can see or understand, we'll miss experiencing so much of God's plan and inexplicable wonders for us. *"As the heavens are higher than the earth, so are My ways higher than your ways and My thoughts than your thoughts"* (Isaiah 55:9).

We can't possibly know the full picture of what God is doing, and we need to give up our demand to understand in order to accept whatever we are given or facing. *"Trust in the Lord with all your heart, and lean not on your own understanding; in all your ways submit to Him, and He will make your paths straight"* (Proverbs 3:5-6).

We never know the whole picture, but God does. Are we willing to let God be God, and believe He will do what He says He will do? *In their hearts humans plan their course, but the Lord establishes their steps* (Proverbs 16:9). God is the One who guides our path, and we can trust God in His direction, while we rest in His presence.

Lord, thank You for using all things to grow us. May our trust in You not hinge on our understanding but on our faith in who You are and what You do and say. May we "live by faith, not by sight" (2 Corinthians 5:7). Thank You, Jesus! Amen.

OCTOBER 24TH

You desire but do not have, so you kill. You covet but you cannot get what you want, so you quarrel and fight. You do not have because you do not ask God. When you ask, you do not receive, because you ask with wrong motives, that you may spend what you get on your pleasures.

JAMES 4:2-3

Good morning! God desires for us to live in a place where we lack nothing. Sounds impossible? Not when we understand the meaning here: "no thing" or in the Hebrew language, the phrase "lack nothing" literally means "to not be empty." When we are living according to the wisdom of the world, we live in want of things, and we're constantly striving to get and have, to fill up. We're living forever unsatisfied. But God! He gives us good gifts to enjoy and longs for us to "lack nothing." *"How much more will your Father in heaven give good gifts"* (Matthew 7:11).

The pleasures of this world keep us from pleasing God, living according to His will, and receiving His rich bounty of fullness. *For in Christ all the fullness of the Deity lives in bodily form, and in Christ you have been brought to fullness* (Colossians 2:9-10). God was in Christ's humanness. We have everything we need for our salvation and right living in His divine nature in us.

The Lord is my shepherd; I lack nothing (Psalm 23:1). Everything we have, everything we are, is a result of God's loving care. We lack nothing in our Lord Jesus Christ.

Lord, thank You for who You are and all that You have done, continue to do, and always will do. In You, we lack nothing. May we align ourselves to Your truth and promises and find our fullness in and through You. Thank You, Jesus! Amen.

OCTOBER 25TH

*For He chose us in Him before the creation of the world
to be holy and blameless in His sight.*

EPHESIANS 1:4

Good morning! Let God have His way! He chose us. We are answering His call. Our salvation is a gift from God. We were chosen by and belong to Him. God's wisdom and power are so great, He is able to know all things because He created all things. *"Before I formed you in the womb, I knew you; before you were born, I set you apart; I appointed you as a prophet to the nations"* (Jeremiah 1:5). God knows us, as He knew Jeremiah, long before we were born. *For you created my inmost being; you knit me together in my mother's womb. I praise You because I am fearfully and wonderfully made; Your works are wonderful [marvelous], I know that full well* (Psalm 139:13-14).

Do we know and believe that we are marvelously made? It is God who created us, knit us together, and God makes no mistakes! *"For I know the plans I have for you," declares the Lord, "plans to prosper you and not to harm you, plans to give you hope and a future"* (Jeremiah 29:11).

God knows us, and He has plans for us. God has a purpose for each and every person, appointing some with very specific work. Whatever we do, we should do for the glory of God, diligently and cheerfully, so we will be effective and fulfill what God intends. The mission for every believer is to love, obey, and serve God and others, trusting God's plan for our lives.

Lord, as Your chosen ones, may we respond to Your calling with obedience and purpose. We are in awe of Your wisdom, power, and perfection. May we respond to Your love with love, praise, and gratitude. Thank You, Jesus! Amen.

OCTOBER 26TH

"Therefore go and make disciples of all nations, baptizing them in the name of the Father and of the Son and of the Holy Spirit, and teaching them to obey everything I have commanded you. And surely I am with you always, to the very end of the age."

MATTHEW 28:19-20

Good morning! We look around and think, "This world is a mess! So many in need!" But what we should be thinking instead is what Jesus commanded us to do: *"Go and make disciples."* We will never be able to satisfy the needs of people because that's not what Jesus commanded us to do. We are sent by Jesus to share Jesus. That is the real need to be met. People need Jesus! *"A person can receive only what is given them from heaven"* (John 3:27). Our main purpose is to point people to Jesus. He is the One who satisfies all our needs.

Every good gift and every perfect gift is from above, coming down from the Father of lights, with whom there is no variation or shadow due to change (James 1:17). The answer is always Jesus. All of life points to Him. Yes, life is a mess. Which is why we need to share the message of Jesus!

For God so loved the world that He gave His one and only Son, that whoever believes in Him shall not perish but have eternal life. For God did not send His Son into the world to condemn the world, but to save the world through Him (John 3:16-17). There is no better and no other way to fully meet the needs of people than to share the message of Jesus. He is our eternal answer.

Lord, thank You for the high price You paid for our sins and to give us new life. May we share the gospel with others with a sacrificial love like Yours, that others would come to receive Your love and believe. Thank You, Jesus! Amen.

OCTOBER 27TH

"'If you can'?" said Jesus. "Everything is possible for one who believes."

MARK 9:23

Good morning! We will not accomplish the work of making disciples from a watered down faith that doesn't stand firm in the knowledge of the power of God. Nothing happens out of our own ability. It is always the power and presence of God that makes the difference. *I can do all things through Christ who strengthens me* (Philippians 4:13).

Why are we so timid and weak? It is because we don't believe. God's Word is truth. Nothing has changed about Him. What God said and did throughout the pages of Scripture and throughout the ages is what He says and does today. *Jesus Christ is the same yesterday, today, and forever* (Hebrews 13:8). God was, is, and always will be good, loving, and all-powerful. He has not changed.

So what about us? Are we going to join the saints of yesteryear, the heroes of faith who stand firm in God's Word, who responded with an unequivocal *"Here am I! Send me"* (Isaiah 6:8)? God uses ordinary, fallible human beings to accomplish His plans through the power of His Holy Spirit. We need only be willing to surrender ourselves to Him in obedience, trust, and belief. There is nothing and no one greater than our God—no one who can accomplish more. What are we waiting for?

Lord, forgive our fears, doubts, and unbelief. Build into us a faith that emulates that of the saints of old. Make us into a people who believe and stand firm on Your Word, ready to go where You lead us. Equip us for Your work. "Yes, Lord, send me!" Thank You, Jesus! Amen.

OCTOBER 28TH

Do not worship any other god, for the Lord
whose name is Jealous [Jehovah-Kanna], is a jealous God.

EXODUS 34:14

Good morning! Is God our last resort? God's jealousy does not come out of a place of insecurity or possessiveness but out of a place of loving protection. God is fully devoted to us. We are His people. *Once you were not a people, but now you are the people of God; once you had not received mercy, but now you have received mercy* (1 Peter 2:10).

Our relationship with God in Christ should be far more important than anything else—our jobs, successes, wealth, or knowledge. We have been chosen by God as His very own and called to be *His ambassadors* (2 Corinthians 5:20), representing Him to others. Nothing should come before God. *Let your heart therefore be wholly devoted to the Lord our God, to walk in His statutes and to keep His commandments, as on this day* (1 Kings 8:61).

There is nowhere or no one we could go to that will ever provide the strength, peace, or love of God. He is all-seeing, all-knowing, all-loving, truly our All in all. Why would we go anywhere or to anyone else before Him? *"But seek first His kingdom and His righteousness, and all these things will be given you as well"* (Matthew 6:33).

We are greatly loved and treasured by God. He has a passionate love for us that says, *"I will never leave you nor forsake you"* (Hebrews 13:5). God is first, for He is the only One true God.

Lord, forgive us our sins when our priorities diminish our understanding of who You are and take away the devotion only You deserve. Thank You for loving us so much that You prepared the way for us to know You and to spend eternity with You. May we always put You first in our lives. Thank You, Jesus! Amen.

OCTOBER 29TH

And I pray that you, being rooted and established in love, may have power, together with all the Lord's holy people, to grasp how wide and long and high and deep is the love of Christ, and to know this love that surpasses knowledge—that you may be filled to the measure of all the fullness of God.

EPHESIANS 3:17-19

Good morning! Most of us have experienced a love for someone so deep and complete that we can't imagine life without them. That love pales in comparison to the love God has for us, His people. God's love is total, reaching every corner of our lives, filling us to completeness with His fullness. Love comes from God and love is God and should compel us to love others. *Dear friends, let us love one another, for love comes from God. Everyone who loves has been born of God and knows God. Whoever does not love does not know God, because God is love. This is how God showed His love among us: He sent His one and only Son into the world that we might live through Him* (1 John 4:7-9).

God is the source of our love. His love is a sacrificial, unconditional love that demonstrates what love truly is. Love is a choice not based on merit or whether it is deserved but born out of His love for us. *Dear friends, since God so loved us, we also ought to love one another* (1 John 4:11).

God's love is divine. It is sacrificial, undeserved, unfailing, unconditional, everlasting, and transformative. There is nothing that compares to the love of God. And it is out of His love for us that we are able to love others.

Lord, thank You for loving us. While we were yet sinners, You loved us enough to send Your Son to save us. May we live transformed lives in and through Your love, that our love for others would emulate Your love shown to us. Thank You, Jesus! Amen.

OCTOBER 30TH

Those who accepted his message were baptized,
and about three thousand were added to their number that day.

ACTS 2:41

Good morning! We've all heard the expression "all in a day's work," but this brings a whole new meaning to that phrase! Just imagine: three thousand new believers added to God's kingdom after Peter preached the Good News about Jesus Christ!

How many people do we know who need to hear about Jesus? *After they prayed, the place where they were meeting was shaken. And they were all filled with the Holy Spirit and spoke the word of God boldly* (Acts 4:31). Are we being bold enough in sharing the gospel with others?

The definition of biblical boldness is "the act of doing the right thing in the face of fear or barriers, with the conviction that God is in control." It's a Spirit-empowered quality that's grounded in forgiveness and humility. Like the disciples, let's start by praying for the power of the Holy Spirit to give us courage and to open our eyes to the people we are to share the gospel with. We won't need to look far. We are surrounded by people who need to hear about Jesus, as close as our own family, neighbors, and co-workers. True boldness is a mark of faith that comes out of being centered on Christ. It requires humility. We may fear not knowing what to do or say. But as Jesus encouraged His disciples, so should we be encouraged by His words to them: *"Do not worry about what to say or how to say it. At that time you will be given what to say, for it will not be you speaking, but the Spirit of your Father speaking through you"* (Matthew 10:19-20).

Make the most out of every opportunity and have confidence that God's Spirit is also with you. Don't wait until it's too late.

Lord, thank You for the privilege of sharing the gospel with others. Increase our boldness and reveal opportunities before us to share. May we always be prepared to share the hope You've given us so others may come to know and believe in You. Thank You, Jesus! Amen.

OCTOBER 31ST

*"The LORD, the LORD, the compassionate and gracious God,
slow to anger, abounding in love and faithfulness."*

Exodus 34:6-7

Good morning! God is compassionate. This is not simply a description of Him, but it is who God is. He defines compassion! *The Lord is gracious and compassionate, slow to anger and rich in love. The Lord is good to all; He has compassion on all He has made* (Psalm 145:8-9).

What about us? Are we compassionate? As followers of Christ, we are to become more like Him, taking on His character in our lives. *Be kind and compassionate to one another, forgiving each other, just as in Christ God forgave you. Follow God's example, therefore, as dearly loved children* (Ephesians 4:32-5:1).

We are God's children, and we should imitate Him. As we come to understand who He is, and we experience His mercy, love, and compassion, we are to share the same with others. *"Be compassionate [merciful], just as your Father is compassionate [merciful]"* (Luke 6:36). We are to follow His example. Be the Jesus in someone else's life today.

Lord, Your mercies are new every morning! May our hearts be softened by Your compassion and love, that we would in turn share with others that which You have given to us. Our desire is to be more like You, growing in our faith and in Your character. Thank You, Jesus! Amen.

November

NOVEMBER 1ST

*The righteous cry out, and the Lord hears them; He delivers them
from all their troubles. The Lord is close to the brokenhearted
and saves those who are crushed in spirit.*

PSALM 34:17–18

Good morning! Often, the most progress made in our spiritual
maturity has been through the doorway of suffering, for if we
will surrender and let God have His way with us, He will draw us
nearer to Himself. Our deliverance may not be the "end of suffering"
we expect. It is the Lord's strength and presence in our lives that
saves us. We want to escape our pain, suffering, hurt, and loss. But
God! He wants to use our trials for His glory to be revealed in and
through them.

God is our source of power, courage, and strength to withstand all
adversity. Is our faith one that will stand firm in the midst of our
adversity? *Blessed is the one who perseveres under trial because, having
stood the test, that person will receive the crown of life that the Lord has
promised to those who love Him* (James 1:12). The *crown of life* is our
eternal reward—living with God forever.

Don't let the devil steal your hope, your joy, and the promises of God.
Our trials are but momentary in relation to the eternity with Christ that
awaits us.

*Lord, thank You that You use all things for our growth and maturity and for
Your glory. We stand firm in faith and on Your promises. You are with us in the
storms of life. Our strength and hope are found in You. Thank You, Jesus!
Amen.*

NOVEMBER 2ND

For all have sinned and fall short of the glory of God, and all are justified freely by His Grace through the redemption that came by Christ Jesus.

ROMANS 3:23–24

Good morning! We don't get to heaven by living a good life. We all have sin and are in need of a Savior. One sin may appear bigger or seen as worse than a lesser one. Fact is, sin is sin. They all separate us from God. It isn't the measure of the magnitude of the sin, it is the fact of sin and not being surrendered and obedient to God. So what are we to do then? Sin can be forgiven, and the way has been made known to us. *God presented Christ as a sacrifice of atonement, through the shedding of His blood—to be received by faith* (Romans 3:25). Christ died in our place: for all mankind to be reconciled to God.

When we sin, we rebel against God and cut ourselves off from His life-giving power. Sin separates us from God. Christ stands in our place, and His death is the sacrifice for our sin. We are pardoned, delivered, and set free. *For God so loved the world that He gave His One and only Son, that whoever believes in Him shall not perish but have eternal life* (John 3:16). Do we believe?

"So if the Son sets you free, you will be free indeed" (John 8:36). We find our freedom from sin and death through God's Son, Jesus Christ.

Lord, thank You for Your incomprehensible sacrifice, the only way for man to be reconciled to You. Your love reached down to save humanity from sin and death. May we not only believe but accept Your gift and live it out so we become a walking testimony of Your gospel. You set the pattern for love. Help us, Lord, to follow You. Thank You, Jesus! Amen.

NOVEMBER 3RD

Therefore God exalted him to the highest place and gave him the name that is above every name, that at the name of Jesus every knee should bow, in heaven and on earth and under the earth, and every tongue acknowledge that Jesus Christ is Lord, to the glory of God the Father.

PHILIPPIANS 2:9–10

Good morning! We've all been given a birth name; some have even two or three. But there is a name given to us with a far deeper meaning that changes our lives forever. We are named Christians, followers of Christ. There is no greater name than this, and it comes with believing in who Jesus is, what He came to do, and in faithful response, putting our belief into action through our changed behavior. It all starts with knowing who He is. *"But what about you?" Jesus asked. "Who do you say that I am?" Simon Peter answered, "You are the Messiah, the Son of the living God"* (Matthew 16:15–16).

With that knowledge, we surrender ourselves to Him, for Jesus is our priority. Knowing Him and bearing the name of Christian requires action and change. *Therefore, if anyone is in Christ, the new creation has come: The old has gone, the new is here!* (2 Corinthians 5:17). We are a *new creation*, actively trying to live according to the teachings and example of Jesus, including love, forgiveness, compassion, and service to others. *For you have been born again, not of perishable seed, but of imperishable, through the living and enduring Word of God* (1 Peter 1:23). With the name of Christian, we are to be *born again* with the ability to love others with spiritually alive hearts. *Now that you have purified yourselves by obeying the truth so that you have sincere love for each other, love each other deeply, from the heart* (1 Peter 1:22). Others will know we bear the name of Christian by our love (John 13:35).

Lord, thank You for Your name, Jesus Christ, and the privilege of bearing the name Christian. May we glorify Your name by our thoughts, words, deeds and draw others to You, loving them as You first loved us. Thank You, Jesus! Amen.

NOVEMBER 4TH

"Repent, then, and turn to God, so that your sins may be wiped out, that times of refreshing may come from the Lord."

ACTS 3:19

Good morning! We cannot justify our sin based on the excuse of what someone else did or said or something that may have happened to us. There is no excuse for sin. We must acknowledge personal sin, repent—speak of it to the Lord—and leave it behind, turn away from it. The key to forgiveness is confession of and turning away from our sin. And then God gives us a better way. *Let us acknowledge the Lord; let us press on to acknowledge Him. As surely as the sun rises, He will appear; He will come to us like winter rains, like spring rains that water the earth* (Hosea 6:3).

We will never receive the benefits and blessings of knowing and following Jesus when we allow or make excuses for sin in our lives. Take seriously the need to bring all things before the Lord in prayer, admitting our disobedience and turning away from it.

"Repent, then, and turn to God, so that your sins may be wiped out, that times of refreshing may come from the Lord, and that he may send the Messiah, who has been appointed for you—even Jesus" (Acts 3:20). Our repentance is followed by God's refreshment, a cleansing and renewed strength that comes from God. Repentance leads to freedom. It can restore broken relationships. We can learn from it and grow in the character of Christ.

Lord, forgive us for our sins. Help us to take inventory of our sin, to not ignore our thoughts, words, and behaviors that don't reflect who You are and what You have taught us. May we quickly repent of the sin that blocks us from our relationship with You and others. Thank You for Your mercy, grace, love, and forgiveness, for cleansing us and setting us free to live with You. Thank You, Jesus! Amen.

NOVEMBER 5TH

"So in everything, do to others what you would have them do to you,
for this sums up the Law and the Prophets."

MATTHEW 7:12

Good morning! Martin Luther said, "It is the duty of every
Christian to be Christ to His neighbor." A distinguishing mark
of humanity is the ability to exhibit loving kindness to one another,
to display compassion in a meaningful way that can make a
difference in another person's life. What a difference there would be
in this world if everyone treated others in the same way they
themselves wanted to be treated!

God commands us to love. First, to *"love the Lord your God with all
your heart and with all your soul and with all your mind"* (Matthew 22:37).
But He doesn't stop there. *"And the second is like it: 'Love your neighbor as
yourself'"* (Matthew 22:39). When we fulfill these two commandments,
we keep all the others.

We are commanded to love and given the description of what love is
and what love is not. *Love is patient, love is kind. It does not envy, it does not
boast, it is not proud. It does not dishonor others, it is not self-seeking, it is not
easily angered, it keeps no record of wrongs. Love does not delight in evil but
rejoices with the truth. It always protects, always trusts, always hopes, always
perseveres* (1 Corinthians 13:4-7).

We are here to make a difference in the lives of others. God has given
us everything we need in and through Christ in us to love others as He
loved us, the way we want to be loved. Let us follow Christ's example.

*Lord, thank You for Your sacrifice that sets us free to love You and others.
Forgive us when we live out of our selfish desires and self-centeredness. May
we daily seek You and live in a way that honors You and brings glory to Your
name. Thank You, Jesus! Amen.*

NOVEMBER 6TH

*For He will command His angels concerning you
to guard you in all your ways; they will lift you up in their hands,
so that you will not strike your foot against a stone.*

PSALM 91:11-12

Good morning! Do you believe in angels? There are mentions of angels visiting man throughout Scripture. Ultimately, it is God who watches over us (Psalm 121:5), but He employs His angels for His works. The Lord has tremendous ability to protect us, and sometimes that protection comes from angels, who may even be in the form of another human. *Do not forget to show hospitality to strangers, for by so doing some people have shown hospitality to angels without knowing it* (Hebrews 13:2).

What excuses do we make for not being willing to open up our homes and lives to others? It takes very little effort for us to show love to others, to make someone feel welcome and valued. You never know when God's hand is in or on that person's visit to us.

God also uses angels to tell messages of His news. *The angel went to her and said, "Greetings, you who are highly favored! The Lord is with you"* (Luke 1:28). What if Mary had dismissed the angel? Could the birth story of Jesus have been different? *"I am the Lord's servant," Mary answered. "May your word to me be fulfilled." Then the angel left her* (Luke 1:38).

Angels are God's messengers. Don't be so quick to dismiss their existence and purpose. *Are not all angels ministering spirits sent to serve those who will inherit salvation?* (Hebrews 1:14). Angels are spiritual beings created by God and under His authority. God has and will continue to use them to minister to and protect believers, proclaim His messages, and execute His judgment. We must be watchful of our response. We wouldn't want to miss God's angelic visitation to us!

Lord, forgive us for being quick to dismiss what we don't understand. Increase our belief in You, who You are, and the things only You can do. Nothing is impossible for You! Thank You for loving us so much that You would surround us with and send Your angels to us. Thank You, Jesus! Amen.

NOVEMBER 7TH

You have searched me, Lord, and you know me. You know when I sit and when I rise; you perceive my thoughts from afar. You discern my going out and my lying down; you are familiar with all my ways.

PSALM 139:1-3

Good morning! Don't think for a moment that no one understands. That is a lie. The only One who needs to understand does! God understands us completely. He knows everything about us. After all, He is the One who created us. And through every circumstance of our lives, He is with us and waits for us to come to Him. *"Call to Me and I will answer you, and tell you great and unsearchable things you do not know"* (Jeremiah 33:3).

Why would we look to anyone but God for understanding? He is ready to answer our prayers, but we must first be willing (and sometimes humbled) to seek Him and ask. We don't need human understanding as much as we need to acknowledge God is our source for everything. He is our strength, and He brings clarity to confusion and order out of chaos. *Before a word is on my tongue you, Lord, know it completely. You hem me in behind and before, and You lay Your hand upon me. Such knowledge is too wonderful for me, too lofty for me to attain"* (Psalm 33:4-6).

God does more than simply understand us. He loves us unconditionally. He protects us, guides us, and knows us completely. *Great is our Lord and mighty in power; His understanding has no limit* (Psalm 147:5). God understands us fully.

Lord, thank You for the truth that we are fully understood by You. May we shift our minds off ourselves and the need for others to understand and fix our thoughts on You. Lord, our desire is to be more like You. May we continue to seek after You, to grow and mature in our faith, and to prioritize understanding You and Your ways over ourselves. Thank You, Jesus! Amen.

NOVEMBER 8TH

"It is written," He said to them, "My house will be a house of prayer; but you have made it a den of thieves."

MATTHEW 21:13 / LUKE 19:46

Good morning! We are the temple of God. What have we brought into His temple that defiles His holy ground? Jesus cleared His temple of the merchants and money changers. *He drove out all who were buying and selling there and overturned the tables of the money changers and the benches of those selling doves* (Matthew 21:12). Jesus' angry reaction was directed at those who were interfering with His people who came to the temple to pray and worship.

Don't you know that you yourselves are God's temple and that God's Spirit dwells in your midst? (1 Corinthians 3:16). Anything that competes with or draws us away from God is not meant to be in His temple. *If anyone destroys God's temple, God will destroy that person; for God's temple is sacred, and you together are that temple* (1 Corinthians 3:17). We, as brothers and sisters in Christ Jesus, are unified to be His temple. We are an assembly of God, gathered together to reach the world for Him. We are accountable to and for each other. God will "drive out" and "overturn" anything that interferes with prayer and worshiping Him.

The temple of God, His church, is not the building. It is His people. We are a holy place, inhabited by God's Spirit, and we need to take care of ourselves spiritually, physically, and mentally. *"Come out from them and be separate, says the Lord. Touch no unclean thing, and I will receive you"* (2 Corinthians 6:17). We are to separate ourselves from the things of this world that lead to sin and defile His temple. Draw near to God through prayer and fellowship with other believers. Resist anything that interferes with God's plan and purpose in your life.

Lord, thank You for loving us so much that You made a way for us to live with You in eternity. Forgive us when we bring into Your temple anything that is not of You, that interferes with our prayer and worship of You. You are holy and just. May we honor You and live obedient to You. Thank You, Jesus! Amen.

NOVEMBER 9TH

If any of you lacks wisdom, you should ask God who gives generously to all without finding fault, and it will be given to you.

JAMES 1:5

Good morning! We have the greatest source of knowledge literally a prayer away and often totally neglect using it. God is so generous to His people, if we would just humble ourselves and go to Him in prayer. God's wisdom is not just head knowledge, like documented facts in an old encyclopedia. No, His wisdom brings direction, clarity, and peace to every situation. Do we trust God? Then take everything to Him in prayer! *Do not be anxious about anything, but in every situation, by prayer and petition, with thanksgiving, present your requests to God* (Philippians 4:6). There is no better resource available to us than God Himself. There is nothing we can't take to God in prayer. There is no source of wisdom that surpasses His.

Do we believe in God's wisdom, His presence, and His love? *But when you ask [pray], you must believe and not doubt, because the one who doubts is like a wave of the sea, blown and tossed by the wind. That person should not expect to receive anything from the Lord* (James 1:6-7). We must pray in confidence of who God is, that He hears and answers our prayers. *In him and through faith in him we may approach God with freedom and confidence* (Ephesians 3:12).

We have the privilege and invitation to take everything to God in prayer. By faith, we can commune directly with God, seek His wisdom, share our burdens, surrender our sin, offer our praise, and experience His presence. What are we waiting for? Simply pray.

Lord, we thank You for Your invitation to bring everything before You in prayer. You welcome us, as Your children, waiting with open arms to receive and hear from us. Thank You, Jesus! Amen.

NOVEMBER 10TH

Come near to God and He will come near to you.

JAMES 4:8

Good morning! In this hectic world of hurried living, take time to slow down with God in His Word and prayer. There is no greater use of our time than time spent with God. He invites us to fellowship with Him so we can be strengthened and renewed for His purpose. We are given clarity and direction for our lives in time spent in His presence. *"I am the vine; you are the branches. If you remain in Me and I in you, you will have much fruit; apart from Me you can do nothing"* (John 15:5).

What is this fruit Jesus speaks of? When we remain attached to the life-giving power of God, He more than just sustains us with life. He empowers us through His Spirit in new life, abundant life. *"If you remain in Me and My words remain in you, ask whatever you wish, and it will be done for you. This is My Father's glory, that you bear much fruit, showing yourselves to be My disciples"* (John 15:7-8).

The only way we are able to live the life God prepared for us is in and through Him. Apart from Him we are unfruitful, lost, distracted, hurried. We find no real purpose other than through Christ. All else is futile and temporary. We glorify God when we are in the right relationship with Him, and we see the results as His Spirit manifests itself in and through our lives.

Lord, You invited us into an intimate relationship with You, to live with You. Amidst the hustle and bustle of this life, may we stay connected to You, the source of life. You chose us to go and bear fruit that will last, to seek You, and to exhibit Your character through Your love as we love You and others. Thank You, Jesus! Amen.

NOVEMBER 11TH

*But when this Priest [Jesus] had offered for all time one sacrifice for sins,
He sat down at the right hand of God, and since that time He waits for His
enemies to be made His footstool. For by one sacrifice
He has made perfect forever those who are being made holy.*

HEBREWS 10:12-14

Good morning! Today we celebrate Veterans Day in honor of and gratitude for those who have served in the military and to acknowledge their sacrifices and dedication. To each veteran, thank you for your service and may God bless you!

As Christ followers, we are called to imitate Jesus, to pursue a life of seeking after Him and becoming more like Him. Christ intentionally came for the sole purpose of being the ultimate sacrifice for our sins. When we believe in Jesus Christ, we are made whole, one with God. Out of His sacrifice, we are invited to believe and enter into a loving relationship that leads to our surrender to Him. We follow His teachings, willing to live in obedience and service. We are given a new freedom, *being made holy*, perfect in God's sight. All because of Christ's sacrifice—His death and resurrection. *Therefore, I urge you, brothers and sisters, in view of God's mercy, to offer your bodies as a living sacrifice, holy and pleasing to God—this is your true and proper worship* (Romans 12:1-2).

Through Christ's sacrifice, we are given the privilege and opportunity to be transformed into His likeness, new creations for His good purposes. Only in Christ Jesus do we find a way! Let us joyfully give ourselves as living sacrifices to Him.

Lord, while we were still sinners, You willingly came and sacrificed Your life for us. We surrender our lives to You in gratitude for Your free gift, the gift of freedom and new life. Lord, we deliberately seek after You, willingly accepting Your guidance and discipline in our lives, that we would continually grow to be more like You and impact lives for Your kingdom. Thank You, Jesus! Amen.

NOVEMBER 12TH

All of you, clothe yourselves with humility toward one another, because
"God opposes the proud but shows favor to the humble."

1 PETER 5:5

Good morning! No one wants to "eat humble pie"! Yet, humility is a character trait God promotes, and for good reason. Humility is not the way of this world we live in where pride, arrogance, and boasting are used for self-promotion. Pride blocks understanding and compassion between generations. Elders frown upon the youth, and youth mock their elders, both thinking they know more than they actually do about the other. But God! He calls us to be humble. *Humble yourselves, therefore, under God's mighty hand, that He may lift you up in due time* (1 Peter 5:6).

God calls us to have more concern for living in a way He desires, to seek His recognition over any earthly position we could acquire or earn. God will bless us in His timing with benefits that far exceed earthly notoriety. *"For those who exalt themselves will be humbled, and those who humble themselves will be exalted"* (Matthew 23:12).

Jesus challenges the norms of society and promotes servanthood. We are to give of ourselves to God and to others. *He has shown you, O mortal, what is good. And what does the Lord require of you? To act justly and to love mercy and to walk humbly with your God* (Micah 6:8). Our hearts must be humble and set on pleasing God, not ourselves or others. French pastor and reformer John Calvin wrote, "Nothing but the pure knowledge of God can teach us humility."

Spend time with God and in His Word. He will teach you His way—the way of humility.

Lord, teach us to be more like You—to be humble, compassionate, loving, and kind. May we be humble in thought, word, and deed, serving You and others out of a joyful heart and spirit that bring honor to You. Thank You, Jesus! Amen.

NOVEMBER 13TH

You, therefore, have no excuse, you who pass judgment on someone else,
for at whatever point you judge another, you are condemning yourself,
because you who pass judgment do the same things.

ROMANS 2:1

Good morning! How quick we are to point a wagging finger at someone else! We are all guilty, at one point or another, of spouting off about something someone else said or did. Paul puts it right out there—*you*—because Paul knows there are no exceptions. There are some who might be less vocal or boisterous with their judgment, but we're all guilty of judging others. *"Why do you look at the speck of sawdust on your brother's eye and pay no attention to the plank in your own eye? You hypocrite, first take the plank out of your own eye, and then you will see clearly to remove the speck from your brother's eye"* (Matthew 7:3, 5).

Most likely, the very things we see wrong in and criticize about others are the very sins we've either struggled with or are currently in the midst of ourselves. *So, if you think you are standing firm, be careful that you don't fall!* (1 Corinthians 10:12). Our judgment or criticism can come back at us.

If our goal and desire is to encourage a brother or sister out of or away from their sin and wrong doings, we must do so through the heart of God. *Therefore, confess your sins to one another and pray for one another, that you may be healed* (James 5:16). We need to remain faithful and in pursuit of what God instructs us to do. *But encourage one another daily, as long as it is called "Today," so that none of you may be hardened by sin's deceitfulness* (Hebrews 3:13). We must be aware of sin in ourselves and encourage others to do the same, but always with love and concern.

Lord, thank You that we can bring our sin before You and find forgiveness.
Forgive us, Lord, when we are critical of and stand in judgment against others.
Help us to be loving, kind, and compassionate toward others, as You are to us.
Thank You, Jesus! Amen.

NOVEMBER 14TH

*Dear children, let us not love with words or speech
but with actions and in truth.*

1 JOHN 3:18

Good morning! What good is love if it's only a spoken word with no action or deed behind it? Love is more than the warm, fuzzy feeling described in a greeting card. It is action, and it produces selfless, sacrificial acts of giving and service. *If one of you says to them, "Go in peace; keep warm and well fed," but does nothing about their physical needs, what good is it?* (James 2:16). Love looks to bring God into every situation and circumstance. We put faith to work. In the same way faith by itself, if it is not accompanied by action, is dead. *Show me your faith without deeds, and I will show you my faith by my deeds* (James 2:17-18).

What if Jesus had come and not followed through on being the sacrifice God sent Him to be? What if He stopped at just speaking about love? But that is not what real love does. *"My command is this: Love each other as I have loved you. Greater love has no one than this: to lay down one's life for one's friends"* (John 15:12-13).

Love is sacrificial. It gives beyond what we feel like giving. Love is listening, caring, doing, and sharing. It's being a solution and aiding in someone else's needs. *"This is My command: Love each other"* (John 15:17). Are we willing to be uncomfortable, to sacrifice ourselves for the comfort of someone else? *"By this everyone will know that you are My disciples, if you love one another"* (John 13:35). Love reveals itself in our actions. It's being willing to be inconvenienced, to go without, to be more concerned about another's welfare than our own. Yes, real love is hard, and that's why it takes faith in Jesus to produce its action. For it is God's power working in and through us that enables us to love like Jesus.

Lord, thank You for loving us so much with a love that sacrificed Your perfection for our sins. Help us, Lord, to love sacrificially, to love in a way that people will come to know You, that they will be drawn to You through Your love in and through us. Thank You, Jesus!

NOVEMBER 15TH

The Lord is good to all; He has compassion on all He has made.

PSALM 145:9

Good morning! For years, I've ended every daily devotional I send out with "God is good, all the time!" Do we believe it? If we believe that to be true, our lives should reflect our belief. When we think of the goodness of God, we can't help but consider how, despite our rebellion and sin, He still loves and cares for us. *But God demonstrates His own love for us in this: While we were still sinners, Christ died for us* (Romans 5:8). This was God's ultimate sign of His goodness, His great love, and compassion. God's goodness is His character. There is no bad or wrong present in God's being or nature. *The Lord is upright; He is my Rock, and there is no wickedness [unrighteousness] in Him* (Psalm 92:15).

Nothing about God ever changes, from creation through eternity. *Do you not know? Have you not heard? The Lord is the everlasting God, the Creator of the ends of the earth. He will not grow tired or weary, and his understanding no one can fathom* (Isaiah 40:28). God's goodness is demonstrated throughout our lives by His deep love for us. His desire is for not one of us to perish but to live abundant lives with Him in eternity. *The Lord is not slow in keeping his promise, as some understand slowness. Instead He is patient with you, not wanting anyone to perish, but everyone to come to repentance* (2 Peter 3:9).

God's mercy is so vast, extending so wide that all are given the opportunity to turn from sin and live changed lives in His goodness. Yes, indeed, "God is good, all the time." May we choose to live in response to His goodness, mercy, and love.

Lord, forgive us for our willful behavior, our sin and rebellion. We praise You for Your constant love for us, that You never change. Your goodness and mercy always remain. May we repent and turn to you, living to bring glory and honor to Your name. Thank You, Jesus! Amen.

NOVEMBER 16TH

As for God, His way is perfect: The Lord's word is flawless;
He shields all who take refuge in Him. For who is God besides the Lord?
And who is the Rock except our God? It is God who arms me
with strength and keeps my way secure.

PSALM 18:30-32

Good morning! November 16th, 1969, our family said our earthly goodbye to my mother. Throughout the years, I've wondered why such a loving, generous, kind Christian woman would be taken up so young (she was only 47) and how different my life might have been had she lived. Today I know and believe that it is exactly the way God would have it.

Billy Graham was quoted as saying, "We don't always understand why God allows some things to happen but 'we live by faith, not by sight' (2 Corinthians 5:7). We also know, 'All things work together for good for those who love the Lord and are called according to his purpose' (Romans 8:28), which means that God is in control of everything and will use it all for our good. God is perfect in every way. God cannot make mistakes. He doesn't change, and He always accomplishes what He sets out to do!"

While I might think I would like to go back and change some choices and decisions I've made in my life, I wouldn't change a thing about where God has me today. It took all of what I've been through to land me here. So, what about you? Are you trusting God for who He is? God is trustworthy. *Trust in the Lord with all your heart and lean not on your own understanding; in all your ways submit to Him, and He will make your paths straight* (Proverbs 3:5-6). The detours in my life's path are where I stopped trusting, following, obeying, and submitting. Choose to surrender to the One who is Sovereign and good, who knows all.

Lord, forgive us for our sin and rebellion. Draw us near to You, as we surrender ourselves to You. Lead and guide us in the way You would have us to go, and may we live in obedience to You and to Your Word. Thank You, Jesus. Amen.

NOVEMBER 17TH

"If you are willing and obedient, you will eat the good of the land.
But if you refuse and rebel, you will be devoured by the sword."
For the mouth of the Lord has spoken.

ISAIAH 1:19–20

Good morning! When we hear the word *obey*, I doubt that adverbs like *joyfully* and *willingly* are the words that first come to our minds! From tantrum-inclined toddlers to feisty know-it-all teenagers and even into our adulthood, we are more inclined toward self-willed disobedience than joyful and willing obedience. God's desire is for us to know Him and trust Him so deeply that obedience becomes our first response to whatever circumstances we find ourselves in. *But if anyone obeys his word, love for God is truly made complete in them. This is how we know we are in him. Whoever claims to live in him must live as Jesus did* (1 John 2:5-6). Obedience is our response to believing in Jesus, to loving God and choosing to live as Christ lived.

Jesus was always obedient to His Father, even unto death. *"Father, if you are willing, take this cup from me; yet not my will, but yours be done"* (Luke 22:42). Jesus confessed His dread of the task before Him but remained obedient to what His Father set before Him to do. Why? Because He loved and trusted His Father.

Do we love God enough to be obedient to Him? *In fact, this is love for God: to keep His commands* (1 John 5:3). To live joyfully and willingly obedient lives to God, we simply need to filter all our thoughts, words, and deeds through this: Are we demonstrating our love for God and our love for others? If the answer is anything but a resounding "yes," we need to pause and rethink.

Lord, forgive our inclination toward the sins of rebellion and disobedience. Reveal in us anything that is not of You, that we may repent of it. Lord, we want to live for You in joyful, willing obedience that pleases You. Father, Your will be done. Thank You, Jesus! Amen.

NOVEMBER 18TH

Do you not know that your bodies are temples of the Holy Spirit,
who is in you, whom you have received from God? You are not your own;
you were bought with a price. Therefore honor God with your bodies.

1 CORINTHIANS 6:19-20

Good morning! There is more to following Christ than simply loving Him, although that is a reasonable place to start. Our love for Him is a starting point that should manifest itself in a life of obedience and service, driven by full surrender, deep admiration, and commitment to His purpose. Christ's death set us free from sin, and our response is a willingness to serve and let God have His way with us in our heart, body, and soul! The price He paid should break our hearts, and our heartbreaks are the doorway God opens up as ways of fellowship with His Son.

I want to know Christ—yes, to know the power of His resurrection and participation in His sufferings, becoming like Him in His death, and so, somehow, attaining to the resurrection of the dead (Philippians 3:10-11).

We must move past a simple love to being united with Christ by fully trusting in Him and experience the power that raised Him from the dead. There is a freedom that comes from believing in Jesus, but it is not the freedom from suffering. We are to be willing to participate not just in the joys of knowing Christ, but also in the struggles, which sometimes means sacrificing or suffering in order to grow in our faith.

Knowing Christ is worth whatever He places in front of us in order that we would honor Him.

Lord, we were bought with Your blood, a price You willingly paid and a sacrifice no one else could have made. Lord, may we be willing to share in Your sufferings so we can know You. Whatever the sacrifice, it is worth it to know You, Lord. May Your glory be made known. Thank You, Jesus! Amen.

NOVEMBER 19TH

Jesus Christ is the same yesterday and today and forever.

HEBREWS 13:8

Good morning! Some 2500 years ago, the Greek philosopher Heraclitus is credited with saying, "There is nothing permanent except change." Much more recently, author, speaker and pastor John C. Maxwell made famous the quote, "Change is inevitable. Growth is optional." Unless we are talking about Jesus, the only One who never changes. He has been and will continue to be the same through all eternity. *"I the Lord do not change"* (Malachi 3:6).

People, on the other hand, are fickle, blown about like fallen leaves. Our trust must be grounded in the One who is trustworthy and unchanging: the Lord our God. He is the One who possesses immortality, whose years never end. After all the troubles of this life, we can rest our feet of faith on the solid ground of truth, trusting God. *Every good and perfect gift is from above, coming down from the Father of the heavenly lights, who does not change like shifting shadows* (James 1:17).

The same attributes of the God of ancient times still hold true—His power, His wisdom, His justice, His truth—all unchanged. What's more, as if we needed anything more, His love for us never changes. *The Lord appeared to him from far away. "I have loved you with an everlasting love; therefore I have continued to extend faithful love to you"* (Jeremiah 31:3 CSB).

God is eager to do what is best for us, if we let Him. He is motivated by a deep and everlasting love. So while we are surrounded by an unstable world that's constantly exploding with change and the resulting turmoil that change causes, our confidence is found in the assurance that the Lord does not change.

Lord, thank You for the blessed assurance we have in knowing You never change. No matter what, You are constant! You love us. You lead and guide us, making a way for us. When we put our hope and trust in You, we begin to change and to grow to be more like You. Thank You, Jesus! Amen.

NOVEMBER 20TH

Do not conform to the pattern of this world, but be transformed by the renewing of your mind. Then you will be able to test and approve what God's will is—His good, pleasing and perfect will.

ROMANS 12:2

Good morning! Have you ever gotten your car stuck in the mud? Your wheels are spinning, the rut is getting deeper, but you're not going anywhere! The same can be true of us in our lives and our spiritual condition. We can find ourselves stuck in the rut of life. The same old ways, complaints, questions, solutions, and conversations are signs of stagnation—being stuck. We stagnate when we choose to stop learning. We get stuck in a rut of "stinking thinking" that leads to old patterns of behavior, and it steals our joy and our soul.

Instead, we must be eager to learn and discover the new treasures God's Word has in store for us. *We all, who with unveiled faces contemplate the Lord's glory, are being transformed into His image with ever-increasing glory, which comes from the Lord, who is the Spirit* (2 Corinthians 3:18).

The truth about Jesus that is shared in the gospel transforms us to become more like Him. *He brought me up out of a horrible pit, out of the miry clay, and set my feet upon a rock* (Psalm 40:2). We are lifted out of despair and set on solid ground. We are given a firm place to stand.

Lord, You are our path out of being stuck in the ruts of this world! Lord, we want to become more like You—transformed into Your likeness. Reveal to us, Lord, the areas of our lives we need to surrender to You in order that we would be set on Your higher ground. Thank You, Jesus! Amen.

NOVEMBER 21ST

*But He said to me, "My grace is sufficient for you,
for my power is made perfect in weakness."*

2 CORINTHIANS 12:9

Good morning! To serve God with any amount of success, to do God's work well and triumphantly, a primary qualification is a sense of our own weakness. If we are marching into life's battles and boasting in our own might—with an "I've got this" attitude—defeat awaits us right around the corner. *"Not by might nor by power, but by My Spirit," says the Lord Almighty* (Zechariah 4:6).

Our world and our culture believe survival and success are built on our own strength, toughness, having an unbending attitude, possibly even a harsh one. But God! It is only through Him, through His Spirit, that anything of lasting value is accomplished. *For it is God who works in you to will and to act in order to fulfill His good purpose* (Philippians 2:13).

Are you tired, discouraged, disappointed, overwhelmed, sick, poor? Take courage in the strength the Lord Himself provides! We must recognize our weakness before Him, and He will give us the victory found in His strength. Our emptiness is just the preparation necessary for us to be filled by His lasting goodness. *"Let anyone who is thirsty come to Me and drink. Whoever believes in Me, as Scripture has said, rivers of living water will flow within them"* (John 7:37-39).

Our being cast down is only the preparation of God's lifting and filling us up!

Thank You, Lord, for Your power made perfect in our weakness by Your strength and provision. Forgive us for our arrogance and prideful thinking and behavior, boasting of our own ability and skill. Lord, we want to serve You in Your Way and in Your strength. Empty us of ourselves and fill us with Your living water. Thank You, Jesus! Amen.

NOVEMBER 22ND

At that time the disciples came to Jesus and asked, "Who, then, is the greatest in the kingdom of heaven?" He called a little child to Him, and placed the child among them. And He said, "Truly I tell you, unless you change and become like little children, you will never enter the kingdom of heaven."

MATTHEW 18:1-3

Good morning! This was a shocking statement during the time at which Jesus spoke them. Children had no say in the choices that impacted their lives; they were powerless. We, too, may question how is this possible, to *change and become like little children?* Like children, we must recognize that we are powerless over the circumstances of our lives.

With humble and sincere hearts, we trust and obey our Heavenly Father. We exchange our self-centeredness and preoccupation with our status for the purposes of God's earthly kingdom. We grow backward in Jesus' direction, away from ourselves. *"He must become greater; I must become less"* (John 3:30).

We are to humbly follow Jesus, to grow and mature to be prepared for earthly kingdom work. Our growth comes from the knowledge in Christ and for the purpose of His glory. *Grow in the grace and knowledge of our Lord and Savior Jesus Christ. To Him be glory both now and forever* (2 Peter 3:18). As we know more about Jesus, we grow in our understanding of what it means to live in relationship with Him. All glory belongs to Jesus!

Lord, You taught Your disciples to take the lowly position of a child, to be childlike, with humble and sincere hearts. Lord, may we seek our place of service in Your earthly kingdom by seeking after You. Our dependence and trust are on You alone. Thank You, Jesus! Amen.

NOVEMBER 23RD

You need to persevere so that when you have done the will of God,
you will receive what He has promised.

HEBREWS 10:36

Good morning! Are you praying for your cross or your burdens to be lifted from you? Instead, pray God gives you strength to endure, to give only what will serve Him most and best. We must persevere through the impossible, the trials that seem as though they're going to break us. Why? Because God will use them for His glory! Trials sift us and grow us.

Stand firm and live a life worthy of Christ. *Whatever happens, conduct yourselves in a manner worthy of the gospel of Christ* (Philippians 1:27). Jesus predicted the disciples would face persecution, and He promised we would have troubles, but there is hope knowing salvation is ours. God will use life's difficulties to build our character, deepen our trust in Him, and increase our confidence about our future and faith. *Not only so, but we also glory in our sufferings, because we know that suffering produces perseverance; perseverance, character; and character, hope. And hope does not put us to shame, because God's love has been poured out into our hearts through the Holy Spirit, who has been given to us* (Romans 5:3).

We can rejoice in our sufferings only when we believe God is using them to build our character and we have put our full trust in His Ways as being good, right, tried, and true. The promise of eternity awaits those who believe and live for God's honor and glory.

Lord, we trust that You will use all things for Your glory. Strengthen us, Lord, that we would mature in character, deepen our trust, and increase our faith. Thank you for opportunities to grow steadfast in You! Thank You, Jesus! Amen.

NOVEMBER 24TH

"But of that day and hour, no one knows, not even the angels in heaven, nor the Son, but only the Father. Take heed, watch and pray; for you do not know when the time is."

MARK 13:32-33

G ood morning! Jesus was always about His Father's business. *"Why were you searching for me?" He asked. "Didn't you know I had to be in My Father's house?"* (Luke 2:49). Jesus was not trying to figure out His calendar or the timing of what needed to be done when. He wasn't rushing around, pushing to get things done, fretting over meeting a deadline. What about us? With all that is currently going on in the world today, where is our focus and what is our concern? Scripture tells us we will not know the day or time of Christ's return. Our business is not to be wasting time speculating about the when, but that we are to be about God's work and preparing, and we are to be ready. *"So you also must be ready, because the Son of Man will come at an hour when you do not expect Him"* (Matthew 24:44).

When we see a need what is our response? Are we truly willing to be the hands and feet of Jesus? *"Truly I tell you, whatever you did for one of the least of these brothers and sisters of Mine, you did for Me"* (Matthew 25:40). The acts of mercy we perform are not dependent on our wealth, ability or intelligence. They are simple acts freely given and freely received. They are the acts of the Father's business, part of the work we must be about, caring for others' needs. Jesus will return. Are we doing His work?

Lord, may we be a people less concerned about the when of Your return and more about doing Your work. Lord, may we love everyone and serve anyone we can, glorifying You by reflecting Your love. All we have is Yours, freely given to us that we in turn would freely give. Your sacrifice for us was much costlier than any sacrifice we will ever know or have to endure. Thank You, Jesus, for loving us! Amen.

NOVEMBER 25TH

Rejoice always, pray continually, give thanks in all circumstances;
for this is God's will for you in Christ Jesus.

1 THESSALONIANS 5:16–18

Good morning! It's officially here: Thanksgiving week, renewing our focus on gratitude (thanks) and generosity (giving). God's Word is filled with examples of the power of gratitude and its resulting act of generosity. Some of the apostle Paul's most well-known verses are focused on gratitude. *Always giving thanks to God the Father for everything, in the name of our Lord Jesus Christ* (Ephesians 5:20). *And be thankful ... singing to God with gratitude in your hearts. And whatever you do, whether in word or deed, do it all in the name of the Lord Jesus, giving thanks to God the Father through him* (Colossians 3:15b, 16b, 17).

Even in suffering, Paul encouraged glorifying God and a grateful heart, and so did James. *Not only so, but we also glory in our sufferings* (Romans 5:3). *Consider it pure joy, my brothers and sisters, whenever you face trials of many kinds* (James 1:2).

But gratitude must have a resulting action. Generosity must be its outcome. No matter what our circumstances, we all have something—and most of us have much—to be grateful for. Let this Thanksgiving season spur us on to an outward generosity from grateful hearts that share the wealth of God's love, His mercy, His grace, and His forgiveness. May each one of us be willing to share the gifts God has richly blessed us with, that we would bless others in His name.[26]

Lord, thank You for Your generous gifts. All we have and all we are come from You. It all belongs to You. May our hearts be filled with thanks and giving, gratitude and generosity! And we'll be sure to give You all the glory, honor, and praise. Thank You, Jesus! Amen.

---

26. Inspired by Pastor Joel Gregory's "Thanks & Giving" Sermon Series, 2023.

NOVEMBER 26TH

For it is by grace you have been saved, through faith—and this is not from
yourselves, it is the gift of God—not by works, so that no one can boast.

EPHESIANS 2:8-9

Good morning! We are all blessed undeservedly! So, let me ask, how are we responding to God's abundant blessings? Are we acknowledging who He is in our lives? Or are we flirting with our pride ("I did this"), our jealousy ("why not me?"), or a multitude of other judgments and dissatisfactions that misappropriately weigh our lives' "success"? The measure of our blessings has very little (if anything at all) to do with earthly treasures.

For just as through the disobedience of the one man the many were made sinners, so also through the obedience of one Man the many will be made righteous (Romans 5:19). God has made us His children! None of us deserves to be His child, and comparing blessings is futile—we are all blessed beyond what we deserve! A grateful heart lives out joy and contentment. A grateful heart opens itself to sharing God's abundant resources with others out of a rich confidence in the Giver's unlimited grace and generosity.

When we are tempted to question our blessings, we must consider who God is and what He has done, is doing, and will continue to do in our lives IF we simply surrender in obedience to Him.

Lord, we can never thank You enough for Your undeserved blessings. May we live out gratitude through extending Your grace and blessings to others. Thank You, Jesus! Amen.

NOVEMBER 27TH

And I am convinced that nothing can ever separate us from God's love.
Neither death nor life, neither angels nor demons, neither our fears for today
nor our worries about tomorrow—not even the powers of hell
can separate us from God's love. No power in the sky above or in the earth
below—indeed, nothing in all creation will ever be able to separate us from
the love of God that is revealed in Christ Jesus our Lord.

ROMANS 8:38-39 NLT

Good morning! Happy Thanksgiving Week! As we move through this season, we each have so much to be grateful for. Yet there are some who are facing this time in the midst of overwhelming trials or circumstances, and some who are painfully aware of a seat or seats that will be empty at the table this year. May we be sensitive to all people, loving, compassionate and kind. May our gratitude be put into action, sharing God's love with anyone and everyone He puts in our lives.

Lord, Your grace is the undeserved, unearned, and the free gift of Your favor and love to us. Your mercy never fails, it is new every morning. Your love is incomprehensible, unconditional and unending. Where would we be if it weren't for who You are in our lives? Thank You, Lord, that in spite of our sin, You loved us enough to come and make a way for us to have a deep, intimate relationship with You. May our hearts be so filled with Your love that we would in turn share with others in need. Thank You for Your many blessings! May we be equally generous with our family, friends, and all those You put in our lives! Thank You, Jesus! Amen!

NOVEMBER 28TH

Rejoice always, pray continually, give thanks in all circumstances;
for this is God's will for you in Christ Jesus.

1 THESSALONIANS 5:16–18

Good morning! A grateful heart is not predicated on perfect circumstances. Wherever we find ourselves—single or married, in sickness or health, happiness or grief, abundance or lack—all our situations give us an opportunity to praise God for His love, grace, and wisdom. We must not be deceived into thinking we could serve God better if our circumstances were different. They are what they are by design and can be used to glorify God. *And we know that in all things God works for the good of those who love Him, who have been called according to his purpose* (Romans 8:28).

This doesn't mean our circumstances are always good. What it does mean is that God is able to turn every circumstance around for our long-range good. God's goal isn't to make us happy but to fulfill His purpose. This Thanksgiving season, I pray we find peace, love, joy, and purpose in Jesus, and that our hearts would overflow with gratitude for who He is, what He has done, and continues to do in our lives. He is worthy to be praised!

Lord, we thank You for all circumstances, not deeming them good or bad but for building in us Your character and a mindset of patience and gracious acceptance, that our lives would bring glory to Your name. Thank You, Jesus! Amen.

NOVEMBER 29TH

He who calls you is faithful, who also will do it.

1 THESSALONIANS 5:24

Good morning! God is faithful! Whatever our circumstances, whatever we are facing, we can trust in God. He is faithful! When we hit a roadblock, a mountain we can't climb, God will make a way. *This is what the Lord says—He who made a way through the sea, a path through the mighty waters ... "I am making a way in the wilderness and streams in the wasteland"* (Isaiah 43:16,19). The issue is never God. The question lies with us and our believing He is who He says He is. *God said to Moses, "I am who I am"* (Exodus 3:14). He is faithful, and He is our defense amidst whatever we are facing. *But the Lord is faithful, and He will strengthen you and protect you from the evil one* (2 Thessalonians 3:3).

Are we willing to surrender ourselves and all our circumstances fully to God? Trusting in His sovereignty? *But blessed is the one who trusts in the Lord, whose confidence is in him* (Jeremiah 17:7). We must not approach God frivolously, in disrespect of who He is and with insincere hearts. Our God is a holy God, worthy of all honor and praise. And He is faithful! Believe in His goodness and His Word!

Lord, we thank You for who You are in our lives—the Lord of lords, King of kings, the Alpha and Omega. There is none other like You! Thank You for loving us so much, that we are called Your children and You are our faithful Father. May our hearts be set on You, fully trusting in You. Thank You, Jesus! Amen.

NOVEMBER 30TH

Jesus Christ is the same yesterday, today, and forever.

HEBREWS 13:8

Good morning! Our lives can be changed in an instant—a doctor's report, an accident, an unexpected financial burden, or a natural disaster. But God never changes, and He is all we'll ever need. Do we believe this to the core of our being? *His divine power has given us everything we need for a godly life through our knowledge of Him who called us by His own glory and goodness* (2 Peter 1:3).

Everything in our world is temporary and can change without warning. God alone is trustworthy and constant. He continually shows us His grace, love, and compassion. All our material possessions and even our life itself may be stripped away, but God is always still present. It is impossible for us to fully grasp or understand!

Oh, the depth of the riches of the wisdom and knowledge of God! Who has known the mind of the Lord? Or who has been His counselor? Who has ever given to God, that God should repay them? For from Him and through Him and for Him are all things. To Him be the glory forever! Amen (Romans 11:33–36).

God's methods and means are far beyond our comprehension. He is not arbitrary. He governs all things—the universe and our lives—in perfect wisdom, justice, and love. Are we trusting in the One who possesses absolute power and wisdom? The One on whom we can and should fully depend? We must trust in Him with everything we have and all that we are.

Lord, You are the source of all things. You are the Power who sustains and rules the world we live in. And You work all things for good and Your glory. Nothing is unexpected to You. Thank You for never changing! Thank You, Jesus! Amen.

December

DECEMBER 1ST

For to us a child is born, to us a son is given,
and the government will be on his shoulders.
And he will be called Wonderful Counselor, Mighty God,
Everlasting Father, Prince of Peace.

ISAIAH 9:6

Good morning and welcome to December! A month filled with preparation and activity. In the midst of all the hustle and bustle, let's remember the real reason behind this season, the Lord Jesus Christ. It was during a time of great darkness that God promised to send a Light who would shine on everyone living in the shadow of death. He is both *Wonderful Counselor* and *Mighty God*.

This message of hope was fulfilled in the birth of Jesus Christ and the establishment of His eternal kingdom. He came to deliver all people from the slavery of sin, to set the captives free. *You will keep in perfect peace those whose minds are steadfast, because they trust in You. Trust in the Lord forever, for the Lord, the Lord Himself, is the Rock eternal* (Isaiah 26:3-4). In the midst of our turmoil, with God we can know perfect peace.

When we are devoted to Him, the real meaning of Christmas lives in and shines through us all year long. Our whole attitude is stable and strong in Christ. With God's unchanging love and mighty power, we are not shaken by the surrounding chaos. Be the Light this season. Keep your thoughts on and your trust in Christ! Share His message of hope and of His great love for all people.

Lord, thank You for this Advent season, the time leading up to the celebration of Christmas. May we remember its true meaning, that You left Your throne in heaven to become flesh in the form of a baby. All that we believe starts here and in believing that You are who You say You are. Thank You, Jesus! Amen.

DECEMBER 2ND

Because of the Lord's great love, we are not consumed, for his compassions never fail. They are new every morning; great is your faithfulness.

LAMENTATIONS 3:22-23

Good morning! When the burdens or sorrows of life weigh us down and leave us struggling to find our footing, we just might be carrying the weight of troubles that are not intended for us to carry alone! Surrender them to God, for He alone is able and invites us to rely on Him. *Indeed, we felt we had received the sentence of death. But this happened that we might not rely on ourselves but on God, who raises the dead* (2 Corinthians 1:9).

Too often we rely on our own skills and resources, when instead, God invites us to realize our powerlessness and to depend on Him. God is our source of power, and we should consistently take refuge in Him. *The Lord is my rock, my fortress and my deliverer; my God is my rock, in whom I take refuge* (Psalm 18:2).

The Lord is our steady anchor, our firm foundation, and He is the hand that keeps us close. When we develop an attitude of reliance on God, we are driven close to Him during challenging times, and we rest in Him during easier times. *God is our refuge and strength, and ever-present help in trouble* (Psalm 46:1). Even during the darkest of times, God is working things for our good and preparing us for eternity with Him.

Thank You, Lord, for Your faithfulness. In easy times and those times that feel as though we are being crushed, You invite us to always find refuge and strength in You. Forgive us, Lord, when we look to ourselves as a source of power rather than relying on You. May we develop a consistent faith that always looks to You, a grateful attitude of dependence and trust. Thank You, Jesus! Amen.

DECEMBER 3RD

But I have calmed and quieted myself; I am like a weaned child with its mother, like a weaned child I am content.

PSALM 131:2

Good morning! Too often we are all about what God can do for us. We seek Him for His provision and care in our lives, or we move about trying to do His work. But we must not neglect our time to simply rest in His presence and find contentment in just being with our Heavenly Father, enjoying His nearness and love. *Come near to God and He will come near to you* (James 4:8).

When we come close to the Lord through prayer or meditation, we can feel His comforting embrace around us, no matter what we are facing. It is in these intimate moments near our Lord that we open ourselves to hear His voice and experience the comfort of His presence.

David wrote, *You make known to me the path of life; You will fill me with joy in Your presence, with eternal pleasures at Your right hand* (Psalm 16:11). Like David, we too can experience the joy of the Lord when we are in God's presence. It is then that we gain confidence in the intimacy of knowing who God is in our lives. He says, *"Be still, and know that I am God; I will be exalted among the nations, I will be exalted in the earth"* (Psalm 46:10).

We need to take time each day to be still before the Lord and exalt Him for who He is—holy, righteous, and good.

Thank You, Lord, for the privilege of calling You Father, of resting in Your presence. Thank You for the peace and joyful contentment found in simply being with You. The knowledge of who You are, that You are always near, and that Your love never ends fills and sustains us. We praise You, Lord, for You are worthy. Thank You, Jesus. Amen.

DECEMBER 4TH

May the God of hope fill you with all joy as you trust in him,
so that you may overflow with hope by the power of the Holy Spirit.

ROMANS 15:13

G ood morning! God is our source of hope, of trust, and of strength. As we put our trust in the God of hope, our faith increases, our hearts are filled with joy and peace, and we experience the power of His Holy Spirit. God is our source of lasting hope—not an earthly hope but a Spirit-powered hope that man cannot achieve on his own. It is a hope that comes through Christ Jesus' power in us through His Holy Spirit.

In His great mercy He has given us new birth into a living hope through the resurrection of Jesus Christ from the dead, and into an inheritance that can never perish, spoil or fade. This inheritance is kept in heaven for you (1 Peter 1:3-4).

We can surrender ourselves to God because He is trustworthy. He knows our hearts and all our needs. He is our place of refuge. *Trust in him at all times, you people; pour out your hearts to him, for God is our refuge* (Psalm 62:8). We can trust in God always, in all circumstances, for He is faithful and good. *The works of his hands are faithful and just; all his precepts are trustworthy* (Psalm 111:7). God is the source of all goodness in truth and justice. He is righteous and worthy of all trust. *Trust in the Lord* (Psalm 4:5). Our hearts are secure in the Lord and He is trustworthy with every detail of our lives.

Lord, we put our hope and trust in You. You are the author and the perfecter of our faith. Lord, may we set our hearts on You, trusting in all that You have planned for our lives. Today, Lord, we surrender all to You, for You are good. Thank You, Jesus! Amen.

DECEMBER 5TH

But test all things. Hold on to what is good. Stay away from every kind of evil.

1 THESSALONIANS 5:21-22

G ood morning! Are you holding on to what is good? Satan is the relentless enemy of good. As early as Adam and Eve, he saw what God had given them was good and he set about to take it away. *"You will not certainly die," the serpent said to the woman. "For God knows that when you eat from it your eyes will be opened, and you will be like God, knowing good and evil"* (Genesis 3:4-5).

Sin entered the world through the devil's lie. Man and woman chose to do what they knew was wrong, choosing themselves over God. The results were disastrous. Nothing has changed. Satan is set on destroying what is good, and we often choose to please ourselves over obeying God. Don't be fooled by the lie that freedom is ours to do whatever we want. So what is our solution?

Scripture tells us that in order to hold on to good, we must abstain from every evil. Evil robs us of the good, of what God intends for us. *For the Lord God is a sun and shield; the Lord bestows favor and honor; no good thing does he withhold from those who walk blameless* (Psalm 84:11).

God is the source of all that is good. He Himself is good. And He withholds nothing that will help us to serve Him. Trust the One from whom all good things come.

Lord, we pray for Your strength to diligently abstain from evil, to hold tightly to what is good. May we stand firm in faith, never taking the good in our life for granted, but putting Your love in our lives to work for Your glory and honor. Thank You, Jesus! Amen.

DECEMBER 6TH

He withdrew about a stone's throw beyond them, knelt down and prayed,
"Father, if you are willing, take this cup from me;
yet not my will, but yours be done.

LUKE 22:41–42, MATTHEW 26:39

Good morning! We can learn much from the character Christ displayed on this earth. He was loving and kind, humble and intentional, never in a hurry, and always aware of others' needs. His prayer spoken alone in anguish in the garden teaches us how to handle our trials and suffering. Jesus exposed His dread of His coming trials. He knew what lay ahead. But He also affirmed His commitment to do His Father's will.

We don't know what lies ahead of us, not even for this day. But God! We know He is with us, He is for us, and He loves us. *What, then, shall we say in response to these things? If God is for us, who can be against us?* (Romans 8:31).

God gave His Son for us so we would have abundant life in Him. He will not withhold anything we need to live our lives for Him. When we fully surrender our will in exchange for His will, we experience victory over sin and death, because His will is that we would abide in Him and be in fellowship with Him. *"Abide in me, and I in you"* (John 15:4 KJV).

We are His children, the sheep of His pasture, and He cares for us. And He has prepared a future place for us with Him. Whatever we are facing today, good or bad, let us join Jesus in praying, "Father, Your will, not mine, be done."

Lord, we don't know what tomorrow will bring. But we believe in Your Word. You sent Your Son to save us, and for that we thank You. We don't understand this world, but we choose to believe in and follow You. May we abandon ourselves to You. Your will be done. Thank You, Jesus! Amen.

DECEMBER 7TH

Day and night your hand was on me, my strength was sapped as in the heat of summer. Then I acknowledged my sin to you and did not cover up my iniquity. I said, "I will confess my transgressions to the Lord." And you forgave the guilt of my sin.

PSALM 32:4–5

Good morning! This season is filled with bright lights and joyful music celebrating the birth of a baby. But for some, the light needs to be shone inward to reveal hidden shame that saps strength and prevents any kind of celebration or peace. If this speaks to us in any way, let's not let it rule our lives any longer. God desires us to walk in the merciful light of His forgiveness. *But if we walk in the light, as he is in the light, we have fellowship with one another, and the blood of Jesus, his Son, purifies us from all sin* (1 John 1:7).

We are called to live according to God's ways, and Jesus is the Light we need. We are cleansed from our sin. Let us acknowledge where we need the power of God's love to work a miracle, to shine His Light in the darkness. *The Light shines in the darkness, and the darkness has not overcome it* (John 1:5).

Jesus—that baby in the manger we celebrate—is the God of our breakthroughs! There is no shadow He won't brighten with His grace, mercy, love, and forgiveness. May this season be the one that includes the gift of being set free from any and all shadows of doubt, guilt, and shame.

Lord, we are so grateful that You came to set us free. You are all we need. Help us to search out the darkness in us, to repent and confess. You, who are holy, will forgive us. In the Light of Your forgiveness, everything is covered in Your mercy and grace. Thank You, Jesus! Amen.

DECEMBER 8TH

So he said to me, "This is the word of the Lord to Zerubbabel:
'Not by might, nor by power, but by my Spirit,' says the Lord Almighty."

ZECHARIAH 4:6

Good morning! We tend to be all about the big and sensational: "super-size, please." But God! It is only through His Spirit that anything of lasting value happens. God uses the insignificant and broken to make big things happen through His power and love. In the story of David and Goliath, David selected five small stones, small and insignificant objects on their own. But coupled with faith in God, they enabled him to accomplish what seemed impossible— to fell the giant. *Reaching into his bag and taking out a stone, he slung it and struck the Philistine on the forehead. The stone sank into his forehead, and he fell facedown on the ground* (1 Samuel 17:49).

With just 300 hundred soldiers against an army of 135,000, God gave victory to Gideon over the Midianites. Do not take God out of the equation of our lives because of what appears to be small or what we consider insignificant. It isn't the number God starts with, it's the abundance He provides. *"Ah, Sovereign Lord, you have made the heavens and the earth by your great power and outstretched arm. Nothing is too hard for you"* (Jeremiah 32:17).

Anything and everything in the hand of God is sufficient. Don't believe the lie that you are not enough! You are a child of God, valued and loved. *Jesus called the children to himself and told his disciples, "For the kingdom of heaven belongs to such as these"* (Matthew 19:14). Sometimes while we are seeking the spectacular displays of God's power, we miss what He's doing in our lives right now.

Lord, teach us to view success as You do, to see You through the eyes of faith, having confidence that You work through the ordinary, often insignificant, to demonstrate Your love and Your power. Nothing is impossible for and in You. Thank You, Jesus! Amen.

DECEMBER 9TH

For God so loved the world that he gave his one and only Son,
that whoever believes in him shall not perish but have eternal life.

JOHN 3:16

Good morning! We're all looking for the perfect gift for our loved ones, when the only gift that really matters is the One God has already given—His Son Jesus. God gave us the perfect Gift when He gave us Jesus! Jesus reflects the Giver, God the Father. *The Son is the radiance of God's glory and the exact representation of his being* (Hebrews 1:3). Jesus Himself said that anyone who had seen Him had seen the Father (John 14:9). The Father's words were spoken from Jesus' lips, and His abundant provision was demonstrated through Jesus' generosity. The Father's great power and love were revealed to us through Jesus!

Jesus gave them this answer: "Very truly I tell you, the Son can do nothing by himself; he can do only what he sees His Father doing, because whatever the Father does the Son also does" (John 5:19). Jesus is the perfect Gift and the perfect reflection of the One Who gave Him. *He is the image of the invisible God, the firstborn over all creation* (Colossians 1:15).

So as you hustle and bustle about, rushing to find the perfect gift, stop and consider sharing the One gift that truly never stops giving— the gift of Jesus and eternal life with Him.

Lord, in this season that is truly meant to celebrate Your birth, may our hearts be set on You and our lives centered on Your Word, the Truth, the only Gift we'll ever really need. It cost You everything yet is freely given to us. Let us be bold in sharing the true "Reason for the Season" to everyone we see! Thank You, Jesus! Amen.

DECEMBER 10TH

But may the righteous be glad and rejoice before God; may they be happy
and joyful. Sing to God, sing praises of his name, extol him
who rides on the clouds; rejoice before him—his name is the Lord.

PSALM 68:3-4

Good morning! Oh, the fullness of joy that can be felt and
expressed through unrestrained worship! Are we responding to
who we are or lifting loud praises to who Jesus Christ is and what
He's done? Why are we okay with shouting so loud at a sporting
event or singing until we're hoarse at a concert, but we stand before
our God barely audible?

I will exalt you, my God the King; I will praise your name for ever and
ever. Every day I will praise you and extol your name forever and ever. Great
is the Lord and most worthy of praise; his greatness no one can fathom
(Psalm 145:1-3). Our victory has been won in Jesus Christ—He is worthy
of great praise! Lift high your voices today! Fill our churches with the
sound of joyful praise and thanksgiving. Worship our King!

Praise the Lord, you His servants; praise the name of the Lord. Let the
name of the Lord be praised, both now and forevermore. From the rising of
the sun to the place where it sets, the name of the Lord is to be praised
(Psalm 113:1-3).

Come, let us adore Him—worship the Lord our God! There is
ALWAYS a reason to praise Him!

Lord, forgive us for our weak and meager voices, our watered down praises.
You are worthy of our praises—loud and strong, a constant stream of voices
singing and praising You. We will give thanks to You for Your unfailing love
and wonderful deeds. Praise be to God! Thank You, Jesus! Amen.

DECEMBER 11TH

Whatever you do, work heartily, as for the Lord and not for men, knowing that from the Lord you will receive the inheritance as your reward. You are serving the Lord Christ.

COLOSSIANS 3:23-24

Good morning! Would our posture at work or maybe in our own homes be different if our assignments came directly from God? Well, actually they do! Wherever we are and whatever we are doing, our response should honor God and be for His glory. Even our drudgery becomes an act of worship or service to God. Our disposition and attitudes are transformed when we submit all we think, do, and say to God. *But just as he who called you is holy, so be holy in all you do; for it is written: "Be holy, because I am holy"* (1 Peter 1:15).

We are to imitate God no matter where we are and in whatever we are doing. Every place and thing is dedicated to Christ. *And whatever you do, whether in word or deed, do it all in the name of the Lord Jesus, giving thanks to God the Father through him* (Colossians 3:17). God's Word tells us that everything should be done in the name of Jesus and that we are at work for His purposes.

We are given twenty-four hours a day to be a mouthpiece for and the hands and feet of Christ. Let's make the best use of our time and energy, doing everything in excellence for Jesus.

Lord, we offer ourselves to You—all of our days and all of our activities. Thank You for the privilege of work and the opportunity to serve You and those You put before us each day. Change the lens of our eyes and hearts to see our lives as a constant discipleship opportunity and an endless offering to You. Thank You, Jesus! Amen.

DECEMBER 12TH

*"For my thoughts are not your thoughts, neither are your ways my ways,"
declares the Lord. "As the heavens are higher than the earth, so are my ways
higher than your ways and my thoughts than your thoughts."*

Isaiah 55:8-9

Good morning! How many times have we audaciously thought, "Lord, what are You doing?" We're so limited in sight and understanding, and yet we question our place and the circumstances facing us. What disrespectful boldness does it take to question our Creator? We aren't meant to understand. We are to have faith, to trust, to know that He is God and He is good. God is perfect, holy, and sinless. *He committed no sin, and no deceit was found in his mouth* (1 Peter 2:22). He was and still is totally misunderstood by man's reasoning. Yet He loves us and made a way for us. *But you know that he appeared so that he might take away our sins. And in him is no sin. No one who lives in him keeps on sinning* (1 John 3:5-6).

I don't know your circumstances, but God does. And He knows far beyond what we can see or know. Continue on in Him, trusting in His righteousness. *See what great love the Father has lavished on us, that we should be called children of God! And that is what we are!* (1 John 3:1).

Look up, shift your eyes to Him and be encouraged by His Word and His promises. He is our answer to all things.

Lord, forgive us for our sins and doubts and the times we fall short of Your glory. You intend good things for our lives, and we know, Lord, that You are the only answer we need. You are the Giver of Life, and we are victorious only by Your work in and through us. We thank You, Jesus! Amen.

DECEMBER 13TH

"You will seek me and find me when you search for me with all your heart."

JEREMIAH 29:13

Good morning! How many times do we speak of "seeking God's will" as if He's hidden it from us and all of humanity? As if He's lost. This just isn't so! It is more likely that we are simply unaware of God's presence because we are too aware of ourselves and the world surrounding us. We are searching after the wrong things. *"But seek first His kingdom and His righteousness, and all these things will be given to you as well"* (Matthew 6:33).

God isn't hiding from us, but we might be walking around with a divided attention that interferes with our spiritual concentration. *Teach me your way, O Lord, that I may rely on your faithfulness; give me an undivided heart, that I may fear your name* (Psalm 86:11).

We are to have a God-centered purpose in our lives, that our awareness toward Him would increase and our hearts would be fully His. Are we listening for what God's desire is for us and responding to what He is prompting us to do? We need to follow the example Jesus set for us when He walked this earth always in concert with God the Father. *"Very truly I tell you, the Son can do nothing by himself; he can do only what he sees his Father doing, because whatever the Father does the Son also does"* (John 5:19).

When our spiritual eyes are pure and our hearts are centered on Him, we will be amazed by all God will reveal to us.

Thank You, Lord, that You are not hidden or lost from us. Help us, Lord, to seek You with our whole hearts, fully surrendering our lives to You. May we pursue You with passion and fervor, eager to be doers of Your Word, that our lives would be pleasing to You and dedicated to the work You have planned for us. Thank You, Jesus! Amen.

DECEMBER 14TH

Humble yourselves, therefore, under God's mighty hand,
that he may lift you up in due time.

1 PETER 5:6

Good morning! Self-sufficiency is a lie that blocks us from fully experiencing God's love. Self-sufficiency leads us to worry about our position and status, hoping for recognition and advancement, depending on ourselves for everything (and believing we are capable of fulfillment on our own). But God! He alone is the only true source of all that we need. *"For in him we live and move and have our being"* (Acts 17:28).

God's way of living contradicts our world's way. To live for God, we must be ready to say and do things strange and contrary to the world. It's not all about us and self-sufficiency. *"Blessed are the poor in spirit, for theirs is the kingdom of God"* (Matthew 5:3). We give when others take; we love when others hate; we help when others abuse or neglect. We give up individual rights in order to serve others and humble ourselves in obedience to God's will and way. *And God is able to bless you abundantly, so that in all things at all times, having all that you need [all sufficiency], you will abound in every good work* (2 Corinthians 9:8).

God is able and willing to bless us. He will lift us up in due time. Often, those who do not have are the ones who know and understand most the generosity of God. One day, we will receive everything God has prepared for us in our heavenly home.

Lord, may we rely on and be obedient to You. You are our Provider, and You show us the Way we should live. Without You, we are lost, and we are nothing. It is not for us to hold life or the world together but to surrender ourselves to You for Your will to be done. Thank You, Jesus! Amen.

DECEMBER 15TH

Do your best to present yourself to God as one approved, a worker who does not need to be ashamed and who correctly handles the word of truth.

2 TIMOTHY 2:15

Good morning! Recently, I heard a teaching on knowing and applying God's Word to how we live our everyday lives. Paul is urging Timothy to *"Do your best."* How are we doing at applying God's Word in and through our lives? Just as we aim to perform well in our occupations and workplaces, and to meet or exceed expectations, we should view handling God's Word similarly. *Your Word is a lamp for my feet, a light on my path* (Psalm 119:105).

God's Word illuminates the direction He would have us to go, and we are to give ourselves spiritual checkups to measure our progress in following His Word. *Examine yourselves to see whether you are in the faith; test yourselves. Do you not realize that Christ Jesus is in you—unless, of course, you fail the test?* (2 Corinthians 13:5-6). God will examine our lives for what kind of workers we have been for Him. We must study His Word and know it—know what it says so we can be good workers, not ashamed, who correctly handle the Word of Truth.

We should be building our lives on His Word and how we live it out. When judgment comes (and it will), let us be people who have consistently and diligently studied and lived out the Word of God.

Lord, may we "show ourselves approved" by our study, knowledge, and outpouring of Your Word in our lives. Our true purpose for living is to walk in intimate fellowship with You and share Your Word—what it says and who You are—with others. Thank You, Lord, for the privilege of knowing and living with and for You. Thank You, Jesus! Amen.

DECEMBER 16TH

... So that, having been justified by His grace, we might become heirs having the hope of eternal life. This is a trustworthy saying. And I want you to stress these things, so that those who have trusted in God may be careful to devote themselves to doing what is good. These things are excellent and profitable for everyone.

TITUS 3:7-8

Good morning! We are works in progress until the day we die. We are saved by grace and Christ's sacrifice. Our good works weren't required, and they won't make God love us more. They are true indications of our faith in Christ, our love for Him, and what we were created to do. *For by grace you have been saved through faith, and that not of yourselves; it is the gift of God, not of works, lest anyone should boast. For we are his workmanship, created in Christ Jesus for good works, which God prepared beforehand, that we should walk in them* (Ephesians 2:8-10).

When we are disciples of Jesus, we understand good works are faithful service, acts of charity, and involvement in helping to fulfill the needs of others. Everyone who is a Christian should be involved. Service is not optional. We subject ourselves to God fashioning us through His work for others, vessels of His love, mercy, grace, and kindness. We take the words of God and actively build them into our lives as a strong foundation for living (Matthew 7:24).

Lord, may we build Your Truth into our lives, actively pursuing You and serving others. There are no shortcuts to spiritual maturity. It comes only through surrendering our lives to You in obedience and hard work. Lord, may we do what You call us to do until the day You call us home. Thank You, Jesus! Amen.

DECEMBER 17TH

The steadfast love of the Lord never ceases; his mercies never come to an end; they are new every morning; great is your faithfulness.

LAMENTATIONS 3:22–23 ESV

Good morning! Today is a new day. Don't bring in yesterday's problems and troubles or worry about the cares of tomorrow. Rejoice in this day and the newness God has set before us. *The Lord has done it this very day; let us rejoice and be glad* (Psalm 118:24). God's promises are true, and His faithfulness gives us confidence in each new day dawning. *I say to myself, "The Lord is my portion; therefore I will wait for him"* (Lamentations 3:24).

God restores and renews, and He keeps His promises for today and the future. Don't miss the wonder of every morning opening to a new day filled with God's mercies and love. Remember who you are and whose you are!

See what great love the Father has lavished on us, that we should be called children of God! And that is what we are! (1 John 3:1). We are children of God, the most high King! We are chosen and set apart to be clothed in the character of Christ. *Therefore, as God's chosen people, holy and dearly loved, clothe yourselves with compassion, kindness, humility, gentleness, and patience* (Colossians 3:12).

Let us start and end our days with the Lord and give Him everything in between. It's going to be a "good God Almighty" kind of day!

Thank You, Lord, for another new day that You have made. We will rejoice and be glad in it. Yesterday is gone; tomorrow is not yet come. We choose to live in this day, to the fullest in and for You. There is nothing that will keep us from loving and living for You. Thank You, Jesus! Amen.

DECEMBER 18TH

May God himself, the God of peace, sanctify you through and through.
May your whole spirit, soul and body be kept blameless
at the coming of our Lord Jesus Christ.

1 THESSALONIANS 5:23

G ood morning! Is God in control of our lives? Have we fully surrendered to Him? God requires all of us, our entire being and everything about us. There are no boundaries that God stands outside of when it comes to the lives of His people. He is to be the Lord of every aspect of our lives, and He wants to be known to us. We find His peace through fully surrendering to and trusting in our Savior.

The one who calls you is faithful, and he will do it (1 Thessalonians 5:24). God set us apart from the world to be holy and righteous in Him. As we grow in our faith, leading a life that honors God, we become more like Him, conforming to His teachings. In our own strength, we would fail, but He is faithful, and He never fails.

God will work His power through those He chooses who know Him. In union with Christ Jesus and through His Spirit, we are made complete. *And to know this love [of Christ] that surpasses knowledge—that you may be filled to the measure of all the fullness of God* (Ephesians 3:19).

God must be the Lord in every aspect of our lives as we are filled with His love moving in our thoughts and deeds.

Thank You, Lord, for how You work in every aspect of our lives. We pray, Lord, to know You more, that as we nurture our relationship with You in our lives, we will grow in our spiritual maturity by Your power. We are grateful for the privilege of walking with and knowing You. Thank You, Jesus. Amen.

DECEMBER 19TH

Live such good lives among the pagans that, though they accuse you of doing wrong, they may see your good deeds and glorify God on the day he visits us.

1 PETER 2:12

Good morning! Are we living out our faith in a manner that glorifies God and is drawing others to Jesus? We live in a society filled with unbelievers or those who have never been introduced to Christ. Many are living an idolatrous existence distracted from God by worldly things and measures. Time, money, and energy are wasted on temporary possessions, pleasures, and careers.

Dear children, keep yourselves from idols (1 John 5:21). Anything we regard as equal to or greater than God, that we rely on or go to in His place, taking us away from Him, is an idol.

God wants us to be an example to those who have no hope, who are living without the love of Jesus. *"I have set an example that you should do as I have done for you"* (John 13:15). Jesus set the ultimate example of leading in love and service, putting the needs of others before Himself.

We are to be an encouragement to those around us, sharing Christ's love, that they might come to believe. *"In the same way, let your light shine before others, that they may see your good deeds and glorify your Father in heaven"* (Matthew 5:16). Actions speak louder than words. We must demonstrate our faith by living out the abundant life God has given us, sharing the loving kindness of Christ as He works in and through us to draw others to Himself. If we make no effort to impact others and the world around us, we are not doing what God has called us to do.

Lord, may our focus be directed to You, to serving You by loving others, so the difference You've produced in our lives would speak loudly and draw others to You and the abundant life You offer. Lord, may we always be eager to share who You are with those who desperately need You. Thank You, Jesus! Amen.

DECEMBER 20TH

Praise be to the God and Father of our Lord Jesus Christ,
the Father of compassion and the God of all comfort, who comforts us
in all our troubles, so that we can comfort those in any trouble
with the comfort we ourselves receive from God.

2 CORINTHIANS 1:3

Good morning! Many people are hurting, going through intensely difficult and challenging circumstances. Are we being an encouragement to them by demonstrating the love of Christ Jesus? We have all experienced moments in our lives when we were overwhelmed, afraid, exhausted, and simply did not know how we were going to continue or make it through. Our only answer is Jesus! And sometimes it is another person who reminds us of this truth. They bring Jesus to us in human form. Be that person to another in need today. *"The King will reply, 'Truly I tell you, whatever you did for one of the least of these brothers and sisters of mine, you did for me'"* (Matthew 25:40).

We won't need to look far. There are many struggling through this time of year, preferring it would just be over. Make their Christmas bright by bringing the Light of Christ to them, illuminating their hearts with His love. Simple gestures like a hug, a prayer, a conversation, a plate of cookies, a meal, a shared verse, an invitation to visit—the list is endless. Don't sit idly by, hoping they'll "get over it." Surround them with the love and joy of the Lord.

Lord, it grieves us to see so many lost and hurting people, particularly during a season when we are rejoicing in the celebration of Your birth. Open our eyes to see and our hearts to love those who are particularly in need of Your love, hope, strength, and peace. Show us how and give us the capacity to love well, to truly give them hope, not just to sustain, but to find victory in this life in and through You! Thank You, Jesus! Amen.

DECEMBER 21ST

The one who calls you is faithful, and he will do it.

1 THESSALONIANS 5:24

Good morning! God is faithful. God's faithfulness is secure, unchanging, and demonstrated by His power in and around us. He is faithful to deliver, heal, set free, bless, and protect us through His omnipotence. There is no power on earth greater than the Almighty God who is in control of our lives. *But the Lord is faithful, and he will strengthen you and protect you from the evil one* (2 Thessalonians 3:3).

But what about us? Are we faithful? Our faithfulness is a reflection of our relationship with God. *Only fear the Lord and serve him faithfully with all your heart. For consider what great things he has done for you* (1 Samuel 12:24 ESV). Our faithfulness to God means trusting in Him and loving Him through all circumstances. Our faithfulness shows how we strive to honor God in all aspects of our lives, including our thoughts, words, and actions. *Now it is required that those who have been given a trust must prove faithful* (1 Corinthians 4:2).

God presents us with needs and opportunities that challenge us, but we must be faithful to Him and do what is right. *Let love and faithfulness never leave you; bind them around your neck, write them on the tablet of your heart. Then you will win favor and a good name in the sight of God and man* (Proverbs 3:3-4).

It is through faithfulness that we demonstrate our love for God and our desire to walk in His ways.

Lord, may we faithfully seek after You and honor You in thought, word, and deed. Just as You are faithful in all things, Lord, may we be ever faithful in response to You and in pursuit of others for Your kingdom. Thank You, Jesus! Amen.

DECEMBER 22ND

And there were shepherds living out in the fields nearby, keeping watch over their flocks at night. An angel of the Lord appeared to them, and the glory of the Lord shone around them, and they were terrified.
But the angel said to them, "Do not be afraid. I bring you good news that will cause great joy for all the people. Today in the town of David a Savior has been born to you; He is the Messiah, the Lord.
This will be a sign to you: you will find a baby wrapped in cloths and lying in a manger. Suddenly a great company of the heavenly host appeared with the angel, praising God and saying, "Glory to God in the highest heaven, and on earth peace to those on whom His favor rests."

LUKE 2:8-14

Good morning! As we draw near to Christmas and a time of family gatherings with gifts being exchanged, we have a unique opportunity to share the gospel with family and friends. It's not about the presents but His Presence! We celebrate Christ's birth— His first coming. If we don't get that right, how can we be prepared for His second coming? And that is what Christmas is all about! Just as Linus dropped his security blanket in the 1965 TV movie *A Charlie Brown Christmas*, I pray we release all our fears and find security in something—someONE—so much greater than ourselves. May this Christmas season be one that is filled with the celebration and love of Jesus!

Thank You, Lord, for becoming man in the form of a baby, to rescue us and set us free for all eternity. Lord, prepare us, our hearts and minds. May we repent and return to You, wholly surrendered and obedient to You. And may this be the Christmas season for many to boldly share the Good News of who You are and that You are coming back again! Thank You, Jesus! Amen.

DECEMBER 23RD

And Jesus grew in wisdom and stature, and in favor with God and man.

LUKE 2:52

Good morning! We can learn so much about our own spiritual journey by studying the earthly life of Jesus. The Bible doesn't offer us details of Jesus' teen or young adult life, but Luke tells us that even Jesus experienced a time of learning and maturing . Although Jesus was certainly unique, He still had to go through childhood and adolescence, to grow physically and mentally. A full human life was part of Jesus' time on earth. But Jesus also grew in His relationship with His Heavenly Father, and He continued to please Him in obedience to the calling in which He was sent.

There is nothing wrong with spiritual immaturity as a new believer, but we are intended to increase in knowledge and faith. *For this very reason, make every effort to add to your faith goodness; and to goodness, knowledge; and to knowledge, self-control; and to self-control, perseverance; and to perseverance, godliness; and to godliness, mutual affection; and to mutual affection, love. For if you possess these qualities in increasing measure, they will keep you from being ineffective and unproductive in your knowledge of our Lord Jesus Christ* (2 Peter 1:5-8).

Faith must be more than an initial belief in certain facts. It must result in action, in growth in Christian character, and the practice of moral discipline. Peter listed several of faith's actions that require intentional focus and work and that are a continual part of our Christian life to grow us and mature us for God's good purposes.

Lord, thank You for the responsibility to learn and grow more like You every day. Thank You for empowering and enabling us. Lord, evaluate our spiritual maturity and reveal to us our weaknesses, where we fall short of what You desire for and of us. May we never settle for anything less than a fully developed relationship with You. Thank You, Jesus! Amen.

DECEMBER 24TH

"Glory to God in the highest heaven,
and on earth peace to those on whom his favor rests."

LUKE 2:14

Good morning! It's still dark outside and quiet in the house. My thoughts have wandered to what it must have been like for those *shepherds living out in the fields* (Luke 2:8) that first Christmas. They were terrified! The very angels of God invited them to greet the Lamb of God—now that's a birth announcement! Their fear quickly turned to joy—and their response was to hurry to see the baby and then to spread the word.

What is our response to the message of Christmas this year? If there is anything that should cause us to respond in joy, praise, and worship, it is the birth of *"the Messiah, the Lord"* (Luke 2:11). Just as the wise men, upon finding Jesus, *bowed down and worshiped him* (Matthew 2:11), let us honor Him for who He is—*He was named Jesus, the name the angel had given him before he was conceived* (Luke 2:21).

The angels' song that first Christmas has inspired composers for over 2,000 years! Let it move us to praise and worship the Savior— Jesus—Messiah—Immanuel! *"Glory to God in the highest heaven, and on earth peace to those on whom his favor rests"* (Luke 2:14).

Lord, we pause this Christmas season to meditate on Your Word, to respond with urgency and passion for what it says, for who You are, and all that You have done and continue to do in our lives. Lord, may we be among those who hurry to seek You and share the Good News—Jesus Christ is born! You came to save us, lost and broken sinners. We praise and worship You, our Savior and King! Hallelujah! Thank You, Jesus! Amen.

DECEMBER 25TH

For to us a child is born, to us a son is given, and the government will be
on his shoulders. And he will be called Wonderful Counselor,
Mighty God, Everlasting Father, Prince of Peace.

ISAIAH 9:6

Good Morning! And Merry Christmas! The birth of a baby over 2,000 years ago is still celebrated as if He were born this very day. The circumstances around this baby were like none other before Him and none other ever again. *This is how the birth of Jesus the Messiah came about (Matthew 1:18). All this took place to fulfill what the Lord has said through the prophet: "The virgin will conceive and give birth to a son, and they will call him Immanuel" (which means "God with us") (Matthew 1:22).*

This baby was conceived and born to a virgin, prophesied hundreds of years prior to His birth. Angels appeared to tell of the baby's coming and announce His birth. A new star appeared in the sky. The location of His birth (Bethlehem) was foretold. His life and death were prophesied. He was born a man but was God. Immanuel—God with us!

Our Savior, though truly a man, was by His human nature the Holy One of God. He is truly the only gift we will ever need and should be the only gift we desire: the gift of God's Son, Jesus!

Share the gift of Jesus! The gift that never stops giving!

Lord, we thank You! We praise You and glorify You! You are Immanuel! The Majestic One! All we ever need. We celebrate Your birth, Your first coming to this earth, to save us in a way no one else could. And we await Your return. May we be all about Your business and may we also be prepared, faithful, and true! Thank You, Jesus! Amen.

DECEMBER 26TH

"For nothing is impossible with God."

LUKE 1:37

Good morning! Are we living in full realization and belief that God is God? A power-packed verse that we reject by disputing it with comments like "But I don't think He'll do that for me." Why not? God can perform miracles. *You are the God who performs miracles; you display your power among the peoples* (Psalm 77:14). And if we truly believe *"nothing is impossible for God,"* why do we exclude that belief from our own lives?

What if Mary had not believed what the Archangel Gabriel told her? What if she had said, "No, thank you"?

God desires to perform His miraculous works through His people. *We have different gifts, according to the grace given to each of us* (Romans 12:6). We in turn must believe. *Jesus answered, "The work of God is this: to believe in the one he has sent"* (John 6:29).

We must be prepared by studying His Word and knowing the signs. *For everything that was written in the past was written to teach us, so that through the endurance taught in the Scriptures and the encouragement they provide we might have hope* (Romans 15:4).

We must be in relationship with the One for whom nothing is impossible. As we near the close of another year, let us take time to reflect back over God's miracles in our own lives and others we know. Prayerfully consider the changes necessary to grow deeper in walking with Jesus and to join Him in His miraculous works in and through our lives.

Lord, remove from us any doubt or unbelief we have. Continue to work in and through us, as You choose. Show us, teach us, grow and mature us, Lord, that we would be faithful kingdom workers for Your glory to be made known. We are here solely for one purpose: to magnify and worship You. Thank You, Jesus! Amen.

DECEMBER 27TH

Search me, O God, and know my heart; test me and know my anxious thoughts. See if there is any offensive [wicked] way in me, and lead me in the way everlasting.

PSALM 139:23–24

Good morning! As we come to the close of yet another year, let us take time to reflect on what God has done and where we've fallen short. If we are to continue to grow in our faith, we must be willing to examine ourselves and invite God to reveal our sins and to correct us. In asking God to search us, we are inviting Him also to open our hearts so we might receive the conviction of His Spirit. We are saying, "Point out anything in us that offends You, and we will listen to You!"

The Lord knows everything about us. Nothing can be hidden from Him, and we cannot escape Him. He knit us together in our mother's womb (Psalm 139:13); He will never leave or forsake us (Hebrews 13:5); nothing will be able to separate us from His love (Romans 8:38–39).

His desire is for us to have a deep, abiding relationship with Him, that we would one day be with Him in eternity. Are we living surrendered lives in obedience to His Word and with His purpose as our goal? *I eagerly expect and hope that I will in no way be ashamed, but will have sufficient courage so that now as always Christ will be exalted in my body, whether by life or death* (Philippians 1:20). Like Paul, our life view must be from an eternal perspective—to live means to develop eternal values, to live for, become more like, and to speak boldly for Christ.

Lord, teach us and show us. Reveal to us any sin, evil, or wickedness that is preventing us from being the people You designed and created us to be. Lord, we want to be wholly Yours, instruments of Your love and peace, Your Light in the darkness. Examine us, Lord, that we might be cleansed of unrighteousness for Your Name's sake. Thank You, Jesus! Amen.

DECEMBER 28TH

Jesus said, "Truly I tell you, unless you change and become like little children, you will never enter the kingdom of heaven."

MATTHEW 18:2-3

Good morning! What is the barrier that blocks us from surrendering our whole lives to God? Our time and our finances are often at the root of our stubbornness. Any time we say the words, "I won't," we are a hindrance to our own spiritual life. Oh, how self-centered and delusional we can be! What childishness are we struggling with? Do we really believe we know more, can provide better, accomplish more than our Lord? We become so preoccupied with our earthly "kingdoms" that we lose our eternal perspective.

It is so difficult for adults to identify with children—but God! That's what He tells us to do! *"For my thoughts are not your thoughts, neither are your ways my ways," declares the Lord. "As the heavens are higher than the earth, so are my ways higher than your ways and my thoughts than your thoughts"* (Isaiah 55:8-9).

We are weak and dependent, with no status or influence without our Lord Jesus Christ in and directing our lives. He is the power working in us to live and to love. We must continually bring our natural lives to the spiritual through the Spirit of God in us. We must remove our prideful ways, humble ourselves, and submit fully to the Lord.

God sees and thinks differently from us because He knows ALL! He has the full picture, all the details. As we make plans for this upcoming year, let's start by surrendering our all to Him who knows THE plan—His plan—for our lives.

Thank You, Lord, that You are in control of all things. We surrender our lives to You, to guide us in the way You would have us to go. We trust in Your plan for our lives, for You have a purpose in mind for each one of us, for Your kingdom and Your glory. Thank You, Jesus! Amen.

DECEMBER 29TH

Jesus said to him, "I am the way, and the truth, and the life.
No one comes to the Father except through me."

JOHN 14:6

G ood morning! As we reflect on this year and consider the year
ahead, consider how we would answer Jesus' question: *"What do*
you think about the Messiah?" (Matthew 22:42). Here's the thing:
Without Jesus, our lives are meaningless and directionless. We can
make our plans and negotiate our way through life, but without Jesus
as our Savior, it is all for naught—worthless. Everything we are
looking for and everything we need can be found in Him. All of our
questions can be answered by Him.

"You do not want to leave too, do you?" Jesus asked the Twelve. Simon
Peter answered Him, "Lord, to whom shall we go? You have the words of
eternal life. We have come to believe and to know that you are the Holy One of
God" (John 6:67-69).

If we are looking to the world or counting on ourselves for the
answers we seek, we will be sorely mistaken and lost. *Then Jesus declared,*
"I am the bread of life. Whoever comes to me will never go hungry, and
whoever believes in me will never be thirsty. For my Father's will is that
everyone who looks to the Son and believes in him shall have eternal life, and
I will raise them up at the last day" (John 6:35, 40).

Jesus is our source of spiritual nourishment and eternal life. Anyone
who believes in Him will find abundant and everlasting life.

Lord, as another year ends and we get ready to start a new year, may we have
a renewed fervor and passion for knowing You. May the time we spend with
You increase as we go deeper in Your Word and a more intimate relationship
with You. Teach us Your Ways and lead us in Your Truth, that we may have
abundant and everlasting life with You. Thank You, Jesus! Amen.

DECEMBER 30TH

Not that I have already obtained all this, or have already arrived at my goal,
but I press on to take hold of that for which Christ Jesus took hold of me.

PHILIPPIANS 3:12

Good morning! There is always much to consider about our faith, but certain seasons increase the likelihood of our seriousness. The New Year dawning is one of those times. But God! Let this year be different—more meaningful, life-changing. Our goal, like Paul's, must be to know Jesus Christ, to be like Christ, and to be all Christ has in mind for us to be. This goal should be our primary focus and absorb most of our energy. What good is it for us to attend church every Sunday to listen to a message we never allow to have any impact on our lives whatsoever? Or worse yet, never hear, listen to, or study God's Word?

I press on toward the goal to win the prize for which God has called me heavenward in Christ Jesus (Philippians 3:14). We should not let anything take our eyes off our goal—knowing Christ. With single-minded purpose, we lay aside everything harmful and anything that distracts us from being effective Christians.

Because of our hope in Christ, we can let go of our past guilt and look forward to what God will help us become. But we must take action—be intentional—to grow in the knowledge of God by concentrating on our relationship with Him. Now is the time to move forward in our life of faith and obedience, surrendering our all to Him.

Lord, may we not procrastinate one minute longer but fully commit our lives to knowing and honoring You. Reveal to us the things that block us from knowing You more. Teach us and grow us, Lord, that one day we will meet You face to face and hear the precious words, "Well done My good and faithful servant" (Matthew 25:23). Thank You, Jesus! Amen.

DECEMBER 31ST

On the last day, that great day of the feast, Jesus stood and cried out, saying,
"If anyone thirsts, let him come to me and drink."

JOHN 7:37

Good morning! It's New Year's Eve morning, as another year is about to end. Many will spend it celebrating and waiting for the ball to drop, marking the entrance of another new year. We mustn't let it pass without setting apart time for solitary thought, and if the need of deep repentance is felt in us, that is good, for He is waiting for us to return. Let us renew our faith in Jesus and live a life committed to Him.

Don't end this year in a state of unforgiveness before God. Don't allow the celebration of the New Year to be met and surrounded by a joyless spirit. Jesus is our fountain of hope! He came to save us from our sin and darkness. Oh, what a wonderful invitation and gift He brings!

"We implore you," the apostle Paul said, *"as though God were making his appeal through us"* (2 Corinthians 5:20). Come before the Lord and be reconciled to Him. What are we waiting for? *Taste and see that the Lord is good; blessed is the one who takes refuge in him* (Psalm 34:8). Come and experience God's goodness for yourself. Accept His invitation to personally encounter a life with God and discover the goodness of a relationship with the only One who really matters. The One who gave His life that we might find life—abundant, eternal life.

Lord, as another year closes, we commit our lives to You—some maybe for the first time. You alone are God—the One who saves. Thank You for sending Your Son Jesus to a corrupt and sinful world, that we, by believing, can come to know You and live. We praise You for who You are, all You have done, are doing, and will continue to do in and through our lives. Thank You for yet another new year. May we experience Your revival in our spirits. Thank You, Jesus! Amen.

ABOUT THE AUTHOR

Katherine Merkle is a first-time author with a passion for sharing the transformative power of God in a person's life. Her debut book, *Good Morning Messages,* is a devotional written after nearly a decade of sharing practical spiritual insights with hundreds of people every day. Her passion for devotional encouragement was birthed out of her own personal experience of surrendering herself fully to God and her daily journey that begins with Scripture, reflection, and prayer.

Good Morning Messages is an answer to Katherine's prayer for God to use her in some way to share the freedom found in a deep, unshakeable relationship with the Lord Jesus Christ. She knows firsthand and firmly believes there is no one outside the love of God. His grace, mercy, love, and forgiveness are waiting for every single one of the lost, lonely, and desperate seeking and in need of a Savior. Her prayer is that, like her, readers will start by spending just a few minutes with God and find freedom, salvation, and life—abundant and eternal.

Katherine lives in northeast Ohio with her husband, Ken, and their dog, Raleigh. Their blended family includes six adult children (four are married), three grandchildren (all girls), and several "grandimals." Life is busy and full, and she is grateful to be so blessed.

Retired from a marketing career that spanned nearly fifty years in various capacities, Katherine started working as a server in restaurants until she was hired at a local radio station in production and promotions. In her early twenties, she moved into different advertising agency roles and eventually landed client-side on in-house marketing teams, the most significant portion of her career being with the Sherwin-Williams Company corporate headquarters in Cleveland.

Katherine served as part-time administrator for her church, Grace Brethren Barberton Campus, up until her final retirement in spring of 2025 and continues to serve on the First Impressions Team and in community outreach opportunities. She enjoys putting her spiritual gift of hospitality to good use during fall and winter months by hosting a large Grace Life Group weekly at their home.

Her favorite time is spent with family and friends, walking in the park behind their home, and an occasional vacation on a beach or in the woods. And every morning you will find her either on the front porch, back deck, or in her recliner with Bible in hand, a collection of devotionals, and still writing and sending out a daily devotional message.

Website: https://authorkatherinemerkle.com

Email: ksmerk@authorkatherinemerkle.com

www.ingramcontent.com/pod-product-compliance
Lightning Source LLC
Chambersburg PA
CBHW060757120626
46557CB00001B/10